Language is Power

Professor John Honey is a graduate of Cambridge and Oxford, and trained in linguistics at the University of Newcastle-upon-Tyne under the celebrated historian of the English language, Barbara Strang. He has taught at the Universities of Durham and Cambridge, in Singapore, and at three universities in Africa. Until 1985 he was Professor and Dean of Education at what is now De Montfort University, Leicester, and for seven years until 1996 he was a Professor of English in Japan, latterly at Osaka International University. His book *Does Accent Matter?* provoked widespread discussion on its publication in 1989. In addition to his concern with issues surrounding the concept of standard English, he has a special interest in interpreting British social history and institutions, and the classics of English literature, to foreign students of English. He was elected F.R.Hist.S. in 1978.

LANGUAGE IS POWER John Honey

The Story of Standard English and its Enemies

faber and faber
LONDON · BOSTON

First published in 1997
by Faber and Faber Limited
3 Queen Square London WC1N 3AU

Typeset by RefineCatch Ltd, Bungay
Printed in England by Mackays of Chatham plc, Chatham, Kent

A CIP record for this book
is available from the British Library

ISBN 0–571–19047–2

10 9 8 7 6 5 4 3 2 1

For my wife Emma

who, like all foreign learners,
has struggled with the complexities of standard English

CONTENTS

Preface ix

PREFACE

Parts of this book have been so long in gestation that it is difficult
to name all those who contributed to its final state, but they are
legion. They necessarily include my colleagues and advanced
students at institutions where I have taught either as a member of
staff or as a visitor within the past fifteen years, including De
Montfort University (Leicester Polytechnic); the (National) Institute of Education, Singapore; the University of the North West
(Bophuthatswana); Kumamoto University; Osaka International
University; and University College ('Castle') in the University of
Durham, where I had the privilege of a visiting fellowship in 1994.
My Leicester colleague Dr Valerie Marett supplied invaluable
source material on UK education while I was abroad. Among
many others who gave help on specific points I record my debt to
Valerie and Michael Grosvenor-Myer, Professor Peter Titlestad,
Professor Roy Holland, Professor Patrick Collinson, Professor
Adrian Roscoe, Professor Peter Mühlhäusler, Dr Sylvia Adamson,
Peter Longhurst, Margaret Sharpe, Dr Christopher Rollason, Pro-
fessor D. E. Cooper, Professor William Samarin, Dr Chris Stray,
Dr George Silberbauer, Peter Bassett and Dr Graeme Cane. My
considerable indebtedness to Professor David Tomlinson of
Kumamoto Prefectural University is made clear in the relevant part
of Chapter 8. I am grateful for formal permission to print passages
of extended direct quotation from books by the Rt Hon. Alan
Clark and by Dr Bernice Martin. My text also incorporates short
stretches of material by me, previously published in articles or
reviews in the journal *English Today* (1995, on pronoun case), in
Etudes Anglaises (1993, on word-stress), in *Applied Linguistics*
(1996, on Pinker), in the *Times Higher Education Supplement*
(1993, on American English) and in that interesting new Scandina-
vian journal *RASK* (1994, on Phillipson).

I should admit in advance that in my zeal to clarify the implications of the arguments I criticise, I have not always followed the

convention of indicating when emphasis is the author's or was added by me. I will also forestall the inevitable criticism of those waggish journalists who will think to score easy shots by claiming that here is yet another linguistic 'expert' whose own sentences are too long for comprehension by the simple-minded, and above all contain too many examples of unfamiliar jargon. The lack of any popular and widely understood terminology by which to describe the way the English language works is one of the specific deficiencies of our educational system to which my book seeks to draw attention.

CHAPTER ONE Introduction

Linguistics is a notoriously schismatic subject.
Sir Kenneth Dover

This book is all about standard English and the educational and political controversies which have arisen about it in recent years. By standard English I mean the language in which this book is written, which is essentially the same form of English used in books and newspapers all over the world. There are a few differences, but these are relatively small. A writer in an American newspaper or book would use a slightly different spelling system (*honor* for honour, *plow* for plough, *center* for centre, and so on), and use a few different vocabulary items (such as *gotten* for got, *envision* for envisage, *elevator* for lift) and a grammar which may be slightly different on particular points, for example in the verb tense used with certain adverbials (I *did* it already for I *have done* it already). In a book or newspaper article written in India or West Africa or Australia, the reader might be able to detect a few traces of the local form of educated written English, though often an extract from such a book or newspaper will carry no indication at all of its regional origin – very unlike the voice of its writer, which may reveal within the first few words that its speaker is Indian or Nigerian or Australian. In Britain itself, a piece of writing in, say, Cockney or West Country English (probably a letter or poem – it would not usually be a book on an academic or educational topic) would reveal its local origins by the use of distinctive vocabulary and grammatical forms. Standard English can be used in a wide variety of styles, from the most formal to the most informal, but because this book is most likely to be read by people with a certain level of basic education and with a serious interest in this aspect of the English language, its style will tend to be more formal than colloquial.

This standardised form of written English has its origins in a particular variety of written language which began to become the common means of communication for literate people in the south-east of England in the fifteenth century. At that time, people in different parts of Britain spoke in very different *dialects*, whose different vocabularies in many cases used different words for the same thing, and whose grammatical rules might be very different from each other. In addition, they used different *accents* (patterns of pronunciation) so that even when they were using similar vocabulary and grammar, speakers from (say) the north and the south of England would have had great difficulty in understanding each other. Though these considerable differences have greatly reduced over four centuries, and especially during the past hundred years, many people in different regions of Britain today still use different pronoun forms (e.g. *yous* or *yees* as the plural of you); different grammar of verbs (as in *he shouldn't have drank it, my sister come yesterday* and, especially in Tyneside, whose rich dialect forms are a living reality, *me and me marrow wis gannin ti wauk* for 'my friend and I were going to work'); and past tense forms *tret* (treated) and *putten* (put). Some dialects have *jock* or *snap* for lunch; Yorkshire has *jannock* for a good person, and that useful word *truntlements* for 'odds and ends', and hundreds of other such words which sound picturesque to speakers of standard English.

Each of these dialects has its distinctive accent, and you do not have to be an expert to tell whether a person comes from the north, or from the south, of England by their pronunciation of words like bath or cup . This is *not a book about accent* – I have already written a quite different book on that, which gave rise to much public discussion in 1989 because it described the way people react to different accents. In this book we are concerned with dialect (i.e., a variety distinguished mainly by its forms of vocabulary and grammar) and only incidentally with accent. In theory, at least, standard English can be spoken in any accent of English, though in practice it is seldom (indeed perhaps never) spoken in the broadest forms of regional accent. It is important to be clear about the distinction between accent and dialect, whose main components are as follows:

DIALECT	ACCENT
pronunciation	pronunciation
vocabulary	
grammar	
idiom	

The first defining characteristic of standard English, then, is its *generality* or *commonality* – the widespread nature of its use. The second is its relative *uniformity*: in very similar form, it is used all over the world, though there are small differences, as we have seen, between the two main forms of English that are learned internationally, British English and American English. Other forms derive from one of these – for example, Canadian and Philippine English are closely related to American English, while Indian and Australian Englishes, and the Englishes of different parts of Africa, come from British English, and all of these regional varieties in turn have some distinctive vocabulary and grammar features. The forces which help to maintain the relative uniformity of standard English will be examined in this book, whose main concern is with the standard British dialect rather than the standard American dialect of English. Those forces contribute to the third defining characteristic: the fact that standard English is subject to standards of *correctness* which are, for the most part, 'codified', i.e., embodied in dictionaries and in a set of rules taught in schools, both to children whose native language is English, and to those learning English as a foreign language.

Standard English is now a battlefield. For more than a decade, it has been a controversial issue on both sides of the Atlantic. Despite its fifteenth-century origins, despite the fact that for five

I have held this view to be a horrid and silly aberration for a long time. Teachers who hold it shortchange their charges.

4

Language is Power

centuries speakers have been very aware of its existence, and that during that time it has been a crucial element in an education system which began by teaching a small proportion and then extended to embrace the whole population, there are those who today question the appropriateness of teaching standard English in schools, and they include not just academics but politicians, and indeed ordinary citizens. To promote one form (standard English) in schools is felt to involve the disparagement of non-standard forms, and for this reason "discussions about standard and non-standard English can quickly become a highly charged emotional issue". As Randolph Quirk pointed out in 1994, standard English has, for a generation or more, been "insidiously demonised as class-biased, at best fit only to be put in dismissive quotation marks". In the same year, as Lord Quirk pointed out, the head of Britain's National Curriculum, Sir Ron Dearing, was sharply warned by the Council of University Teachers of English against any proposals that showed a concern to "privilege standard English"; the prime purpose of those who advocated this form of English was (the Council claimed) to "enhance the traditional power base of a particular social élite". Sociologists and linguists in Britain and the USA can now write of "the standard English ideology" and imply a direct connexion between the teaching of standard English and various forms of 'coercion' and 'oppression'.

From the mid-1960s to the mid-1980s I was involved in teacher-education and I was also briefly a government inspector of schools – an HMI, following in the footsteps of Matthew Arnold. From around the early 1970s onwards I began to encounter statements from practising teachers that they did not see it as their duty to require their pupils to use standard English – which, they explained, is of course just one among many dialects of English, all equally good; moreover, for a teacher to require a pupil to use it must constitute an *act of oppression*. In some cases teachers claimed to have been told this by other HMIs, by their teacher-education lecturers, or by local authority inspectors. At Sussex University, English literature critic Alan Sinfield complained in 1994 that the

Conservative government's National Curriculum proposals "require students to undergo tests in standard English", which he identified simply as "the variant used by many white, middle-class people in the south east of England".

This book examines – and exposes – the kinds of argument that have been put forward against the emphasis on standard English in schools and indeed in society, and it maintains the opposite position, namely that standard English is not merely one variety among many, but instead is a specially important and valuable variety which derives its value from a set of qualities which are not shared by other, non-standard dialects. It follows that to give access to standard English to those members of society who have not acquired facility in it through their parents, is an important priority in any society concerned with social justice and the reduction of educational inequalities.

It must be recognised squarely, however, that there exists an almost insuperable obstacle to my contention about the special qualities of standard English. This obstacle is the consensus that has has existed among linguists (i.e., specialists in linguistic theory) for at least three decades now, around the hypothesis that I will call 'linguistic equality', the notion that that all languages, and all dialects of any language, are equally good. This hypothesis has been of fundamental importance in shaping the whole of the debate over the use of standard languages and dialects in educational systems, and over and over again it has been appealed to as the clinching argument for resisting the requirement that schoolchildren should be given maximum access to standard English. Because it has been so central to the whole discussion, I ask the indulgence of my readers if I take them on a detour during the next chapter, in order to show them how this theory about languages and dialects came to pervade Western linguistics, and how far the theory can still be regarded as a credible support for the wide-ranging ideological case against standard English that has been built upon it.

CHAPTER TWO

The Language Myth

What I tell you three times is true.
Lewis Carroll,
The Hunting of the Snark

Versions of the 'linguistic equality' hypothesis have been around in linguistics and anthropology on both sides of the Atlantic since early this century, but it it was essentially during the period of rapid growth of linguistics as a discipline, especially in the USA, from the 1960s onwards, that this doctrine began to be enshrined, as a matter of dogma, in many texts designed for students. Moreover, it was not long before this dogma began to influence what was being taught to teachers in training.

"Essentially, any language is as good as any other language," wrote three distinguished British linguists (Professors Halliday, McIntosh and Strevens) in 1964, and they went on to explain that "every language is equally well adapted to the uses to which the community puts it". For this reason, "there is no such thing as a 'primitive' language"; moreover, "among the languages in the world today, there is no recognized dimension of linguistic progress". This means, they said, that "no language can be identified as representing a more highly developed state of language than any other". They have an interesting comment on those who disagree, observing that the "misapprehension" that some languages are intrinsically better than others "cannot be dismissed as ignorance or prejudice", since "it is held by people who are both intelligent and serious, and can bring forward evidence to support it". Nevertheless, they say "it is *wholly false* and can do a great deal of harm".

Listen now to Professor David Crystal, a leading authority on the English language, in a book published in 1968 and reprinted many times since then: "We cannot measure one language against the yardstick provided by another . . . It is ridiculous to think that a language could exist where there were insufficient words for the people to talk about any aspect of the environment they wished." Instead, he insisted, "language always keeps pace with the social development of its users".

I have noted down more than twenty examples of such statements, made between the 1960s and the present, which I happen to have come across; if I had instituted a thoroughgoing search I could have found dozens more, in books read by students of linguistics, anthropology or education. They apply both to separate languages and to different dialects or varieties of a language. "Every language has sufficiently rich vocabulary for the expression of all the distinctions that are important in the society using it" (Lyons, 1970). "All languages and dialects are adequate as communicative systems" (Wolfram, 1973). "All varieties of a language are structured, complex, rule-governed systems which are entirely adequate for the needs of their speakers" (Trudgill, 1974). "It is an established fact that no language or dialect is superior to another" (Edwards, 1979). "All languages are equally complex and equally capable of expressing any idea in the universe" (Fromkin and Rodman, 1974/78/83). "There is virtually unanimous recognition among linguists that one language or dialect is as good as another" (Sutcliffe, 1982).

Several of these authorities deal specifically with the way languages are able to cope with the need for expanding vocabulary in response to social change. Listen to one of the great figures in American sociolinguistics: "Every language, dialect, patois or lingo is a structurally complete framework into which can be poured any subtlety of emotion or thought that its users are capable of experiencing. Whatever it lacks at any given time or place in the way of vocabulary or syntax can be supplied in very short order by borrowing or imitation from other languages" (Haugen, 1974). Then this, from a widely used American textbook in linguistics: "The vocabulary of any language can be expanded to include new words for new concepts" (Fromkin and Rodman,

1974 etc). Next, an Australian anthropologist working with Pidgin and other languages in Papua New Guinea: "All languages have within them the capacity for expression of all concepts that could possibly occur to human beings; all have the possibility of change and adaptation, of absorbing new concepts, without the language thereby being altered out of all recognition" (Laycock, 1976). If this were not the case, he claims, French would have been inadequate to discuss the French Revolution, German to discuss the Blitzkrieg, and English to cope with the Space Age. These languages found ways of dealing with new concepts "without their speakers being aware of the change", because any language can deal with anything required of it: "it is in fact *axiomatic* that any language can handle anything its speakers wish to talk about" (Laycock, 1976).

A very significant quotation comes from Ken Livingstone, a Labour Member of Parliament since 1987, whose own experience of higher education was at a teacher-training college in precisely the period when this new linguistic orthodoxy was establishing itself; he was soon to become an influential figure in local government, and thus in educational policy, in the Greater London area. On a BBC discussion programme in 1982 he declared, "No one system of language is better than any other."

Elsewhere – in a detailed article in the academic journal of German specialists in English, *Anglistik* – I have set out more than twenty such statements illustrating the new dogma, published between 1964 and the early 1990s. For our present purposes, I have distilled the essence of them into five propositions which are stated explicitly by one or more of them and which, taken together, represent the consensus of opinion which developed in that period among linguists, anthropologists and educationists about the nature of 'linguistic equality':

a) there is no valid basis for the *comparison* of languages or dialects;

b) no language or dialect is more *developed* than another, nor more *efficient* or *expressive*;

c) no intellectual *handicaps* can attach to speakers in virtue of speaking one language or dialect rather than another;

d) all languages and dialects are perfectly adapted to the *present* needs of all their speakers, and have the power to adapt virtually instantaneously in order to meet *new* needs.

e) those who argue otherwise are reprehensible/harmful/ridiculous, even if their arguments are supported by *evidence*.

Anyone who doubts the claim that these views represent a consensus among linguists and others on both sides of the Atlantic should reflect on the identity of the authors of the works from which those twenty-odd quotations are derived. They include 'household names' in British linguistics such as Professors Michael Halliday, Angus McIntosh and Peter Strevens, Sir John Lyons, Peter Trudgill, Jenny Cheshire, Michael Stubbs, James Milroy, David Crystal, and Dr Viv Edwards, and, among American linguists, Walt Wolfram, Einar Haugen and the best-selling textbook authors Fromkin and Rodman.

One of these quotations (Sutcliffe, 1982) refers to *virtually* unanimous recognition among linguists of the principle of linguistic equality, and that word of qualification is important. So far as I know, only one major figure in linguistics in Britain or America has publicly queried this consensus, and this was the distinguished US sociolinguist, Professor Dell Hymes, who was an early campaigner for the *principle* of equality but always insisted that it must be hedged around with serious *ifs* and *buts*. An early statement of his views came in a huge anthology of seminal articles, *Language in Culture and Society*, which he edited in 1964. In his own contribution to that volume, his essential concern was to dispel the misconceptions and stereotypes surrounding 'primitive' languages, and to emphasise that "we know of no natural languages with vocabularies so small that their speakers must eke them out by gestures . . .; which lack definite systems of sounds and grammar; which lack standards of usage; which, because of lack of system or of writing, change more rapidly in structure than other languages;

which lack abstract terms or capacity for forming them; which cannot serve significant intellectual and aesthetic expression". Hymes's concern, then, was to assert, against a background of racist disparagement (especially by laypersons, but even by some scholars) of the language and culture of preliterate societies, that instead preliterate languages have proper vocabularies, systematic, consistent and stable grammars, standards of usage, and some capacity to express abstraction.

Even as he asserted this, however, Hymes felt it necessary to issue a warning that the proper recognition of these qualities carried the "subtler hazard" of meeting a stereotyped error with a similarly fallacious counter-stereotype which would involve "the denial of any functional differences at all", since "we do NOT [he emphasised] know that all languages are equal in every respect", nor do we know "that they cannot be measured and compared as to complexity or as to adequacy for particular purposes". Yet he recognised the danger that an admission that languages might indeed be susceptible to a valid system of ranking for certain purposes might involve "lending aid and comfort to the enemy" (i.e., to those who seek excuses for discriminating against preliterate peoples).

But, as is clear from the quotations, Hymes's highly significant warnings in 1964 did nothing to stop the elaboration and perpetuation of the unqualified or 'strong' theory of linguistic equality over the next thirty years. Yet we must have at least three serious reservations about this 'strong' theory. First, it is true – and important – that linguists have, in general, demonstrated that the languages of primitive communities are not in fact the debased vehicles of childlike simplicity which some descriptions suggested; none has been shown to be lacking in stable and systematic grammar. For most (though not necessarily all) 'primitive' languages, what has been demonstrated is in fact the opposite: that they exhibit a grammatical complexity of fearsome proportions, with multiplex 'case' systems for nouns, and elaborate aspectual systems for verbs requiring the highest degree of specificity – so great a complexity indeed as to suggest overload, or over-kill, in relation to what might be thought to be the present-day needs of their speakers, and certainly in comparison with the relatively far simpler grammar of the languages of modernised societies. (The history of English, and to a lesser extent of the Romance languages, for example, has generally been one of a great levelling of inflections – in other words, verb-endings and most noun-endings have been simplified.) For the languages of primitive communities, their much-vaunted complexity may be shown, in fact, as now conferring no clear functional advantage.

The implications of complexity

What do we mean when we say that a language might have an 'overload' of specificity? In most Western European languages, grammatical tense – indicating the time of the action of the verb – is important, though it was not always so (Old English, for example, had very limited grammatical means of expressing futurity). This importance reflects accurately the relative emphasis on time in our modern way of living and thinking. But many other languages, including Chinese and Japanese, have strictly limited grammatical methods of expressing tense, which has to be deduced from the context. If we look at a language such as Navaho (spoken by Indians in North America), we find that in using a verb, tense is less important than specifying the type of action involved, in respect of whether it is momentary, progressing, continuing, or customary. More important than when an action took place is whether it is complete or incomplete. Thus the grammar is less precise than English on 'time when', but far more specific in indicating 'completedness'.

Nor does the complexity stop there. What we regard as simple statements must in Navaho indicate four kinds of detail: (1) whether the 'it' described is definite, or an indefinite 'something'; (2) whether an object involved is round, long, fluid, animate, or falls into yet other categories; (3) whether (in accordance with the

A fine argument. It favors the American
impulse to simply verb forms as being
more sophisticated than too much specific...

12 · Language is Power

emphasis on 'completedness') the act is in progress, about to begin, about to end, habitually carried on, repeatedly carried on, etc.; (4) the extent to which the 'I' involved controls the action described. To this extent, it can be said that Navaho cannot express a thought in a way parallel to English, and translating between English and Navaho is an almost impossible exercise. So, too, with the Nootka Indians, for whom a sentence, simple enough in English, like 'He invites people to a feast' becomes 'Someone (impersonal) goes in order to get (i.e., invite) those who engage in the activity of eating boiled food'. The sentence 'He will give it to you' is expressed in Navaho in the form *thee-to-(transitive marker)-will-roundthing-in future*, and in Yano, a language of north-east California, as *roundthing-away-to-does(or will)-done unto-thou-in future*. In the languages of many preliterate peoples, there is a wealth of grammatical forms by which the speaker is obliged to specify degrees of physical distance involving the 'actors' or objects in a sentence, and whether they are here, near, far away, very far away, etc. The range of 'aspectual' complexity of the verb may be vast: the Sotho language of a Bantu people in Southern Africa is reported as having a verb system with 38 affirmative forms, 22 'potential' forms, four 'optatives', and 40 conditionals. We may question the appropriateness of all this specific detail to the efficiency of communication in a modern society, but we can never doubt the subtlety and intellectual refinement which these languages represent, alongside which our own languages may look crude and impoverished.

Our first objection, then, to these formulations of the linguistic equality theory is that complexity, though proof of mental profundity, does not necessarily lead to functional efficiency in all contexts. Our second objection is this: it simply is not true that there are no criteria for comparing the development of languages – that, as Crystal puts it, "we cannot measure one language by the yardstick provided by another"; or that "there is no recognizable dimension of linguistic progress" (Halliday et al.). Two very obvious criteria or yardsticks present themselves. First, vocabulary size:

a language with half a million words, many of which possess many distinct meanings, can usefully be compared with a preliterate tribal language with a total vocabulary of a few thousand words, most of which carry only one meaning; and, secondly, the development of more sophisticated ways of representing abstraction, a quality which may have limited representation in the languages of some known preliterate peoples. We do not know for sure how far (if at all) the absence of a word prevents a speaker from using a concept; what we do know is that the existence of a word in a vocabulary available to such speakers greatly *facilitates* their using that concept, both for their own use and in communicating that concept to others. (The American psycholinguist Steven Pinker describes an Australian aboriginal language of only 200 words which he claims, though without citing any evidence, can express the full range of concepts in everyday speech – he does not say how much abstraction is discussed in such everyday speech.) I. A. Richards's system of Basic English in the 1930s presupposed 850 words, and it must be relevant that Basic English never caught on. Small and simple vocabularies involve what, in a different book, Crystal himself has called "unwieldy, lengthy circumlocution" if they are to represent new items or concepts, and this involves a very significant loss of efficiency and economy.

The ability of members of a community to "discuss any aspect of their community they wish" (as Crystal put it) implies adequacy within a static community: this may be the case, but what happens if they want, or need, to step outside the intellectual bounds of their own community? Trudgill's reference to "needs" implies the same static reference to present needs. We can see that what Crystal called the "*ridiculous* supposition" that the tiny vocabulary of a given language might involve cognitive limitations for its speakers must indeed be entertained, unless we are prepared to accept that those speakers are to be denied access to centuries of modern knowledge.

Instant adaptability

When challenged on these implications, these and other linguists usually fall back on the 'instant adaptability' argument, well stated by Laycock and explicit also in Haugen. This brings us, however, to our third reservation. The potential for adaptation of such preliterate languages may be a much more serious problem than these statements acknowledge. The examples of adaptation usually given emphasise English – whose vocabulary expanded dramatically after the Norman Conquest, again at the Renaissance and again in the Space Age – or French or German. Hebrew, Arabic, and Bahasa Indonesia/Malaysia are also examples of languages whose vocabularies have expanded substantially, and at great cost in effort and money, to respond to modern forms of knowledge. But we may be comparing, on the one hand, the language of a small isolated preliterate community with a few thousand words, nearly all with single meanings, and on the other hand the hundreds of thousands of words, many with multiple meanings, of a modern written language. The vocabulary of a preliterate society with no numbering system beyond two, three, or four – whose members may, *pace* Hymes, indeed have to resort to gesture to indicate greater numbers – and which has no distinction between cardinals and ordinals and no way of indicating distance other than 'quite a long way' and 'very nearby', cannot by itself cope with the elementary mathematics or science or indeed many aspects of the modern world, other than by incorporating a number system wholesale, together with a vast infusion of foreign words. We nowadays believe that the brains of members of a Stone Age tribe have exactly the same potential as the brains of members of the most advanced societies for complex, sophisticated, abstract thought, but they lack the terminology which saves them from having constantly to rediscover what we, through literate language, already know. This belief is supported by the fact that when children from such tribes are offered a modern mathematical education, some of them quickly develop great proficiency in it.

For one language simply to incorporate elements essential to modernisation from another language sounds easy – but in practice it presents special difficulties which I will typify as (1) scale, (2) pace, and (3) congruence.

As we have seen, arguments for the ability of languages to incorporate large quantities of new vocabulary typically use the examples of English or German or French (cf. Laycock) at critical phases of their past history, or more recently of Hebrew, Arabic, etc. But these are all cases of incorporation into an already huge lexicon; the proportions involved in transforming a language of a few thousand words present a different problem. In addition, the quoted examples typically involve long periods of time – many generations, even several centuries – whereas the argument of linguistic equality presupposes a far shorter period than this: we noted Haugen's comment about the ability of all languages to adapt "in very short order". Indeed, we know what happens to 'small' languages when faced with incorporating change on this scale and at this pace: they are *swamped* – young speakers turn instead to powerful languages like English, the indigenous language dies, and the world is losing languages at an alarming rate (in 1995 the American linguist Michael Krauss was reported as predicting that between 5 and 10 per cent of the world's 6,000 languages will become extinct within the next century). In any case there is also evidence that where languages do incorporate foreign vocabulary, there always tends to be a time-lag which can seriously disadvantage the current generation of speakers.

[handwritten marginal note: Too many new words too fast (yet still not fast enough to update)]

There is a third important factor at work, which I have called *congruence.* Speakers do not automatically allow their language to make certain adaptations. There are obstacles which are technically called *phonotactic* or *phonaesthetic* barriers – some languages cannot cope with, or cannot regard as aesthetically acceptable, particular vowels or consonants or combinations. English has around 40 phonemes (distinctive sounds): a language with only eleven phonemes cannot easily accommodate words involving the

sound system of a language with 40, or 100, or 140 phonemes. In
the case of the vast incorporation of Graeco-Latinate vocabulary at
the time of the Renaissance, there were running battles (some
stages of which were known as the 'inkhorn' controversy) for nearly
a century among educated English speakers, many of whom
fiercely contested the admissibility of these new forms. Moreover,
languages differ in their existing resources for word-formation –
some preliterate languages are immensely productive of newly
derived words, some have few existing mechanisms for this. No
less serious are what might be called psychological obstacles: of
two closely allied tribal languages, one may welcome word-
borrowings from outside languages, the other may staunchly resist
them, raising barriers against what are apparently felt by speakers
to be 'incongruent' elements.

Bludgeons and rapiers

Linguistic equality, in the formulations we have cited, is thus seen
to be a very unhelpful hypothesis. We can recognise that 'primitive' languages are not deficient in respect of complexity – often
quite the reverse – though they may be unequal, in their present
form, in their ability to perform certain functions; and that their
powers of absorption and adaptation may be limited. The most
obvious area of inequality between the languages of preliterate
and advanced societies is in the vocabulary needed to describe
modern knowledge, including science and technology. Some
features of the grammatical system, such as the absence of a passive
voice or of specific tenses, or of mechanisms for 'relativisation'
(linking elements in a sentence, by 'who', 'which', etc.), may also
present difficulties. This inequality of specific function, however,
is only one of many which may exist between different languages,
and they are certainly not always to the advantage of 'advanced'
languages. The languages of preliterate societies often have much
more refined vocabularies for the description of certain natural
phenomena (plants, animals), or for the expression of emotions,

than any major modern language. One linguist colleague tells me that a Bantu language spoken in Zaire has a far more expressive adverbial system than any European language known to him, and we can readily understand the claim to me by an anthropologist that the Bushman language of the Kalahari has a more more elaborate and expressive vocabulary for the expression of 'intimate affect' – a close and positive emotional relationship – than any other language he knows. Similar claims of specific kinds of functional superiority have been made for particular languages in the Americas and Caribbean, and the famous Benjamin Lee Whorf said of the Hopi language of Northern Arizona, that in its capacity to describe certain phenomena, "English compared to Hopi is like a bludgeon compared to a rapier." Even here, however, we must not be carried away. The statement by J. E. Joseph that linguists have believed since the nineteenth century that gaps in one language or dialect are always compensated for by "some other richness of structure" is given without offering any justification whatever for that belief. Significantly, Joseph, who in the same book appears to endorse both the linguistic equality hypothesis and the instant adaptability hypothesis, is reluctant to accept that intellectual functions add any special quality to standard languages, on the grounds that to do so would be implicitly to prize Western languages and cultures above others, and would thus be culturocentric.

Meanwhile, the lone voice of Dell Hymes continued to issue warnings against the misrepresentation of the theory of linguistic equality. In three publications in the year 1974 – by which time the doctrine was a fully established orthodoxy – Professor Hymes challenged various unqualified assertions of the egalitarians, including the distinguished British linguist Sir John Lyons. "To say," wrote Hymes, "that every language has a sufficiently rich vocabulary for the expression of all the distinctions that are important in the society using it, is to beg a host of questions." Moreover, to claim, as Lyons had also done, that all languages are of roughly equal complexity is simply wrong – and an example of the triumph of what he called "ideological confidence" over empirical knowledge.

Nine years later, when I published in Britain a critique of some of the most popular formulations of the linguistic equality dogma, I was subjected to blistering attacks, both personal and professional, which are referred to in a later chapter. Two of the most powerful of my critics mounted a defence of that dogma, to which we must briefly give attention. Their argument was that these propositions about all languages being equal referred, not to language as it is actually used by its speakers in real life, but to language in its theoretical sense as an abstract 'system'. There are several objections to this, the most compelling being that the strict severance between a language as an abstract system and its speakers' use of it is a nonsense, as is now increasingly recognised by linguists – indeed, one of them has recently labelled the theory that language somehow has a life of its own, which is independent of its speakers, as 'the organic fallacy'.

However, since then, some linguists have become more cautious in the way they have stated the dogma. They have tended to use terms like 'inherently' or 'intrinsically' equal, or 'linguistically' equal. In the layperson, the use of these phrases creates the impression that (as some of these theorists actually believe) all languages or varieties are *of equal value to their speakers* – an implication which, as will be explored in the rest of this book, is, for many crucial purposes, simply not true. Moreover, there is always the further implication that, whatever the present state of a language's resources of grammar, vocabulary, etc., all these can adapt instantaneously to meet new needs. As we have seen, this is simply not so.

A recent reformulation of the dogma is highly significant. In his book attacking the worldwide teaching of English as a process of 'linguistic imperialism', Robert Phillipson bases his argument that English has appropriated an unfair share of resources on the fact that "linguists are trained to see any language as potentially fulfilling any function", thus any advantages enjoyed by English must be due to a sinister plot to create cultural inequalities between it and other languages. The key word is, of course, *potentially* – a very important change in the way the dogma is now to be defined. Whether that potential can be turned into actual, and what would be required for this to become possible, constitute major problems in Phillipson's account, which we will return to in the last part of this book.

In his authoritative and widely read *Cambridge Encyclopedia of Language* (1987), Professor David Crystal elaborates, and essentially confirms, his 1968 position that "All languages meet the social and psychological needs of their speakers." He then repeats a point made by Dell Hymes, that it cannot be true that speakers of preliterate languages rely on gestures, since this would prevent communication at night. However, on this specific point Hymes was misled, since we know that there are in fact languages whose number systems rely substantially on gesture. Also, says Crystal, they cannot be without abstract terms, since how could they possibly develop moral or religious beliefs? Yet their ability to discuss and reflect on those beliefs may indeed be limited by the range of abstract terms available; and many religious beliefs of preliterate peoples are in fact expressed in terms of what, to them, are concrete realities, not supernatural abstractions at all. Crystal's conclusion that "there is no evidence to suggest that primitive peoples are in any sense 'handicapped' by their language when they are using it within their own community" simply begs again the whole question of its serviceability for a wider set of needs, and the adaptability of languages to social change – though it is noteworthy that he now no longer repeats his claim that there exist no 'yardsticks' by which languages can be compared, whereas Trudgill can still refer to "the *invidious* comparison of linguistic varieties on grounds of adequacy" (my emphasis). It is disappointing that there has been so little progress in twenty years. The pall of dogma still hangs heavily over British linguistics.

It is time to move the argument on to a further stage, in the next chapter. Meanwhile, we may summarise our investigation so far by saying that the consensus among linguists and others about 'linguistic equality', which was illustrated by the five propositions (a) to (e) on pages 8–9, is based upon seriously questionable premisses. There are, indeed, valid criteria for the comparison of languages, and by some of these criteria some languages are shown to be, in their present state, more serviceable than others for certain functions. Because of this, the speakers of certain languages may experience disadvantages in relation to forms of knowledge which are not yet well established in their existing culture. Not all languages appear to be able to adapt quickly in response to rapid social change. However, those who attempt to argue against the consensus view continue to be regarded as reprehensible.

CHAPTER THREE

The Dialect Trap

There is no merit in equality, unless it be equality with the best.
John Lancaster Spalding

Our finding that languages are not all equally 'good', and that speakers of some languages may be at a big disadvantage in handling certain types of knowledge or skill, has important implications for the way we plan methods of helping the developing countries to make the best use of their resources, and reduce their inequalities, in a fast-changing world. But this book is not about the Third World, important though it is. It is about the way the linguistic equality dogma has been used in order to oppose an emphasis on standard English in school systems in Britain and North America. Assumptions about the special value of standard English cannot be supported if, as the dogma goes on to state, not only all languages, but *all varieties* of a language, are equally good.

Many people can, despite the insistence of the linguistic equality theorists, see the force of a common-sense argument about the functional disadvantages, in the modern world, of speaking only a preliterate language with a tiny vocabulary. But the differences between a standard language and a dialect – surely they must be so small that the suggestion of any intellectual implications for their speakers is improbable? And is this not especially so when we recognise the very arbitrary criteria which in centuries past helped to cause one dialect rather than another to assume the status of a standard language?

Nevertheless, the suggestion used to be confidently made that the use of a standard language, like English, confers intellectual advantages on those who speak and write it, while the speakers of non-standard social and regional dialect forms suffer comparable forms of disadvantage. In both Britain and the United States, psychologists and sociologists in the 1950s and 1960s sought to relate the persistent patterns of educational under-achievement of working-class or ethnic minority students to different patterns of language use by those groups – in America these included Bereiter and Engelmann, in Britain the London University sociologist Basil Bernstein. Bernstein's theory of linguistic codes – which distinguished between an 'elaborated' code, mainly associated with middle-class children, and a 'restricted' (and supposedly linguistically and intellectually deficient) code, mainly associated with working-class children – seemed to teachers to help explain the relative academic performance of these students, and during the 1960s and early 1970s Bernstein's ideas of these two 'codes' passed, sometimes in highly garbled form, into the theoretical apparatus of training-college students.

Bernstein's own account of his theory has changed over the past thirty years, and has in general suffered from a relative paucity of empirical verification of the grammatical and other ingredients which he has claimed as characteristic of his two codes. Among features of the 'restricted' code are short, grammatically simple and often unfinished sentences, with little use of subordinate clauses; repetitive use of a few simple conjunctions like *because*, *then*, *so*; a rigid and limited use of adverbs; and a number of features which suggest confusion between reason and conclusion and so threaten the logical force of the sentence. Elaborated code speakers are said to use more complex sentence constructions, employ more discriminating varieties of adverb and adjective, and to make use of specific grammatical elements like prepositions and other techniques of cohesion to indicate logical and other relationships. For restricted code speakers, meanings are commonly *implicit*, whereas for elaborated code speakers they are *explicit*. The restricted code is 'particularistic', expressing the values and concerns of a local group, while the elaborated code is 'universalistic', looking to the wider society. The restricted code is 'context-bound', and utterances can often be interpreted only by reference to prior knowledge or to signals provided within its group of speakers. The elaborated code tends to be 'context-free', and less dependent on such knowledge or signals.

The viability of such explanations, however, came to a sudden halt with the reception by the linguistics community of a powerful argument by a man regarded (with some justification) as the high priest of modern sociolinguistics, the American scholar William Labov. In a famous paper widely reprinted from 1972 onwards, *The Logic of Non-standard English*, Labov examined the assumption underlying many American educational programmes (especially remedial ones) that the vernacular English of American Blacks involved a cognitive (i.e., intellectual) deficit, which caused them to do badly at all subjects in the school system – with, for example, scores in reading which were two years behind the national norm in the first school years and which then fell even further behind during the Black child's later school career. In his paper Labov offered a devastating rebuttal of such assumptions.

Labov set out in that paper to explode the notion of verbal deprivation altogether, as being an "imaginary defect" of the ghetto child which simply "diverts attention from the real defects of our educational system". To achieve this aim, he employs several strategies. The first is to show that that the poor perform-ance in oral tests of Black children from the ghettos is due to the "hostile, threatening" atmosphere in which the tests are normally conducted, which produces "defensive, monosyllabic" verbal responses from the Black children. Labov shows that this can be changed by using unthreatening Black adults as interviewers, making the interview situation totally informal, using taboo language, etc. In these conditions the child's contribution to the interview will reveal verbal fluency of a rare order. So far so good: educationists have learned a useful lesson on how to arrange genuinely productive oral interviews.

Labov's second strategy is to prove that the Black English Vernacular (BEV) is in no way inferior to standard English as a vehicle of logical argument. At this point he uses two interviews which have become famous, one with Larry, a 15-year-old gang member, on the topic of life after death, and the other with Charles, a young, middle-class, college-educated Black adult, on the subject of belief in witchcraft. Larry is said to be a typical speaker of the Black English Vernacular as opposed to standard English: his contribution to the interview requires a full grammatical explication by Labov, and also an extensive re-ordering by Labov of Larry's arguments into logical form. The tenor of that presentation can be judged from Labov's treatment of one stage of Larry's discourse, when the interviewer takes the initiative in probing Larry's apparent assertion that if God exists, he would be white. Larry says:

> Why? I'll tell you why. 'Cause the average whitey out here got everything, you dig? And the nigger ain't got shit, y'know? Y'unnerstan'? So – um, for – in order for *that* to happen, you know it ain't no black God that's doin' that bullshit.

Labov's comment on this is typical of his approach to Black English in this paper: "No one can hear Larry's answer to this question without being convinced they they are in the presence of a skilled speaker with great 'verbal presence of mind', who can use the English language expertly for many purposes." Larry's answer, he says, is "a complex argument". The formulation is, he admits, not standard English, "but it is clear and effective even for those not familiar with the vernacular. The nearest standard English equivalent might be: 'So you know that God isn't black, because if he were, he wouldn't have arranged things like that.'" By contrast, the young middle-class Black adult speaker of standard English, Charles, is quoted as having delivered one paragraph on witchcraft which (Labov claims) shows him to be intelligent and sincere, but tending to use more moderate and tempered language than Larry, and making more effort to qualify his opinions. This endows Charles's quoted answer with what for Labov is its "primary characteristic" – its verbosity.

There we have it, then. The comparison of these two interviews is used as the central pillar supporting the key contention of Labov's article about the logic of non-standard English. So far from being deficient in logic, speakers like Larry present their argument in ways which show them to be "quick, ingenious and decisive", where standard English speakers like Charles are "enmeshed in verbiage", "simultaneously overparticular and vague", cluttering up their assertions with qualifications like "I think", with modal verbs like *may* and *might*, and humming and hawing, and using "uncommon words", so that in the end "words take the place of thoughts". The contrast is between the *precision* of the Black English Vernacular and the *empty pretension* of standard English.

With this demonstration, Labov claims to have exploded two myths: that lower-class Black children suffer any kind of linguistic deficit; and that the standard English of the middle classes and of the school system "is in itself better suited for dealing with abstract, logically complex, or hypothetical questions". Indeed, Labov takes his claim further still. This non-standard variety of English is not merely proved to be every bit as usable for the expression of logical argument as standard English, it is indeed superior: its speakers are "*more effective* narrators, reasoners and debaters" than many speakers of standard English.

There were two immediate results of Labov's paper. First, it was accepted with acclaim by linguists and by many educational theorists in Britain as well as in America. By 1979 a British textbook on language could rightly point out that the work of Labov on the Black English Vernacular "has been accepted without much criticism"; the central argument of his most famous paper had been swallowed whole, and uncritically, by the British linguistics professor Peter Trudgill, and elaborated with reference to British classrooms, in his book *Accent, Dialect and the School* (1975). This work, which became an Open University set book, was greeted by a reviewer in the *Times Educational Supplement* as "a salutary antidote to the obsession with standard English which has been a

feature of our educational system", and in it Trudgill cited Labov's
Logic of Non-standard English as "essential reading". Another
popular textbook of the later 1970s on language and education put
this paper at the top of its list of 'recommended reading', accompanied by the comment "A very important paper. Highly recommended." From 1972 onwards this paper was quoted widely,
unremittingly, and uncritically as if it definitively succeeded, as
Labov claimed, in demolishing for all time the notion that any
intellectual handicaps could attach to the speaking of this or
indeed any non-standard variety of English. Its case was used as
crucial support by groups in the USA promoting the school use of
the form of Black English labelled 'Ebonics' (a fusion of the terms
'ebony' and 'phonics') from 1975 onwards, in place of standard
English.*

The second immediate effect was to dethrone Bernstein and his
theories: his high academic reputation went into sudden eclipse,
and in any linguistic context the word 'deficit', or its very implication, became an index of the worst form of political incorrectness.
More than twenty years after Labov's paper, a large group of
teachers of English as a foreign language from countries like
China, the former USSR, and states in South America were
discussing at an international conference in the USA the difficulties of having to make use in their countries of teachers of English
(in some systems they were forcibly 'converted' ex-teachers of
Russian) whose own knowledge of English was seriously limited.
Several of the discussants used the term 'deficit' to describe their
colleagues' dangerously inadequate use of English. Up jumped
two white American professors, in a knee-jerk reaction, to protest
against the use of the word 'deficit' in this or any linguistic
context.

---

* Though by the mid-1990s both Black and white political leaders were
united in rejecting its use as the main dialect for teaching, many also pointed
to its value as a *bridge* to standard English, and to the advantages to such
pupils if all teachers understood its differences from the standard.

Looking at Labov's methods

Because Labov's case has been so enormously influential among specialists in linguistics, among educationists, and on educational policies in the USA, and has in turn had considerable influence in Britain, we must remind ourselves of the research methods which underpin these conclusions. What Labov gives us is a comparison of the edited extracts of *two* taped interviews, followed by his own interpretation and comments. No *evidence* is presented on whether the interviews, or their subjects, can be regarded as representative. The interpretation of what he claims is the essence of the argument of each speaker is entirely Labov's own, and purely subjective. Given Labov's earlier insistence on the atmosphere of the interview as being crucial to its success in eliciting behaviour that is genuinely typical of the speaker, it is odd that we are given no evidence on how far these conditions were satisfied in the case of the interview with Charles, the speaker of standard English. It is very noticeable that the development of the supposed 'logic' of Larry's brilliant argument (as interpreted for us by Labov) depends heavily on answers elicited from Larry in the course of a sustained two-way exchange in which it is the interviewer who opens up a number of key stages of the argument. But in the interview with the standard English speaker, the whole of the argument attributed to Charles (and analysed adversely by Labov) is a sustained and extended answer to a single question from the interviewer, and the development of its argument does not depend on constant prompts from the interviewer. Yet it is Larry, whose 'argument' does require such prompts, who is credited with "great verbal presence of mind".

We are simply not comparing like with like. With a disingenuousness so colossal that it almost disarms, Labov at one point concedes that he is not offering systematic quantitative evidence, yet the whole of the rest of his article presupposes that his analysis of these two interviews proves his case; and indeed the whole of his attempt to assert the 'logic of non-standard English' depends on the comparison of just these two interviews. At a later stage in the article he uses his admission that these interviews are not controlled experiments as though it were some kind of merit, because this will help convince the reader that controlled experiments which have been offered in support of his *opponents'* case are misleading.

What we have seen here is a travesty of scientific method. But even if Labov had provided proof of properly conducted experiments using representative sampling techniques under controlled interview conditions, he might still have come up with evidence suggesting that, in comparison with less educated speakers of whatever variety of English, those who have experienced more education tend to indulge in longer sentences, with longer stretches of extended and unprompted explanation. He might also have found that part of this length and apparent 'verbosity' is contributed by forms such as *I think*, the use of modal verbs like *may* and *might*, and many other signs of hesitation and, above all, of the need to qualify stated opinions. Everyone knows that it is easy to be 'spontaneous', 'direct', and 'precise' in your arguments if your education has not given you a knowledge of the complexity which surrounds any of the great issues – such as the existence of the supernatural – on which there is no consensus either among the uneducated or among the world's greatest thinkers. It is those who, like Charles, are at an intermediate but advancing stage of their intellectual development who are most given to hesitation, qualification, repetition, and thus verbosity. They have enough knowledge to perceive that a bold and precise answer is open to dissection and possible ridicule, yet their intellectual maturity has not yet reached the stage where they can expound a case which acknowledges both their own opinions and their awareness of possible intellectual objections to their case, and other subtleties. A 15-year-old gang member who has turned his back on education and the things of the mind is only too ready to rush in with dogmatic statements which may merely reflect his own ignorance and prejudice.

Labov's influential article was also defective from another point of view. Crucial to its argument is its supposed demonstration of the superiority of the Black English Vernacular as a vehicle of logical argument. But in 1984 the Oxford philosopher and logician David E. Cooper, by now professor of philosophy at Durham University, subjected Labov's re-ordering of Larry's allegedly impressive logic to a devastating critique, showing that what purported to be a logical argument simply did not hold water in the way that was claimed. My own objections to Labov's findings in terms of scientific method were published in 1983, but neither they nor Cooper's in the following year served to dent the authority with which the Labov article had come to be regarded in the linguistics and educational communities, and, as we shall see later in this book, strenuous attempts were made to prevent some of these criticisms from being more widely known.

Indeed, the way in which one hitherto influential paradigm was overthrown by another, to the extent that the first fell into almost universal discredit, not by a process of extended discussion and empirical investigation but simply by the strength of an ideology, is one of the more remarkable features of the intellectual landscape of the post-1960 period. The Bernstein 'deficit' model was rejected, and dismissed as unacceptable, simply because enough established figures in linguistics declared it to be so, and their most important single piece of evidence was the famous Labov paper.

Students of mine whose attention has been drawn to possible criticisms of Labov's methodology and his concept of logic have in some cases reacted by writing as if Labov's achievement were comparable with the case of Piltdown Man, or the fraudulent Soviet geneticist Lysenko. But I think such criticism is over-severe. What Labov has demonstrated so far is highly unconvincing, but, precisely because of the 'unscientific' character of his single experiment, we cannot exclude the possibility that some other proof might be found that demonstrates the equality, or superiority, of the Black English Vernacular. Yet, as I will show, there are plenty of reasons to believe that this will not happen.

A re-examination of these issues is long overdue. The core question is how significant are the differences between standard English and other dialects. We can all agree that originally – at some point in past time – all dialects everywhere were equally fitted to be candidates to become a standard language. By a combination of fairly arbitrary factors (like geography) and more pertinent factors (political, economic, educational) one dialect emerges as the standard language, and once that takes places this dialect assumes a number of special characteristics which the others do not have. For English this took place in the fifteenth century, when changes in the language of central government records were soon followed by other changes which will be described in Chapter 5, and by a snowball effect standard English assumed functions which set it apart from other dialects. The most crucial functions are its use as the written language and in connexion with education, since the vehicle of communication and the object of transmission in schools and universities always tend to be the the standard language. It was this written language which developed the massive vocabulary which is a distinctive feature of major languages like English: written languages, and *a fortiori* printed ones, have special power to perpetuate new linguistic forms beyond the lifetime of individual speakers.

The advent of mass education extended access to standard English to every corner of the kingdom, and schools were rightly perceived by nineteenth-century observers as a steam-roller which threatened to obliterate local dialects. Why, then, did this not happen completely, even when assisted by the new mass media of a standard-English popular press, and then from the 1920s and 1930s onwards by radio and television? Given the huge power and influence of these institutions, why did – why *do* – non-standard dialects and their distinctive grammatical and other uses, often strongly stigmatised by teachers, by employers and others, persist in the late twentieth century, to the extent that a majority of native speakers in the UK can probably be said to be habitual domestic users of at least some non-standard spoken forms? It seems as though the remorseless processes of language standardisation hit a barrier which prevents the total eradication of certain forms of dialect (and, even more, accent) and ensures their survival, in some degree, despite the obvious advantages – in terms of social prestige, and judgments about one's own educatedness and competence – of adapting to the widely accessible standard. So why do large numbers of people cling to spoken forms which receive so many kinds of negative evaluations – adverse judgments which these speakers themselves often share?

Language and values

The starting point of our explanation must be the principle that different linguistic features, including grammar and accent, encode *systems of values*. For all speakers, the dialect and accent they use provide signals of the value system that they identify with. It was the same American sociolinguist William Labov who, in another classic paper, drew attention to systematic differences in the pronunciation of certain vowels among the inhabitants of Martha's Vineyard, an island off the coast of Massachusetts used as a holiday resort by the citizens of the adjacent New England mainland. Labov demonstrates – in this case convincingly – that the locals who use these sounds appear to do so unconsciously, but their function is to assert the fact that these speakers belong to the island, and that it is to them, rather than the outsiders, that Martha's Vineyard really 'belongs'. Similarly, many speakers of French use dialect or accent features to signal a *regional* identity, and in Britain, Scottish, Welsh and Northern Irish speakers also do this, more often with accent than dialect, and for educated speakers often with only tiny traces of a regional accent – what I have called a 'close paralect' of Received Pronunciation (RP) – and they thereby indicate some kind of 'nationalism', or ethnic or regional allegiance.

The most commonly proposed motivation has to do with the equation linking standard dialects and accents with *status* as a function of power (political and economic), and non-standard ones with *solidarity* with a local community or with a low social class, and findings in many evaluation experiments strongly support the latter, insofar as they show friendliness, humour, kind-heartedness, etc., to be stereotypical for speakers who use non-standard dialect or accent. This account is vulnerable in making use of a fairly crude concept of power which reflects Mao's famous image of power issuing from the barrel of a gun – a concept whose *coercive* (as opposed to persuasive or authoritative) connotations are inappropriate to the way the standard dialect and accent are used by many in the population without access to significant power, nor indeed enjoying significant economic privilege.

A more finely tuned account of the notion of solidarity is provided by the sociolinguist Lesley Milroy, whose analysis of *social networks* examines 'the informal social relationships contracted by an individual' as a way of explaining more precisely the patterns of non-standard usage of individuals in certain close-knit communities. By tracing observable interactive links between people, the sociolinguist is able to explore, with greater accuracy than is possible by the use of blunt sociological categories like social class, the way factors such as social cohesion in such communities operate to create, reinforce and alter individuals' speech patterns. The result provides a persuasive explanation of why and how non-standard speech forms persist in such environments, which is essentially because of the strength of individuals' identification with such communities, and the force of the coerciveness of local public opinion which sees the use of non-local forms as some kind of disloyalty to the social group. We see here the strength of an alternative value-system, which places a higher value on the feeling of community supportiveness than on membership of the mainstream society.

Another explanation of the persistence of both non-standard dialects and accents is offered by an alternative description of the two sets of values which are involved in the choice of either form. By this analysis, standard forms are the expression of a complex of values associated with being in the mainstream of society, and with educatedness, which is in its turn associated with literacy. In contrast, non-standard forms express local or regional particularism (with some of the functions of what in other contexts is called 'tribalism') and the rejection of (or dissociation from) a high regard for education. As many scholars have shown, the process of modernisation which involves urbanisation and mass education also tends to promote the establishment of widely accepted or 'mainstream' norms and values. Life in modernised societies puts an ever greater premium on qualities of occupational competence which are also increasingly tied to educatedness. Underlying a respect for educatedness is a set of attitudes towards literacy:* as the linguist David Barton has put it, "every person, adult or child, has a view of literacy, about what it is and what it can do for them, about its importance and its limitations."

Since the work of Goody, McLuhan and Ong from the 1960s, literacy as a historical phenomenon has been explored by many scholars, and though its implications have in particular respects been exaggerated, its general cognitive implications, over time, are so important as to mark it out as a catalyst which has helped to "transform human consciousness" and to open up new forms of logic and other thought processes. (We shall return to an examination of these implications in a later chapter.) Since literacy is embedded in language, standard forms of language tend to be perceived as the only appropriate vehicles for education and literacy, while non-standard forms thrive among those who have been disappointed in their own experience of formal education. Add to this a generational factor and the characteristic anti-authority phase of adolescence, and we are not surprised to find non-standard accent and dialect forms adopted (indeed learned) as

---

* The term literacy covers a wide spectrum, ranging from basic functional literacy to the most elaborate literary forms: the spectrum reflects a tendency for the less literate always to feel respect for the more advanced forms. Readers should have no serious difficulty in deciding which level of literacy is implied in any specific reference in this book.

a badge among adolescents, including Black American gang members, British teenagers in Reading, or young Blacks in London and other parts of Britain – indeed Black English speech forms are also adopted by children of other ethnic groups such as Greeks and Turks in London. Among some such peer-groups, especially males, the value system which this non-standard language encodes includes attitudes which as well as rejecting or disparaging mainstream deference to 'educatedness', are demeaning to women and glorify criminality, violence and drug use. Labov found a regular relationship between, on the one hand, peer-group membership and status, and on the other hand reading failure. We do not, of course, make the mistake of assuming that all users of such non-standard forms share these anti-social values, but it is obviously a powerful form of motivation for many such speakers, especially at a formative period in their lives.

Whereas such varieties frequently celebrate 'macho' values, many studies report that, in general, women have a stronger tendency than men to adapt their speech to the standard variety, and also to evaluate standard accents more highly. Professor Trudgill has proposed a useful distinction between *overt prestige*, which involves respect for mainstream norms, and *covert prestige*, which reflects the scale of values within a smaller social group, in which there is nevertheless a kind of respect for the mainstream forms (often perceived as 'upper-class') as being in some sense 'right'. Such conflicting motivations help explain why these close-knit communities may have to be more blatantly coercive than any school system in trying to maintain their own prescriptive norms, so that (as Milroy shows) physical violence may be invoked to discipline deviations like the use of a standard rather than local non-standard linguistic form. The Milroy research was carried out in Belfast, where loyalty to community is underpinned by, and in turn subserves, fierce sectarian allegiances.

There is the further point that research has suggested that English-speaking illiterates experience special difficulties in understanding standard English grammar – for example, they tend to interpret sentences spoken to them solely from the words which happen to come next to each other, rather than to be grammatically connected to each other – difficulties which they share with very young children, the hearing-impaired, and those who have lost their power of speech through brain damage. This facet of illiteracy contributes further to the difficulty of expecting equal respect for the forms of language associated respectively with illiterates and with literate people.

Literacy and educatedness

It appears, then, that standard English is perceived by all – and resisted by some – as the language of literacy and of educatedness. But does it follow that the vast lexical riches of standard English, and indeed its distinctive grammatical forms, are not available to dialect speakers? Why not just incorporate the vocabulary and grammatical forms of standard English into dialect? The notion of congruence, which we examined in the previous chapter, is a clue. The educationist David Corson has shown, first, that a high proportion of the words used in the specialist discourse of the main disciplines of the school and university curriculum are based on classical Latin or Greek roots. Family background gives the children of more educated parents distinct advantages in handling these, simply from the way they tend to speak and the things they tend to read, and quite apart from any specific grounding in a classical education. Peer group and home pressures may actually serve to discourage use of such words by working-class children – a use which is perceived as incongruous, even though these specialist words are not just highbrow synonyms for ordinary words. Corson analysed the use by groups of schoolchildren of key words typically used in seven semantic fields which are proposed by education professor Paul Hirst as being central to modern knowledge, of which 90 per cent happened to be of Greek or Latin origin. Compared with their peers, poorer working-class children are not disposed to use specialist Graeco-Latin words widely in any of the

I am not sure congruence is the operative impulse. I think genuineness (being true to who one is) operates in retaining one's accent + dialect. The "upper circles" have no such division of loyalty.

four contexts examined in these academic studies; differences in active vocabularies are very pronounced by age 15. In the resistance to the use of certain linguistic forms by certain social groups, what seems to be at work is an aspect of psychological reality: loyalties to a local or a generational value-system constitute a psychological barrier to the use of standard forms perceived as incongruent. This helps to explain why, in practice, Cockney-born physicists do not discuss quantum theory among themselves in Cockney grammar and idiom. It is partly because the incorporation of the specialist terminology into their dialect is perceived as not congruent, and also because for dialects to be used for such very different functions is to risk losing their *raison d'être*, which is the communication of a value-system in which high-falutin' intellectual discussion is inappropriate.

yes

That non-standard speakers may encounter difficulties in handling the standard English grammar on which schools operate is illustrated by an example from my own teaching experience in a largely working-class grammar school around 1960, before any of us had ever heard of Bernstein. A senior colleague, fresh from marking a huge pile of pupils' work, declared in the staff-room his conclusion that in many homes in our catchment area children were unused to forming sentences using the word 'although'. I explored this hypothesis informally and found it plausible that many of our pupils were unfamiliar, from their own background, with certain grammatical constructions such as concessive clauses, or the future perfect tense.

In another essay published elsewhere, I have made a comparison between standard and non-standard dialects and listed twenty characteristic functions which distinguish the two. Here I will summarise a few of these. First, standard languages are multifunctional, whereas dialects tend to serve limited functions. Secondly, among the most important functions of standard are as the language of writing and of formal education and of the processing of all the forms of information required in a modernised society. Thus it acquires its third function, as the carrier of a far

Sartre's distinction between pre-reflective (direct) experience, and reflective (conscious awareness & evaluation) may be useful here to differentiate non-standard from standard.

greater range of abstract meanings, and with a vaster overall vocabulary. Fourthly, standard is codified (i.e., its rules are formally set down), whereas non-standard is uncodified, enabling the former to be formally taught and learned, whereas non-standard is not in practice available to be formally learned. Fifthly, this makes standard inclusive and open, whereas non-standard is *exclusive* and closed, the language of narrow particularism – the ghetto, the in-group. Sixthly, standard has, to a noticeable extent, the capacity to be regulated so to restrain undesired tendencies such as racism or sexism, whereas non-standard has little such capacity.

Yet another feature of non-standard forms of English causes difficulty: their relative instability, compared with standard English whose forms are kept in check by measures which include mechanisms for 'codification'. The term 'dialect' in a country like Britain covers a huge range of variation. There are parts of Britain – for example in County Durham or Northumberland, and perhaps also further north along the east coast and deep into Scotland – where dialect differences are so distinctive that a resident of one village who visits the adjoining one may be instantly identifiable as an 'outsider'. In parts of Yorkshire (and adjoining Derbyshire and Nottinghamshire), Lancashire and the West Country, for example, dialects with a wide range of distinctive grammar and vocabulary are used in almost every informal encounter of daily life. By contrast, large numbers of speakers of non-standard English all over Britain use a fairly small proportion of fragmentary forms – usually grammatical forms rather than special vocabulary – which are the scattered shards of the once proud regional dialects which competed, centuries ago, to become standard English. They are in many cases less regional than social dialects, whose only defining characteristic is that they are typical of speakers with least formal education. These 'ghost' dialects (or residual 'sociolects') are typified, not by any riches of local vocabulary, but by about a dozen kinds of grammatical difference illustrated by *he ain't the one what done it so nice*, or *we was over by them trees*, etc. and by the absence of some of the more sophisticated grammatical options available in standard English.

Even with the more 'complete' varieties of dialect there are great difficulties of identification. For example, it might be thought, from the proliferation of books on the 'Yorkshire' dialect and the claims of its supporters, that there existed for this identifiable geographical area a 'Yorkshire English' which is distinctive in respect of certain chunks of its vocabulary. But, as scholars at Leeds University have found, when correlating 12 items of 'Yorkshire' vocabulary with 34 'Yorkshire' locations, "no one location produced the complete set of items, only two locations shared the same subset, and some locations had no shared items at all". As Cambridge's Dr Sylvia Adamson has commented, "So how are we to define 'Yorkshire' as a stable and coherent entity?"* Even greater problems exist with 'ghost' dialects, the non-standard grammatical forms heard among the residents of amorphous urban agglomerations all over Britain.

Standard English: quality and functions

Several different linguists have been credited with the original observation that "a standard language is a dialect with an army and a navy". This statement has more wit than truth, since it implies that, in the last analysis, standard languages have greater authority in society than non-standard dialects essentially because of the application of brute force. We have seen that this is not so: standard English, for example, has a whole range of features, qualitative (for example, facilitating various cognitive processes) and functional; the full range of the intellectual implications of using it has not yet been fully explored, and this question deserves to be reopened, once we have broken down the taboo on the discussion

---

*The nineteenth-century poet William Barnes tried to popularise the literary use of the Dorset dialect, but it showed itself to be notoriously unstable. "The first difficulty," a modern editor of his work has written, "is deciding what the Dorset dialect is."

of 'deficit' which settled upon this topic following Labov's 1972 article.

At present, we do not know for sure what consequences there might be for the intellectual progress of a pupil in Britain who spoke a non-standard variety of English, though it has been pointed out that difficulties can arise for such speakers in the early stages of learning to read, from the greater mismatch between their pronunciation system and the orthography of standard English. There is a clearly established correspondence between a child's ability to learn to read and write, and his linguistic ability, but we just do not know how far that correspondence may be adversely affected by the child's speaking a non-standard dialect.

But some things we do know: for example, that the whole of our educational system, as it is at present constituted, presupposes the ability to handle standard English. This is the variety of English used by teachers themselves and it is the one in relation to which they tend, rightly or wrongly, to make judgments about their pupils. Among innumerable powerful pressures in this direction are the public examination system, the fact that all textbooks are written in standard English, and the general point, from which it seems impossible to escape, that there is a long-standing and now overwhelming association, right across British society, between the use of the grammar, vocabulary and idioms of standard English, and the concept of 'educatedness'.

Some of the linguistic experts whose statements we have examined would wish to challenge this – to dispute, not the fact that this *is* so, but that it *should be* so. They advocate the use of dialects and creoles in public examinations such as GCSE and 'A' levels and for university degrees. Professor Peter Trudgill, for example, has claimed that a high-level discussion of the poetry of Keats, written in a non-standard dialect, is *just as good* as one written in standard English. This point is also made by David Sutcliffe, whose study of the varieties of Jamaican patois spoken in Britain likewise presupposes the unanimous agreement among linguists about all languages and dialects being equally good (see above,

page 5). In order to demonstrate that Jamaican creole is, like any
other non-standard variety of English, capable of conveying the
same nuances, and of entering into the same degree of abstraction,
as standard English, Sutcliffe shows how an academic thesis presented for a Master's degree at a British university could be written
in Jamaican creole. Few readers of this book will understand the
whole extract, but a few lines from it will illustrate some of its
features:

> Bika demya pikni naa du gud iina skuul, rait?
>
> Bot wi kyaan se fi-dem langwij du dat-de. Wi kyaan se a hou
> di wod-dem komin an di piipl-dem yuusin dem fi stailin an dis
> an dat mek dem chupid. But eniwie disya aagument gat tuu
> said, yu nuo, Bernstein-dem main gi dem se fi-wi langwij
> mashop, jyaan giud fi wi edyukieshan. Baratz an Labov an
> Stewart an Shuy se i no mashop i dis difran. A dis bika dem no
> taak laik fi-dem tiicha mekin plenti blak pikni kyaan gud iina
> skuul.

To anyone conversant with Jamaican creole this rendition is
charming, but it also reveals a number of limitations that are
involved in using this dialect for this academic function. One of
the advantages of standard English is its range of styles, from the
most colloquial (and slangy) to the most stiffly formal.* This
passage exposes the apparently very limited stylistic register of this
dialect: the use of forms of 'sympathetic circularity' as in *rait?* and
yu nuo (you know), which are characteristic of colloquial speech
rather than of academic writing. Most speakers of this dialect
would regard it as 'incongruent' to discuss technical linguistic
ideas in this way. There is a further difficulty, in that like many
non-standard dialects, many of its usages, both pronunciation

---

* Textbooks indicate this range of style, from the most formal to the least
formal, by labels such as Poetic, Formal, Neutral, Colloquial, Vulgar, and
illustrate 'Poetic' by the line *Anon the damsel waxed wroth*, which in 'Vulgar'
becomes *In a jiffy the chick got good and sore*. The 'neutral' form would be *At
once the girl became angry*.

forms and grammatical uses, resemble those of small children or the least educated (*dis an dat; mek dem chupid*), and, however admirable the speaker, her or his language may be devalued when it is sounds like baby-talk or appears in any other way incompatible with educatedness. It is noteworthy that Caribbean and Black American universities do not normally use such forms of Black English as the main vehicle for their teaching, for the very good reason that graduates who could only handle this dialect might find few chances of employment.

Barbara Jordan was in 1972 the first Black woman from the the American South to win a seat in Congress since Reconstruction: in her hard-won position she became famous as "a voice of righteous authority". Her accomplishments, wrote an obituarist on her death in 1996, "defied race and gender bias and the burden of physical disability"; she was a woman who "seemed comfortably familiar, but was also majestic in her bearing and beliefs". For this reason, many Blacks looked up to her as an inspiring role model; in the words of one young Black woman's tribute: "When she spoke, she was speaking for the rights of women, Black women like me." Others said Barbara Jordan also spoke for Black men, and for all Americans who struggled with a difficult, often unfair world; and, of course, she spoke out in standard English. In fact, most public figures from the Black American community who aspire to be role models for their fellow-Blacks are conspicuous for their ability to exploit the rich resources of standard English. This applies to Jesse Jackson and Colin Powell, and no less to figures as different from each other in their message as Louis Farrakhan and the late Martin Luther King – indeed the latter's historic speech 'I have a dream' achieved its impact because it was in standard English. All this is equally true for Judge Clarence Thomas and Professor Anita Hill – though probably most of these figures are 'bilectal', that is, they could readily switch into a Black English dialect when appropriate.

As I have insisted, we cannot be sure of the intellectual consequences of speaking a non-standard dialect rather than standard English, though we can point to many obstacles which such a speaker will face in any context connected with formal education. The social consequences, however, are well known. Because of those inescapable associations which have grown up between the ability to handle standard English and the concept of 'educatedness', the non-standard speaker, whether in Britain or in North America, is put at an unfair disadvantage in any crucial encounter outside their own speech-community, and increasingly often within their speech-community as well. Since our citizens no longer live out their lives in the village, or even region, in which they grew up, they are constantly involved in exchanges – spoken or written – in which their ability to be articulate in standard English is of vital importance to them. This may be at the trivial level of ordering a meal in a restaurant or, more seriously, having to ask for credit in a shop, being stopped by a policeman or arguing with an official, voicing a grievance or making an effective complaint, giving evidence in a court of law or just generally asserting one's rights – indeed, in any situation where authority, respectability or credibility are at issue. (A relative of my wife's speaks the rich dialect of an old-established British mining community. In any encounter with officialdom when he travels round the world, he compensates for the limitations of his native dialect by the use of two strategies: he shouts, and if that fails, he swears.)

This brings us straight back to the connexion between language and power. As we have seen, standard English is often represented by its critics as the language of the power élite, and requiring children to learn it is represented as an act of oppression. The real truth is the opposite: causing children to learn standard English is an act of empowerment which will give them access to a whole world of knowledge and to an assurance of greater authority in their dealings with the world outside their own homes, in a way which is genuinely liberating. When we have grasped this, we can understand the rage of those Black parents, in both the United States and Britain, who react with passion to the efforts of linguistic theorists on both sides of the Atlantic who promote the use of dialect – including (in the US) Labov's 'Black English

Vernacular', or 'Ebonics' – in schools. There is resistance from both teachers and parents to the idea of using teaching materials which have been translated from standard English into Black English, which seems to them to reinforce forms which are unacceptable when used both by those who speak them and by the children who are exposed to them. According to radical British linguist Dr Deborah Cameron, some of Labov's bitterest opponents have been Afro-American intellectuals – "Black scholars with radical credentials" – who believe that the effect of his work on Black English will be to disadvantage inner-city children. Indeed, we note that what further increases their suspicion and hostility is that they notice that the white liberals who wish this dialect upon them go to great lengths to insulate their own children from any taint of non-standard dialect. Asked about the standard English issue in schools, African-American poet Maya Angelou said, "I think they should teach the English language, primarily." She went on to point out how fundamental standard English is in every environment, "because the language is so flexible"; it is, moreover, "the language which one needs in the market-place". As an American high-school teacher, Daniel Heller, has observed, "Language is power, and those who can enter into the political and economic conversation with skill can attain power."

But perhaps the issue is more complicated than that. Perhaps it is *inappropriate* that the knowledge, power and privileges which are accessible through standard English should be on offer to the underprivileged, whether Black or white. As we shall see in the following chapters, there are linguists and educationists who argue precisely that.

CHAPTER FOUR

Some Enemies of Standard English

*There is nothing so absurd or incredible that it has not
been asserted by one philosopher or other.*

Descartes

In this chapter we begin the examination of some of the main
currents of thought in linguistics and in education which have
contributed to the disparagement of standard English and of the
emphasis which some educationists have wanted to place on it
within the school system.

One undoubted influence has been the work of Noam
Chomsky, who has been the most powerful and influential figure
in twentieth-century linguistics, though in the past decade much
of his theory, which has itself undergone progressive and major
redefinition in the forty years since it burst upon the academic
world in 1957, has lost a great deal of its authority outside a
narrowing band of pure theorists. The aspect of Chomskyan
linguistics which most concerns us here is his distinctive view of
how children acquire language in the first place, which makes it
essentially due to the child's having inherited genetically a piece of
complex fixed mental machinery, a "set of mental tramlines programmed into our brain since birth". Thus, language capacity is
essentially inborn, and all the speech produced by the young child
is a matter of interaction between the sounds that child hears
in its environment and this innate mechanism. Moreover, in
Chomskyan theory, certain aspects of grammar and sound systems
are universal in all languages, and for Chomskyans "it is only by
assuming that a child is born with the highly restrictive principles
of universal grammar, and the predisposition to make use of them
in analysing the utterances he hears about him", that we can make
sense of the process of language learning. An important corollary

of Chomsky's theory of essentially innate linguistic capacity is the assumption that all human languages are cut to a common pattern, since they are all, of course, determined by that psychological structuring which is innate to our species.

It is easy to see how such beliefs (and they are essentially a matter of belief, rather than of empirical proof), which have become powerfully entrenched in the linguistics establishment, should have lent support to the notion that all human languages and dialects are 'equally good'. If all human societies are composed of individuals born with the same kind of programming device designed to enable them to learn to speak in ways which, whatever their apparent differences, reveal the same underlying 'universal' grammar and sound system, then qualitative judgments about different languages or dialects are as inadmissible, for many scholars in the social sciences, as are qualitative judgments about different kinds of human society or the specific social institutions which characterise them.

Sociolinguists like Labov, however, are less concerned with questions about the theoretical mechanisms by which children acquire language, than about the enormous variations among languages and dialects in the real world. Chomsky's theory does not profess to be about the real world of variant forms which real-life speakers actually use. Rather, it is entirely based on the theoretical model of the 'ideal' speaker-listener in an (imaginary) completely homogeneous speech community, of a kind which we all know exists nowhere, but which is conjured up in order to develop rules about the supposed 'underlying' grammar which every speaker possesses.

At particular points, however, Chomskyan theorists and real-world sociolinguists come together. Thus, for example, both the sociolinguist Labov and, more recently, Chomsky's psycholinguist colleague Steven Pinker in his 1994 bestseller *The Language Instinct* insist that the speakers of all non-standard dialects are "bathed in verbal stimulus from morning to night". But if we can no longer accept Labov's claim (to which it appears Pinker also subscribes) that where such language is non-standard it can never involve any 'deficit' to its speakers, then we can see that simply being 'bathed' in language may be of little help for the development of certain functions: everything depends on the quality of the language in which one is bathed.

It is worth devoting some space to Pinker's book, since it has had astonishing sales success and has achieved something of a cult following, with some reviewers daring to compare it, in its own field, with Stephen Hawking's bestselling but largely unread book on the universe (Pinker's is, at any rate, much easier to understand).

The recurrent theme of Pinker's book, stated repeatedly and emphatically, is that language is not a cultural artefact – a product of living in a particular society – but instead a biological *instinct*. Children, he says, don't have to learn the rules of grammar. Since these rules derive from 'super-rules' which are innately programmed into the mind of each child, they are acquired spontaneously by the time the child turns four, and in the next eleven years each child will also go on to acquire a vocabulary of 20,000 words without any intervention from its parents. In this sense, argues Pinker, every child of three is a genius.

What he really means is that the language *instinct* – the innate part of language, the facility for universal grammar which, following Chomsky, he presupposes – is inbuilt into every human being and does not depend upon the particular culture or language in which the individual is brought up. But his certainty about this leads leads him to jump to the next stage – the belief that all languages and dialects are equal, and that all their speakers speak them correctly. For linguists, as for the ordinary reader, these presuppositions raise some crucial problems, and his unawareness of these constitutes a major criticism of his book.

For though Pinker does not tell his readers this, in fact the Chomskyan theory of language and the 'transformational' grammar system that is based on it both presuppose, as we have seen, the existence of "an ideal speaker-listener, in a completely homo-

geneous speech community, who knows its language perfectly".
No such speaker exists, of course, in real life, and indeed the
underlying grammatical competence of each individual – the
theoretical capacity for language which is hypothesised by
Chomsky and his followers – needs to be translated into a practical
performing skill within an *actual* variety of an *actual* language in a
whole set of *real-life* situations. Since the 1960s a whole industry of
linguistics has grown up, known as sociolinguistics, which has
explored the implications of an individual's having to learn how
a hypothetical underlying theoretical knowledge of grammar
(Chomsky's 'competence') can be turned into the skills of
'performance' – knowing how (and when) to speak, according to
the often highly delicate norms of speech usage in any given community, which vary vastly even between modern societies like
Japan and the United States, and no less so between (say) Britain
or France, and an aboriginal tribe in Papua.

Pinker's account fails at two levels: he fails to explain how the
underlying capacity, the innate 'instinct' for language, translates
into actual ability to use the grammar, phonology, and vocabulary
of one specific language; and he fails to explain the relationship of
that innate ability to the acquisition of the working rules which
guide us in handling language in socially sensitive ways.

We can accept, as a working hypothesis, the notion that each
newborn child has an inherited tendency to acquire and to use
language in certain ways. What that language is, how it works,
how that language is acquired and how it is used, will each depend
upon the specific culture in which the child is brought up, and the
resulting language use is thus indeed a 'cultural artefact'. This
language which the individual has acquired will be one of a huge
variety of languages whose variations reflect history and geography, and which are not equally well adapted (or adaptable) to
fulfil all the same functions. The Chomsky/Pinker theory tells us
nothing definitive about the conditions in which the individual's
acquisition of language will be completely successful, nor about
the factors determining how language is used in real-life

situations. In their claim that all languages are 'equal', these theorists actually obscure much that can be observed about linguistic
behaviour.

The Pinker Fallacy

For Pinker, it is a short step from the Language Myth to the Pinker
Fallacy – the assumption that just as everyday language (which
may indeed be governed by an innate linguistic faculty) follows
spontaneous, not socially imposed, rules, the same is true for the
standard (written) language. Standard English is treated by Pinker
as simply another variety of language, rather than a specialised
variety which has to be learned and whose complete rules are *not*
acquired, like an ordinary mother-tongue dialect, at one's
mother's knee by the interaction of an innate language-acquisition
mechanism with whatever happens to be the speech of the home
and peer-group. Because of Pinker's insistence that language is not
the product of living in a particular society, but is instead a biological instinct, and that children are innately programmed to
acquire all the required rules of grammar spontaneously by the
time the child is three or four, he has trouble explaining the problems some children have in speaking or writing acceptable English.
If learning such rules of grammar is as instinctive as a spider's
tendency to spin its web, and if the design of syntax is coded in our
DNA, then how does it come about (he asks) that so many
speakers and writers of English are accused of committing
grammatical and other 'errors'?

  In answer to his own question, Pinker tells us that these so-called
'errors' are the 'inconsequential little decorations' invented by
faddists, and are comparable with the criteria designed for judging
the animals exhibited at cat shows. Nowhere does he tell us that
there are crucial differences between 'everyday' or 'natural'
language and a standard written language, and that the latter is
a special form representing a superimposition upon natural
language, one which develops its own structures, vocabulary,

[Margin note, left:] I have always disapproved the word instinct for the language mechanism

[Handwritten note, bottom:] Honey is not doing well with this — the language propensity is not perfect and it must depend partly on the language

styles, qualities and functions, all of which need to be specially learnt. Indeed he explicitly rejects this notion, when he follows the Language Myth in asserting that there are no meaningful differences between standard English and local dialects, claiming that therefore it is misleading to call them 'dialects'.

But at several points in his argument confusion creeps in. On one page he admits that "although language is an instinct, written language is not"; in another context he appears to concede that there is a distinction between "the ability to converse normally in everyday English" and "the ability to learn the standard written dialect in school". Elsewhere again, he notes that there are some "rare", predominantly written, grammatical constructions, that a child may not have mastered by age four. But the implications of this difference are never faced. His difficulty is compounded because he does not make it clear that while 'language' might be a biological rather than a social artefact, *a* language – i.e., any one specific language – is not, and is very much the product of a particular culture at a given point in time; and he never defines the boundaries between the two.

His failure to spell out a clear distinction between the 'natural', 'everyday', 'spontaneous' language of children and that other special variety – standard English, whose users, especially writers, require an extended period of prolonged exposure, formal instruction, and careful attention to rules – is at the root of several absurdities in Pinker's book.

For Pinker, every speaker uses the grammar of his or her dialect correctly – and (he implies) articulates distinctly, because what sounds like slurring cannot be slovenliness, since all speakers slur their speech in systematic ways. Therefore it cannot be right for a teacher to 'correct' such a speaker for their *I ain't done nothing*, or *he don't see them birds*, or their dangling participle. That would be equivalent, he says, to claiming that a group of birds are singing, or building their nests – or performing some other instinctive operation – 'incorrectly'. Just as the test of 'correctness' for bird or animal behaviour must always be 'ask the bird', so all speakers of

they are born into, just as the Standard form does
Doesn't he see a difference between speaking + writing.

To be fair, Pinker is concentrating on the issue of the propensity for language common to all, on which the acquisition of the specific language of the culture hinges. He

English must instinctively know what is correct use of the language, and employ it. He devotes a whole chapter to the demolition of *prescriptivism* – the tendency to insist on certain linguistic forms as being 'correct' – which he claims began in eighteenth-century England, and he wastes much powder and shot in attacking the fads and shibboleths which are the stock-in-trade of present-day language 'mavens', as he calls them – language 'experts', gurus, watchdogs, usually self-appointed, who lay down the law about correct English usage.

Presumably because of his neglect of the sociolinguistic literature, he is unaware of the anthropological evidence suggesting that for all languages, even in the most 'primitive' societies, there exist standards of usage and that in such societies certain individuals are considered to be better models of speech than others – though at one point Pinker is indeed forced to recognise that speakers may differ in their ability to communicate effectively; and also that grammars of different languages or dialects have degrees of complexity. When he does quote anthropological evidence, it is to point out the fact that tribal chiefs are often both gifted orators and highly polygynous (i.e., have many sexual partners) which, he says, implies a long-term evolutionary benefit to 'good' speakers of a language. The sillier and more arrogant among the popular journalist-prescriptivists are easy targets; and the earnest language-watchers whose newspaper columns try to educate readers on the historical origins of words or idiomatic phrases are dismissed by Pinker as just boring. Recurrent complaints by university teachers and by employers that young people have problems in expressing themselves grammatically, or indeed with any kind of written accuracy, are dismissed with a simple argument: the howlers quoted in support of such complaints are, he says, simply invented.

This is not the last of his surprises. At a very late stage in his argument, Pinker suddenly reveals that, despite the whole tenor of his book, he himself is a closet prescriptivist: he is *enraged*, he says, by the incorrect use of words like 'disinterested', for the very good reason that they make it difficult to communicate the useful sense he intends. And in a section which appears to violate the whole of the case he has been building up in the previous 400 pages about the need to recognise the "dignity of vernacular language" and the indistinguishability of dialects from standard English, he sets out the case for students to have intensive exposure – by "practice, instruction, and feedback" – to examples of "good" prose writing. Why? Because "expository writing requires language to express *far more complex trains of thought* than it was biologically designed to do". So written standard English *is* something crucially different from everyday English after all!

In discussing Steven Pinker's widely read book, we have touched on a number of issues which are central to the case for and against standard English. They include, in addition to linguistic equality, the question of whether standards of English usage are really declining, as they are so often said to be; the question of whether standard English is just another dialect, or instead a special one whose forms need to be specially learnt; and the whole issue of that insistence on 'correct' forms which we call prescriptivism. We will return to all these core issues again in the course of this book. At this point, however, we must briefly examine an implication of one of Pinker's most serious errors, his use of the (mistaken) assumption that every child uses his native language correctly, in order to ridicule those who would ever presume to correct or improve that use of English. Though, as we saw, he shows awareness in a few places that written standard language is not the same as a child's native language, he never explores these differences, yet they are crucial.

The influential American linguist Leonard Bloomfield wrote that children born into homes of privilege "in the way of wealth, tradition, *or education,* become native speakers of what is popularly called 'good English'" – what linguists, he says, prefer to call 'standard English'. There are, however, some linguists who claim that "it is probably not uncommon for some standard languages to have no native speakers", and standard German is cited as an example – a matter of some surprise to educated Germans. When

Oxford linguistics professor Suzanne Romaine says that standard English (of the kind that we write) is nobody's mother-tongue, we take her to mean that even that minority in the population who are born into a home where this variety is spoken have to build on that foundation by systematic instruction. Indeed, we know that every single child to whom standard English is available needs to develop its use of the multiplex semantic resources of standard – its huge vocabulary of words and phrases often with multiple meanings, its generally greater sentence complexity, its distinctive grammatical forms (which may include relativisation and passivisation), the availablity of a fuller range of styles than non-standard varieties typically have – and to do this by constant exposure to written forms, to educated speech, and to explicit teaching. How this development can be fostered among pupils, and specifically whether it is best done by teaching grammar explicitly, have been highly contentious issues among educational theorists and English teachers for several decades now, with the dominant view supporting the position that grammar cannot be explicitly taught, only 'caught' by exposure to good models. This too, is something that we must examine in closer detail in a later chapter. For the present, however, we must deal with an influential school of thought about the relevance or otherwise of standard English to the majority of schoolchildren.

A 'class' dialect?

Some linguists argue that for non-standard-speaking children to learn to use standard is wrong because standard English is *not for them*. It is not for them because standard English is a *class dialect*. Since the 1960s a number of writers, including the literary critic Raymond Williams and, in his train, a group of British linguists whose names became prominent in students' reading lists in the 1980s and 1990s, have preached the doctrine that standard English is the exclusive preserve of the upper classes. One of them, Deborah Cameron, in her 1995 book, quotes approvingly the conclusions of a school of "revisionist historians" – academics like Dick Leith (1983) and Tony Crowley (1989) who explain, she says, that standard English was "the authoritarian creation of a small and self-serving élite". For Leith, standard English was essentially created in the sixteenth century by government functionaries and small groups of literati, a term he uses to mean an exclusive and snobbish group of intellectuals, the cream of the intelligentsia. All these historical claims about the nature of standard English are examined in the next chapter, and found to be grossly misleading. But if we consider only references to the contemporary situation, we note that for the University of Southern California linguistics professor James Gee, the idea of associating standard English with "well educated people" is "a naive social belief". Another "naive social belief" for Gee is the notion that some people use language better than others; and indeed it is a commonplace among these authors to imply, as Pinker also does, that there is no such thing as sloppy or lazy speech. Anyone who suggests otherwise is considered to be using a linguistically invalid social judgment.

The concern of all these critics is to show that standard English is the property of the privileged, whereas the more important point could be argued with equal force that standard English *confers* privilege. Leith and Crowley are concerned to show that the processes at work in the history of English are still present, and continue to operate through the agency of educational institutions and the mass media, to "maintain oppressive class relations in Britain". Dr Cameron in particular attacks traditional accounts of the history of English which claim that standard English served society as a whole, whereas in fact, she says, it served the interests of a dominant social class by reinforcing their cultural, economic and social privilege. Specifically, she is angered by the statement in the 1988 Kingman Report on English teaching that standard English constitutes a great social bank on which we can all draw and to which we all contribute. This, she says firmly, "perpetrates a falsehood", since "Standard English *is, and always has been, a class variety*", and the Kingman committee's vision of national 'unity' (to which English teaching may contribute) simply means every-body subscribing to the values and attitudes of a particular class. Standard English is a form of language which "covertly represents the particular standpoint" of a homogeneous social group – *male*, *white* (indeed Anglo-Saxon), *heterosexual*, and originating from the *most privileged social class*.

That 1988 Report of the Kingman Committee on English teaching is likewise attacked by University of Washington lin-guistics professor James Tollefson (1991) for ignoring standard English's *class* basis and the fact that it is essentially associated with "hegemonic domination of society by groups having control of economic resources and political power". He further criticises its *unwarranted* assumption that participation in British society is dependent upon knowledge of standard English. He disputes the Report's assumption that standard English is 'normal': instead the standard is "the arbitrary result of domination by its speakers". Nowhere is there any consideration of whether stand-ard English has any special qualities which may benefit its speakers in fulfilling specific functions, or of what changes would be need-ed to enable non-standard varieties to fulfil those functions. Tollefson goes on to complain that making standard English cen-tral for school instruction gives *unfair advantage* to children whose home language is standard English. (If this were true, then we would all have to give attention to ways of diminishing the importance of standard English in society.) Also in America, Leon Botstein has attacked colleges and their teaching staffs for having become, like the professions, collectively dependent on their ability to "manipulate and communicate a narrow, non-common language officially regarded as legitimate and essential for most academic careers".

The 'power élite'

According to the American sociolinguist Robert St Clair (1982), standard English is used selfishly by the power élite to *deny* minorities full access to mainstream culture, and he, too, claims that the insistence on standard syntax in US schools represents an attempt to guarantee the success of those children whose home language coincides with the arbitrarily chosen dialect of the school system, i.e. standard English. The American linguistics professor Arthur Brakel (1978) says that allowing the lower classes to learn standard English was simply a mechanism by which "the power élite skimmed off the most dynamic of the underprivileged classes for membership in the leisure class", thus strengthening the élite in two ways, by adding 'new blood' and by depleting the lower classes of their most favoured members. In Britain, the linguist Dick Leith identifies the historical evolution of standard English with the manipulation of power, and predominantly with power as based on the ownership of capital: it was due to the deliberate cultivation, by a small élite, of a variety that could be regarded as *exclusive*, leading to the creation of what was essentially "a class dialect, that [was] imposed on an often resentful, and sometimes bewildered, populace". Several British linguists, including Professor Peter Trudgill, have indeed shown strong correlations between the use of specific linguistic forms and membership of specific social classes, but in all of these studies education itself is a factor, often a crucial factor, in classifying for social class, so it is virtually impossible to isolate class as an independent variable.

Professor John E. Joseph likewise explains the essentially class basis of standard English. The prestige of a standard language is an 'incidental' transfer of the prestige which attaches to quantifiable and scarce *physical or material power* – i.e., to brute strength or financial clout. Because, for Joseph, "the intrinsic qualities of language are undetectable, language is highly sensitive to prestige transfer". But the qualities of prestigious forms of language, whether labelled by linguists as intrinsic or as social, *are* detectable: ordinary people *can* judge that one variety of their own language possesses richer resources of vocabulary and grammar than another, and is better fitted to perform a wider range of functions. Joseph does not consider the possibility that the language is transferred direct from educated people whose prestige is due to their education, nor that the 'scarcity' factor attaching to standard language is due to the fact that becoming fully educated in the skills of modern knowledge is not successfully achieved by the majority, but that all respect it in others and count on being able to make use of others' such skills in some way.

Nevertheless, for Professor Joseph, individuals learn standard languages essentially in order to increase their personal standing. 'Eloquence' in the use of language, he says, almost universally functions as a *mantle* of power – the *covert* and *shady* connotations of the word 'mantle' being emphasised here. And he adds that while the fact of acquiring standard English "can aid an individual in improving personal status, on the macrocosmic level it can aid in *maintaining the overall social status quo.*" That failure to precipitate social revolution may be the ultimate crime of teachers of standard English.

Tollefson's rejection of the assumption that access to standard language is necessary for participation in a modern society was similar to Leith's judgment that "the use of [standard English] may be required in certain *prestigious* occupations, but these are *few* in number". Perhaps the most extreme example of this "standard English is *not for them*" argument was by the American linguist James Sledd, who in a famous paper in 1969 argued that the arbitrary requirement in American schools of standard English (which he called "middle-class mid-Western speech") is merely a cloak for white supremacy, and he quotes a chilling phrase to liken the process to "turning black trash into white trash". There is no point, he says, in trying by way of standard English to offer Blacks upward mobility because white power will always frustrate that. Requiring standard English of Black children is "only another mode of exploitation, another way of making blacks behave as whites would like them to". And anyway, he says, it won't work. Yet it is well known that in the days of the slave trade between West Africa and North America, measures were taken to ensure that boatloads of slaves did not all speak the same language, since linguistic diversity put them more readily at the mercy of the slavers; and Sledd appears to recognise this history when he claims that American society uses language difference in order to keep members of minority groups under control, so it seems wildly inconsistent for him now to deny access for those groups to linguistic forms which would offer them an escape from a diversity which historically has rendered them so vulnerable.

Furthermore, during the the nearly three decades since 1969 Black Americans, particularly educated Black women, have made substantial progress on a large number of indicators and especially in education, raising serious doubts about the underlying assumptions of Sledd's argument. Despite the persistence of shameful forms of racism, collectively Blacks continue to make strides in politics, in the professions and in education, that would have seemed staggering thirty years ago. On the other hand, class inequality has grown enormously since the 1970s, with Black people still vastly over-represented in the bottom fifth of the incomes table.

Some, at least, of these writers are influenced by the basic Marxist notion of social class. Non-standard English is part of the integrity and solidarity of the working class: allowing some working-class children to adopt the speech-forms of the more educated classes crucially weakens that solidarity and political power. However, as the changing economic conditions of countries like Britain have weakened the old forms of class-consciousness, Marxist theorists have argued (as we shall see in the next chapter) that where classes do not appear to exist, they must be created – manufactured – by political activity in order to help produce the conditions for a Marxist revolution. If escape routes out of the working class and into the middle class can be blocked off, for example by denying access to the speech forms associated with the mainstream of society, the process of creating an aggrieved and deprived lower class – the tinder-box to ignite the hoped-for revolution – is assisted. Others on the far left may argue simply that anything which prevents a liberal capitalist society from working should be sabotaged, since it is not 'right' that a non-socialist way of life should be seen to work. So we can see good *ideological* reasons why a number of those with a deep commitment to the political left – and several of these writers identify themselves clearly as 'socialists' – should want to denigrate standard English and curtail access to it among non-standard speakers.

The history of standard English is at the core of these controversies, which is why the next chapter is dedicated to a detailed look at that history, and at the way some of these ideological issues have influenced the way the history of standard English has been re-written.

CHAPTER FIVE Re-writing History

*It's a beautiful thing, the destruction of words . . . Don't you see
that the whole aim of Newspeak is to narrow the range of thought?*
George Orwell

This chapter deals with a group of influential writers on aspects of
the English language who, from the 1960s on, have each tried to
re-interpret the story of the origins, spread and functions of standard English. (Because we are dealing with the precise meaning of
significant terms, these pages will bear an even larger number than
usual of words or phrases which are italicised or put in quotation
marks.)

The story begins with the Cambridge don Raymond Williams
(1921–88), whose seminal books *The Long Revolution, Culture and
History, Keywords: A Vocabulary of Culture and Society* and *Marxism and Literature* achieved a very large readership and established
him as one of the most prominent left-wing thinkers of post-war
Britain, and a key figure in the history of the criticism of modern
British literature and culture.

What specifically concerns us here is Williams's account of the
rise of standard English. This is encapsulated by his statement in
Keywords (1983) that "in the nineteenth century there was the
curious case of Standard English, a selected (class-based) use taken
as an authoritative example of correctness, which, widely backed by
educational institutions, attempted to convict a majority of native
speakers of English of speaking their own language 'incorrectly'."

This conclusion had been established twenty years before, at
least to Williams's own satisfaction, by his chapter on 'The growth
of standard English' in his book *The Long Revolution* (1961). Here
he claimed that by the nineteenth century "the effort of the rising
middle class to establish its own common speech had been

achieved, and it is then that we first hear of 'Standard English', by which is meant speech". This, he claims, was a very different thing from the written standard which, he recognised, was established very much earlier. Indeed, he claims, giving it the label 'standard' – "with the implication no longer of a common but of a *model* language – represents the *full coming to consciousness* of a new concept of *class speech*". This was now no longer just "the functional convenience of a metropolitan class, but the *means and emphasis of social distinction*".

Looking at the detail on which Williams bases these conclusions, we note that Williams draws attention to changes in 'standard' (or 'received') pronunciation (RP) in the period 1775–1850, involving certain vowel sounds and the loss of post-vocalic 'r' (the 'r' which BBC newsreaders do not pronounce in words like *farm* and *cord*). These and similar changes, he says, were spread by improved communications, "but the main agency, undoubtedly, in *fixing them as class speech* was the new cult of uniformity in the public schools. It was a mixture of 'correctness', natural development, and affectation, but it became, as it were, embalmed." As a result, he claims, there was "no longer one kind of English, or even a *useful common dialect,* but 'correct English', 'good English', 'pure English', 'standard English'". Then, with the spread of education mainly under the direction of the middle class, this attitude spread from being "simply a class distinction" to the stage where "it was possible to identify the making of these *new sounds* with being educated, and thousands of teachers and learners, from poor homes, became ashamed of the speech of their fathers".

There are at least two crucial defects in Raymond Williams's account. First, it is simply not true that standard English, as an identifiable variety which carried the prestige which caused it to be taken as a model, came into being in the nineteenth century – as we shall see when we return to investigate the detailed facts on this, later in this chapter. Secondly, Williams has confused the form of standard *accent* which indeed became widely established among the English middle classes around the middle of the nineteenth century, with the *spoken standard dialect*, i.e., standard English in its spoken form, which had long been accessible to people with any degree of education and continued to be so throughout this period, though the degree of local *accent* in which they spoke it may have modified. In yet a further respect Williams's account is unsatisfactory, if one is unable to accept his supposition, stated in his book, that the widespread perceptions among quite ordinary people in nineteenth-century Britain that there existed some form of national identity or national 'unity' was simply a 'silly' ideal, in the light of the class divisions which, for a Marxist, are the only way of truly understanding society.

'There is no standard English'

We must next consider the views of Roy Harris, who was professor first of Romance languages, and then from 1978 of general linguistics, at Oxford; Professor Harris is widely respected among linguists (other than supporters of Chomsky, of whom he has been a severe critic), and his views on standard English are seen by some as a kind of aberration. In public utterances in the early 1980s, Professor Harris disputed the notion that a 'standard English' existed, though at that stage he gave no developed arguments in support of his contention. Some linguists may have assumed that he shared the rather extreme view of an American linguist C. J. N. Bailey, who has argued that although the concept of a standard language – which he takes to mean "a single (i.e., invariant for age, style, etc.), classless language form imposed by authority as a requirement for every school child to get familiar with and be able to use on call"– is found in many European countries, it is found in no English-speaking country. This is because there are "no generally accepted authorities to create language norms" in any English-speaking country. Bailey's verdict ignores more than two hundred years of strong prescriptive tradition in the way English has been taught in all such countries, quite apart from the dictionaries, grammar books and other texts, and the manuals of correct usage and style, which abound in our own day.

It is perfectly true that, with or without an accepted authority such as the French Academy, no language is ever *completely* standardised, but this does not prevent people from perceiving the existence of a standard form of British English even if they cannot describe absolutely all its forms or rules. We should not fall into the trap of denying the existence of a 'standard' version of anything simply because in its purest firm it is difficult to define or measure. It is, after all, many years since Sir Karl Popper, and before him, another philosopher of science, Tarski, demonstrated the nature of 'regulative ideas' which do not correspond to precise measurement: even the most exact measurement in millionths of a centimetre is likely to be inexact, and the fact that a millionth of a centimetre is unlikely to be met with in practical human experience does not invalidate the *concept* of a millionth of a centimetre.

But in his book *The Language Machine* (1987) and in an essay published in the following year, Professor Harris goes beyond C. J. N. Bailey in doubting the existence of standard English: he queries whether it is possible "to determine what standard usage is, either in the English or any other linguistic community". In a chapter explicitly about "the *myth* of standard English", Harris claims that before the publication of the famous multi-volume *Oxford English Dictionary* from 1882 onwards, "hardly anyone had heard of standard English at all", and he ridicules the belief, which was held by all the members of the team of scholars who planned the *OED* in the 1850s and 1860s, "that a standard language had long existed in England, even if" – as those scholars may have believed – "no one had been quite sure what it included". Around 1900, he claims, there was a generally accepted 'official view' of the English language, formulated in the nineteenth century in response to the historically unprecedented social and educational demands of the previous half-century. "The central tenet of this 'official view' was that beneath the extreme diversity of English usage, both in present and in former times, there lay – contrary to superficial appearances – a single national language. This language was called standard English."

So we have the 'paradox', says Harris, that "what was, socio-linguistically, a *very restricted* form of English [was] being passed off, under the label 'standard', as an optimal form of English tran-scending mere class, geographical, individual or other differences: that is to say, as a *single national norm*, an 'English par excellence' " (emphasis added). From this false premiss, alleges Harris, the *OED*'s editor-in-chief J. A. H. Murray (a largely self-taught Scot of humble origins) proceeded to ignore "the fact that the usage of the cultural élite in the nineteenth century simply did not function as an English 'par excellence' for the majority of his fellow country-men, because *they neither spoke nor wrote it.*" For Harris, the very term *standard English* was a neologism (newly coined term) devised by the 1850s planners of the *OED* themselves. It is not just a matter of standard English being a class dialect, says Harris, it was a class dialect which, thanks to the myth created by these and other nineteenth-century linguistic scholars, "had 'become' something neologistically called 'standard English' ".

Professor Harris had never claimed to be a specialist in the his-tory of the English language, and he did not attempt, in his short treatment of the 'standard English myth' (which is indeed almost identical in the two books discussed) to provide detailed historical evidence for his contention, so it was difficult for others who were specialists in the history of English to challenge his account. Never-theless, his conclusions rapidly passed into the armoury of those who attacked the emphasis on standard English in the school system, which became a much politicised issue in the late 1980s.

The Crowley thesis

It was left to a young British academic, Dr Tony Crowley (whose views were quoted in the last chapter), to take up and develop the ideas of Raymond Williams and Roy Harris, and to provide a detailed theoretical and historical justification for them, in his book *The Politics of Discourse* (1989), published in the United States as *The Politics of Standard English*. Because of the importance which has become attached to that book, and the regularity with which it – and especially its general conclusions – are now cited, it will be useful for this chapter to examine in some detail the way he develops his argument, and to scrutinise examples of his use of evidence, the way he uses language, and the ideological presuppositions of some of that language.

In his introduction, Crowley makes clear that his book is grounded in the work of three Marxist theorists, the Frenchman Michel Foucault and two Soviet linguists, Voloshinov and Bakhtin, the combined influence of whose work gave him the "direction in which to proceed". For Foucault, language – and more generally *discourse*, by which he tends to mean the kinds of knowledge that can be discussed, and the way in which they can be discussed – are subject to a set of 'prohibitions' in a complex and unceasing process of permission and denial, "an ordering of what can be said and what not, of who can speak and who is to remain in silence". We know that there are many societies, both traditional and modern, in which speakers (especially children, and often women) have been, or are, subjected to strict rules and expectations about what they can say and when, but in countries like present-day France, Britain or America any vestiges of such 'prohibitions' are surely but a shadow of what they once were. Nevertheless, for Foucault, in *every* society the production of discourse is controlled, selected, organised and redistributed according to a certain number of procedures. Since Foucault never specifies who is doing this controlling, organising, etc., or in whose interest it is being done, there is an element of mystery – or mystification – in all this. But, says Crowley, what Foucault is really trying to point out is the way the education system in countries like Britain organises and presents the different branches of knowledge. Whereas in theory there is a presumption that schools provide open access to discourse and free choice in what learning takes place, and in what way, radical educationists reveal the essential *naivety* of such a view

DBP
general agreement over matters of language usage is comparable to the way we accept

by pointing out "the limitations that operate upon discourse and the ways in which discourse is not open, but delimited and constrained". Such radicals argue that it is often not free choice that operates, but sometimes no choice at all.

What is Crowley talking about here? Does he mean the lack of parental choice in Britain's state school system, which successive Conservative governments tried hard to remedy but without complete success? Not at all: Foucault is quoted to show that what is meant is the fact that while in theory the individual has the right of access to "any kind of discourse", in fact what they get "follows the well-trodden battle-lines of social conflict", which simply "reflects the *distribution of knowledge and power* which is characteristic of modern societies more generally" – a distribution "according to the principles of exclusion and inequality".

Our immediate response is that though there is still much inequality in our educational system, there is vastly more equality now than there was (say) fifty years ago; and also that equality of opportunity seems to many people a more valid objective than the expectation of full social equality. In respect of language as a fundamental form of 'discourse', it is relevant to ask whether the ideal of equality (or equality of opportunity) is likely to be better served by offering access to standard English or by denying it. As to the 'principle of exclusion', we have already seen (Chapter 3) that it is standard forms of language which are the more open, and it is the non-standard varieties which operate to exclude.

V. L. Voloshinov, writing at the height of Stalin's reign of terror, provided Dr Crowley with two main concepts. The first, deriving from the Marxist notion of class struggle, is that the ruling class always strives to remove from the various aspects of social life (and the 'discourse' by which they are discussed) the knowledge of the social and historical processes from which those aspects and institutions, according to Marxist analysis, have actually derived; and secondly that the ruling class does this by pretending that those aspects of life – and the discourse surrounding them – are "natural and given", whereas (it is implied) Marxists

language itself -- as given, but subject to personal
test by individuals after acquisition

alone understand the underlying class conflicts whence they really derive.

A fundamental concept for the Soviet theorist M. M. Bakhtin was that language is so extensively the subject of stratification by these social forces that the very notion of "a language" – a single and unified language – must be accounted a fiction reflecting the "active process of repression" which produced it. A fiction, because in reality language is heterogeneous "from top to bottom", with a vast number of different forms reflecting the past and the present, and differing "socio-ideological groups", all co-existing in a state of constant tension. This tension is related to the fact that centrifugal forces are constantly operating to produce new languages, in opposition to the centripetal forces of language which attempt to unify and centralise by processes of repression. The "unitary" language, which can be identified in such forms as the literary language, and in 'correct language', imposes itself on the new forms, forcing limits to their growth, exercising discipline on them, and finally by acts of violence and repression brings about the victory of one reigning language or dialect, the "enslavement" of the other varieties, and the "incorporation of barbarian and lower social-class strata into a unitary language of culture and truth" as the lowest rungs of a hierarchy whose top place is reserved for the unchallengeable "authoritative word".

If we applied these ideas to the history of Marxist regimes in, say, the Soviet Union, in Eastern Europe, in China, Vietnam, Kampuchea or North Korea, we might well imagine them to be a parable of what happened to the freedom of discourse under these regimes, a grisly process of repression of all freedom of speech, culminating with the enthronement of the unchallengeable 'authoritative word' of the Party. But when applied to the story of how standard languages came into being in modern states, Bakhtin's analysis is, at least for the student not yet firmly committed to the Marxist dialectic, full of awkward questions. Anyone acquainted with the history of English or other major languages will want to object that Bakhtin's is not an adequate account of the

pattern by which some languages or dialects achieve their dominance: in particular, centrifugal forces are not, at all stages of this
process, significant and recurrent elements, once the standard
form of a language has become established and harnessed to the
mass media; and acts of violence and of oppression are often
absent from the history of the process. Instead, it does seem to be
possible, in contrast to what Voloshinov claimed, to see at work
the operation of "natural" and "given" rules, which we may
indeed regard as *inherent* or *intrinsic* or even *inevitable* in view of
the way all languages appear to respond to functional demands
made of them in any social situation, and which do not necessarily
conform to those rules laid down for all time by Karl Marx.

Nevertheless, it is explicitly within this pattern of Marxist
thought that Crowley sets out to re-write the 'facts' of the history
of standard English. He claims that he is not writing a 'slavish'
account designed to vindicate that theoretical foundation, and
that the 'bleakness' of his account is compensated for by the fact
that it is accurate, by which he means more accurate than traditional accounts. Less committed readers must obviously feel free
to decide for themselves how far he has escaped the slavery of the
ideological system which inspired him, and how much his
re-writing of history renders his account more accurate.

Crowley devotes the whole of an early chapter to the writings of
Richard Trench, who (though he does not tell his readers this)
became Anglican Archbishop of Dublin in 1864. Crowley claims to
demonstrate "the highly political concerns of much of mid-
nineteenth-century work on language in Britain" and that "across
a number of different fields, ranging from theology to the construction of the national identity and social unity, work on the
English language was used to gain specific ends". The idea that
people in that period who did work on the English language *used
their work for specific ends* is to most people a totally unsurprising
notion, and indeed it would have been amazing if they had not
done so; the comment only acquires a tincture of meaning in the
context of the preceding comment about the "highly political

concerns" which were around at that time, and Crowley's main point therefore must be to encourage the reader to wonder if these "specific ends" were in some way disreputable or at least suspect.

Since he specifically mentions theology, it is noteworthy that he discusses no major theological scholar of the nineteenth century, nor indeed any of the great theological debates of the period. Trench himself, a minor figure in terms of his theological output or influence, was however author of several works on the English language in the 1850s, and in his view that language was "a moral barometer", capable of being manipulated for evil purposes, he was in some ways a forerunner of George Orwell. Trench and others are considered as having regarded language as (in Crowley's words) "the political unconscious of the nation" because he (like Edmund Burke sixty years before) drew attention to the cultural continuity of the nation – a partnership between past, present and future generations – which, for Trench and other contemporaries, was expressed and reflected in the English language. Such notions of language and national identity, expressed by De Quincey twenty years before, give Crowley an excuse to imply that one of Trench's books on language, published in 1855 during the Crimean War, was designed to drum up an artificial feeling of patriotism. Other writers on English who in the next fifty years celebrated the undoubted fact of the increasing use of the language world-wide are credited by Dr Crowley with "announcing the global encirclement enacted by the imperialists".

But the association of a national language with the idea of the nation-state is in no way special to Britain. Language was part of the national heritage strenuously appealed to by the dictionary-maker Noah Webster and many of his contemporary writers at the time of American independence, and by Abraham Lincoln's contemporaries when the unity of the federation was threatened. The nineteenth century saw the emergence of many new states, especially in Europe, in which a sense of national identity was based on language. In many states, a standard national language came to be emphasised in competition with a mass of local dialects and minority languages. Comparison with some of these many examples would have been an appropriate commentary on what Crowley is trying to claim for Archbishop Trench, but apart from a brief reference to the French philosopher Renan, and a few lines on the nineteenth-century creation of a national literary language for newly unified Italy, this great area of relevant literature is neglected: we shall return to a consideration of the highly relevant example of France later in this chapter. Yet even that passing mention of Italy is instructive, since it shows how the development of a modern standard form of the Italian language was welcomed by the Marxist theorist Antonio Gramsci, on the grounds that its absence had created friction "particularly among the popular masses". But in Britain, says Crowley, the comparable standard form of English was "not a form around which *radical struggle* was to be focused, though it was *promulgated and acknowledged in various cultural modes for specific ends*". What that last clause means I simply do not know, but I do understand the point that because standard English never became a rallying point for radical struggle, it is has become disreputable for those who are committed to the concept of the class war.

The Crimean War has yet more to account for. The fact that Oxford professor Max Müller was asked by an official from an unidentified government department to write a phrase-book in the languages of the Crimean region for the assistance of British officers, demonstrates for Crowley that the study of language in England was "markedly influenced by political exigencies". But if he had wanted to show that there is a connexion between the particular languages which were studied in Britain in the nineteenth century – or in any period for that matter – he could have found a thousand more compelling examples. The imperial expansion of Britain had already led directly to major advances in the study of Sanskrit and other ancient Indian languages, and until the decline of that Empire after 1945, hundreds of indigenous languages were described and codified in response to the demands of an imperial system which brought British forms of government,

law and schooling to their speakers. Oriental languages were introduced at Cambridge, Oxford and other universities partly as a
reflection of the realities of Britain's place in the world – why
otherwise would a sufficient number of students want to study
them? By the same kind of process, linguistics, formerly a
Cinderella subject in the United States, was to undergo dramatic
expansion in the wake of the 'sputnik' scare which released massive
funds for an academic discipline which, especially in its Chomskyan
form, could be represented as somehow relevant to national
defence. The social and political factors which help to determine
why one language or subject is studied in any educational system
are part of what is called the 'sociology of knowledge'. Crowley
shows little awareness of the sociology of the curriculum of
nineteenth-century schools or universities, into which he is trying
to fit his theories. The question is not *whether* factors that are not
strictly linguistic helped to promote the study of language, but
rather what effect these factors had on the particular language
itself, and on the way it was taught.

More seriously, Trench is taken to task for that fact that in his
writings on the English language, when exploiting notions of
'Englishness', patriotism, and pride in the language, he emphasised an identity or commonality amongst its speakers rather
than stressing differences of economic and cultural status. But this
criticism is, of course, a glaring anachronism: to expect a leading
British churchman to base his argument in the 1850s upon an
assumed social or economic equality, in a nation in which vast
differences of rank and wealth were taken for granted by most
people, and certainly by most educated people, is as realistic as to
expect him to assume a world based on supersonic flight, television or the information highway. A present-day Tory MP has
assumptions about social and economic equality which are
closer to Dr Crowley's than to Archbishop Trench's. Critics like
Professor Terry Eagleton use the word 'presentism' for this kind of
inappropriate projection back into the past of the political and
other concerns of the present.

In one sense, Crowley is correct in drawing attention, in a way he does not intend, to an aspect of the "highly political concerns of much mid-nineteenth-century work on language", for the study of English language and literature came to be regarded, in the second half of that century, as appropriate subjects to be taught to two groups in the population hitherto grossly under-represented in the education system: women, and those working-class adults for whom university extensions and other agencies were established to cater. If Trench's work did in fact contribute to this, then the Archbishop must be given more credit than Crowley allows for his contribution to social and economic equality.

However, Crowley is concerned to show how, in the middle of the nineteenth century, " 'the history of the language' as a specific field of knowledge [was] distinct of course from the history of the language", which might in turn be different from "the historical becoming of language", but in any case led to "the rise to rapid hegemony of the new discourse". Background historical developments included new discourses of reform, "and coetaneous with that shift was the recession of Chartism", though "that is not to say, of course, that the undemocratic constitution of the British social formation was fundamentally altered in this period since political, cultural and economic power was still exclusively exercised".

Having thus established his own credentials for the exact and lucid use of language, Crowley goes on to elaborate the central theme of his book, his contention that the terms 'standard language' and 'standard English', in their current senses which relate to an "*authorised, delimited and unitary literary* form of the language", are essentially the product of the way these terms were used by the (mostly unidentified) proposers of what became known as the *Oxford English Dictionary*, and among the members of Britain's Philological Society generally, in 1850s and 1860s. And indeed, as he says, the earliest citation given for 'standard language' in the 1933 supplement of *OED* was from that society's original *Proposal* for the compilation of such a dictionary, in the year 1858.

But Crowley's extended account of this is doubly wrong. First, the actual term 'standard English' had already been used two decades before by a writer in the *Quarterly Review* in 1836, who followed up that use by pointing out that there was general agreement in labelling our *standard form of speech* as the English language, whereas all provincial deviations from it were to be termed *dialects*. In the same year Benjamin Smart (1786–1872), a private tutor and prolific writer on aspects of the English language, wrote in middle age – again, this was two decades before the deliberations of the *OED* planners – of "the common standard dialect", that of the educated, whose non-local character he compared with other dialects. By 1850 we find a writer of educational texts comparing "dialect" with "standard modes of speech". Moreover, as Professor R. W. Bailey has pointed out in criticism of Raymond Williams's less detailed account, "far from being a nineteenth-century image, standard was applied to a prestige variety of a language as early as 1711, and then the term merely codified a notion already old". This, then, is Crowley's second error: to imagine that the concept only emerged when the present-day word for that concept had begun to come into general use. In fact, all the ingredients of *authorised*, *delimited*, *unitary* and *literary* had played their parts in the widely established concept of a 'standard English' for which that term was not yet used – though speakers had several other words for it – for a period of possibly *four hundred years* before the dates Dr Crowley claims for its emergence.

How it really happened

In order to appreciate the enormity of the misinterpretation that is involved here, we need to remind ourselves of the main outlines of the conventional account of the development of standard English, especially as the finer detail of its origins has been revealed by scholars over the past three decades or so. Out of a great diversity of local standards, a national standard emerged in the fifteenth century. This was not Chaucer's English, which may be taken as representative of 'London English' around 1400, nor was it close to two other types of Middle English previous to Chaucer which may have had a claim to being, in some way, earlier forms of a national standard. Following the replacement of Latin by English in the 1420s as the language of central government records, and the centralisation of these documents in the chancery at Westminster, there developed, within a few years, a 'chancery' type of English, used in day-to-day letters and other government documents, which was distinguished from those earlier potential standards by the presence of what dialectologists recognise as 'central Midland' features (especially Bedfordshire, Northamptonshire and Leicestershire). These writers began by trying to regularise spellings, and by the 1440s and 1450s had achieved a fair degree of regularisation in the direction of those forms which have since become standard (though the full standardisation of spelling was, of course, not achieved for many centuries more). A degree of standardisation of grammar and vocabulary followed, so that from 1450 onwards it becomes almost impossible in literary works, except in distinctly northern texts, to determine with any precision the region in which a given work was written, and in correspondence and local records there was a widespread tendency to conform to this new London standard. Thus, by the time Caxton introduced printing into England in 1476 he had available to him an obvious vehicle, a standard written English, for use in his numerous translations and other printed works which then popularised this form in every corner of the land. The influence of London speech on the emergence of what was coming to be thought of as a standard way of *pronouncing* English was much slower, but even so, it is clear that by the first half of the sixteenth century "there was already a clear idea that there was a correct way of pronouncing English, that some forms of speech had already become a criterion of good birth and education, and that it was deliberately fostered and taught".

For several centuries more, the mass of the population would continue to speak their local dialects with, of course, their own distinctive accents, though the distinctiveness of the grammar, vocabulary and idiom of these dialects would slowly decrease under the increasingly powerful influence of standard English. At the other end of the spectrum, a small percentage of the population would speak and write the grammar and vocabulary of standard English, and speak it with a standard accent (much later to be labelled 'received pronunciation', RP). And an ever-increasing number of others would speak and write standard English, while using in their speech a local accent which might be nearly as strong as that of a pure dialect speaker, but which might also be very close to the standard accent, or more probably somewhere in between.

There was also the complication that by the seventeenth century an aristocratic dialect (or 'hyperlect', comparable with the 'U/non-U' forms discussed in the 1950s), with its own distinctive grammatical forms (like *it don't* and *ain't it?*) and vocabulary and accent, was spoken by some members of the nobility and gentry – Harold Macmillan, prime minister in the 1960s, retained traces of this – and there were also some who spoke with the vocabulary and grammar of standard English but with the *accent* of the hyperlect, i.e., a special form rather like the 'posh' version of RP heard in our own day, especially from older royalty and aristocratic figures. And it was quite common until the 1870s for members of the aristocracy and gentry living in the provinces to speak standard spoken English (in grammar and vocabulary) but with obvious traces of a local accent.

The usages of standard English, which were thus available to be spoken and written, constituted an identifiable standard English which was regarded by the middle of the sixteenth century as the common dialect of educated people, and the model to be taught to children and foreigners, so becoming "a matter of precept as well as practice". The development of a rich literature confirmed that the once despised English language was fit to perform the functions of Latin and French which, for most uses, it had supplanted. From the middle of the sixteenth century onwards for perhaps two hundred years, the progress of this standard English was characterised by a protracted process of assimilation of foreign elements, especially Latin vocabulary, and aspects of a highly ornamental style, in response to the reception of ideas and texts associated with the Renaissance. Estimates vary between 10,000 and 20,000 for the number of new words, mostly from Latin, that entered the English language between 1500 and 1650. The early, and bitterest, phase of the conflict this generated about the appropriateness of such foreign usages in English was nicknamed the 'inkhorn controversy'. The point of this qualification is therefore to affirm that a standard variety of English, both spoken and written, was recognised as existing before the end of the sixteenth century, in the sense of an *authorised*, *delimited* and *unitary* standard, but that recognition of the 'unitary' character of that standard English – i.e., that it involved an essential unity of language – continued to be a matter of contention for a further two centuries. However, in both its rival characters, a more literary one dominated by Latinate forms, and the other one associated more with everyday uses and having a higher proportion of Germanic (i.e., Anglo-Saxon) vocabulary, it was recognised as being clearly distinguishable from all the regional dialects around it.

The key points of distinction between this standard English and its potential rivals – the regional dialects – lay in the groups who were perceived as its typical users, and crucially whether they were metropolitan or provincial, educated or illiterate. Commentators from the sixteenth century onwards were quite clear as to the general profile of the speaker and writer of the approved and admired forms: such users tended to be associated with London, initially with the Court, and later, by extension, to educated groups who participated in the life of the nation's cultural capital, and a further extension was made to include the university towns of Cambridge and Oxford, both within sixty miles of London. Speakers of dialects other than this emergent standard were stigmatised as 'provincial', with its connotations of unsophisticated, rustic, ignorant, vulgar, unfashionable (in the sense of being unworthy of imitation), and were often also referred to as 'barbarous'. These connotations continued to be consistently associated with dialect speakers throughout the seventeenth and eighteenth centuries: the eighteenth century was to be the golden age of 'prescriptivism', when a mass of commentators and teachers attempted to reform the language to purge it of just these 'barbarous' non-standard elements. The most powerful motive for this process of standardising both written and spoken English was the great increase in geographical and social mobility, and the economic opportunities such mobility both offered and reflected.

It is quite true that the term 'standard English', whatever the exact date of its first occurrence, did not pass into general, and generally accepted, use and thus become the 'standard' term for this form of spoken and written English, until some point in the nineteenth century. But earlier generations were quite clear about the concept and had a variety of names for it, some of which changed in popularity between the sixteenth and the nineteenth centuries. One early term was 'the King's English', used by Thomas Wilson in 1553 (and later also by Shakespeare in *Merry Wives*, 1598) to indicate a normative and thus authoritative form of English, not necessarily assumed to be the one actually spoken by the sovereign of the day (there may even have been a Queen on the throne at the moment Wilson wrote, and there certainly was when Shakespeare did) but following a contemporary formula which attached the word *King's* to items to indicate an authentic standard. And in the reign of Elizabeth those who referred to *the Queen's English* meant the English language under the guardianship of the Queen, hence standard English.

As part of his vitriolic war of words with fellow-writer Gabriel Harvey, the Elizabethan satirist Thomas Nashe in 1592 impugned Harvey's use of language. It is not enough, wrote Nashe with forceful crudity, that about twelve years ago Harvey pissed all over his own credibility in three letters which he published, but (he went on) the man keeps on overusing out-of-date literary fads, and "*abusing the Queen's English* without pity or mercy". This was obviously intended to be a savage rebuke, but it would have been emptied of all meaning if there had not existed by that time a fairly clear idea of a 'correct English' whose norms had been violated by the man Nashe attacked.

From the middle of the sixteenth century onwards, writers on aspects of the English language, of whom a large proportion were writers of textbooks for children learning spelling, reading, grammar and composition, indicated the language on which they were commenting or in which they were teaching their pupils to write, as being 'the English tongue', or just simply 'English', or, especially from the eighteenth century onwards, 'the English language', and by all these terms they made it clear they meant the standard form. One of the very earliest, John Hart's book in 1551, offered to expose "the *unreasonable* writing of our English tongue", drawing implications "for the perfect writing thereof"; the notable educationist Richard Mulcaster's 1582 text dealt with the *right writing* of our English tongue, Simon Daines's in 1640 with "right speaking", and Owen Price's in 1668 with "right spelling and writing". But, as even Raymond Williams discovered, one of the earliest and commonest words indicating this 'standardness', and the accuracy required to attain it, was *true*. Thus the anonymous ABC for children in 1561 claimed it would enable children to *write English truly*; Peter Bales's book (1590) was "to write *true* orthography in our English tongue"; Edmund Coote's in 1596, which ran to more than 50 editions in the next century and a half, was for the "*true writing* of our English tongue"; Richard Hodges's in 1644 was "for the *true* spelling and reading of English, as also for the *true-writing* thereof". Similarly, "to read English *truly*" (John Newton, 1699), "*true* English" (Strong, 1674; B. Harris, 1679; H. Care, 1687); Anon, *Writing Scholar's Companion*, 1695; T. R., 1700; Anon, *Guide,* 1703; Anon, *Second Book,* 1704; "*true* spelling", James Ellis, 1719; "*true* spelling and writing", William Baker, 1724. William Ward's grammar of 1767 referred to "true and false English".

From an early date, several such writers were explicit in indicating the alternative forms of the language which were not considered an appropriate linguistic target for their readers. The

Leicestershire schoolmaster John Brinsley wrote his 1622 grammar book "for those of the inferior sort, and all ruder countries and places", among which he specified Ireland, Wales, and the very newly settled Virginia. Although he obviously assumed access within England to a standard English language, pupils in those other countries would need help in achieving the object "that all may speak one and the same language".

Three years before, Alexander Gill, Mulcaster's successor as headmaster of St Paul's School, and Milton's teacher, described (in Latin) the linguistic situation of England at that time as involving six dialects: a *common dialect*, northern, southern, eastern, western, and 'poetic'. Among all of these, "none of them is so flavored with barbarism as the western", he wrote; "among the country folk in the rural parts of Somerset, one can readily question whether they are even speaking English or some foreign idiom." Gill made a contrast between, on the one hand, the "corrupt" forms of the country folk who spoke these dialects, or the "murderous scum" of vagabonds and petty criminals – whose 'dialect'* was in fact no more than the cant of the criminal fraternity – and, on the other hand, the fact that "among those of gentle nature and cultivated upbringing, every place is as one in language and accent and meaning" – though in fact we know that this was not completely true for all of them, since the gentry of the provinces still spoke their standard English with some degree of local *accent*, and would continue to do so until well into the nineteenth century. John Green's *Refutation* of 1615 had expressed a similar view of the unitary character of English, but specified that, following the disruption of Old English by the Norman Conquest, "it was only of late years" that "our English tongue" had been able to "recover a common dialect again", though the way certain learned men were now using it, with all their Greek, Latin and Italian

---

* Even the underworld literature of the Elizabethan period – the tracts and ballads of the beggars, vagrants and professional thieves – was written in what is clearly identifiable as standard English, decorated with a small proportion of vocabulary items drawn from criminal 'cant' (slang).

words, was causing it to become too "refined" for "simple, vulgar people" to understand, indeed a "great mingle-mangle". The really great influx of Greek words, however, was two hundred years into the future, with the development of the terminology needed for the expansion of science after 1800.

Not all teachers were as hostile as Gill to dialect forms. For example, John White's 1701 textbook for "reading and writing true English" gave examples of "the English of our honourable ancestors, and also of our Western dialect", but the anonymous author of the 1705 text which aimed to enable pupils "to read *the whole English tongue*" (later in the page expanded to "the whole body of the English tongue") in practice restricted himself to standard English. The eighteenth century also saw a change from 'true' English as the reference for standard English, to forms such as "good language" (Wilson/Hutchinson, 1724), and, later in the century, ways to correct "bad English" (John Carter, 1773; H. Ward, 1777; A. Murray, 1785) and examples of "good and bad English" (Rhodes, 1795). Two notions now become commonplace in such eighteenth-century texts, *correct (correctness)* and *proper (propriety)*, echoing the growing social concerns of a period of greatly increased social mobility, in which to be able to speak the grammar and vocabulary of the standard dialect with an acceptable accent was to become more important than ever before.

So we find George Shelley's composition book of 1712 is about "correct English", and the concern of William Loughton's 1734 text is with "writing correctly and properly", and Daniel Turner's grammar of 1739 is for "writing the language correctly and handsomely", to "introduce the English scholar to a just notion of the propriety and beauty of the English language". The grammar book by Ann Fisher (1745), living among speakers of the distinctive dialect of the Tyneside area, deals with "speaking and writing the English language properly and correctly". Carter's dictionary of 1764 was designed to give foreigners "the true English accent", and "natives will be enabled to shake off the false and improper dialect (peculiar to any county in the kingdom) and children

will be taught to speak the language with the greatest propriety".
Writing the English language 'correctly' or 'properly and
correctly' was specified by the author of *New & Improved* 1771,
Fenning, 1771, and Pape, 1790.

Elisha Coles's 1674 text had taught the rules of spelling "according to the present proper pronunciation of the language in Oxford
and London", but, as we have seen, accent was the last aspect of
spoken English to be standardised, even within Britain and
certainly for English-speakers elsewhere. A 1766 textbook by the
Surrey schoolmaster James Buchanan aimed towards "establishing
a standard for an elegant and uniform pronunciation of the
English language, throughout the British dominions, as practised
by the most learned and polite speakers". Sheridan's *Rhetorical
Grammar* of 1781 taught "propriety of pronunciation"; two texts
in 1799 (Anon) and 1800 (Angus) taught "the most approved
mode of pronunciation", while that of Thomas Batchelor in 1809,
designed "for provincial schools", offered an analysis of "the
minute varieties [of sound] which constitute a depraved or
provincial pronunciation".

Our last category is a group of words which exploited the connotations of authority associated with royalty, and with the universality, and completeness of coverage, of standard English. Tobias
Ellis's word-list of 1670 began with the title *The English school*, but
later editions up to 1709 appeared variously as The *royal* English
school, or The *true royal* English school. Greenwood's *Royal
English Grammar* appeared in 1737, and in 1754 Farro's *Royal
Universal Grammar and Vocabulary* claimed to offer a 'digestion'
of the entire English language into parts of speech. We note
Fenning's Royal Dictionary of 1761, Chapman's New Universal
and Royal spelling book of 1765, Barclay's *complete* and *universal*
dictionary of 1774. Perry's *Royal Standard Grammar* of 1775,
which enjoyed huge sales, played on the semantic overlap of 'royal
standard' (the flag of kingly authority) and the notion of a 'standard' or model of language.

The study of school textbooks for spelling, reading, writing and speaking makes it abundantly clear that between the sixteenth and the beginning of the nineteenth centuries there was an ever more widely held notion of a standard form of English, all the elements of which except accent were realistically accessible through book-learning. The prestige attaching to this standard form of written and spoken dialect was partly its association with London as the centre of culture and as a site of political and economic power, but that prestige related even more crucially to the admired writers whose literary works had from the first been constantly held up for emulation and required for study, to a limited extent in the sixteenth and seventeenth centuries but as a matter of course by 1770: for much of the eighteenth century these writers included Addison and Steele, whose *Spectator* essays were considered "a Standard of good style" (William Foot, 1747). In addition to the "host of grammar books, with which society has been pestered" during the period *c.*1750–1830 (according to William Hill, 1833), there was a torrent of cheap anthologies of poetry and prose by "the standard authors" (Johnstone, 1818), "approved authors" (Anon, 1818), "most approved standard writers" (Winks, 1834).

Comparisons with America – likewise neglected by Crowley – are instructive. In the immediate aftermath of American Independence, the young Noah Webster was at great pains to emphasise the distinctiveness of standard American English, but later in his life he moderated this line and re-emphasised the essential unity of the two standard forms of the language. In 1824 Webster wrote, during a stay in England, that despite a number of specific points on which "respectable men" are not agreed, yet "in regard to the *great body* of the language, its principles are now settled by usage, and they are uniform in this country [England] and the United States." Later editions (1829 onwards) of his earlier textbooks made clear that the standard of pronunciation he recommended was "the best usage both in England and the United States", which he then specified as "that which is sanctioned by the most general usage of well-bred people both in the United States and in England". This judgment undoubtedly reflected his having spent that year in England in 1824, which led him to record this verdict on the essential similarities of the common standard English: "I have repeatedly conversed with English gentlemen in London, Cambridge and Oxford, for half an hour or an hour, without hearing or using a single word which would distinguish an Englishman from an American." His comment is, of course, mainly about a common pronunciation – the essential identity of grammar and vocabulary between the two forms of standard English did not need even to be stated. The way other commentators discussed the state of the English language in America around 1800 makes it clear that Americans in that period were in no doubt whatsoever that there was a standard British English: the question was how their own language, spoken and written, would develop in relation to it.

Writers like Webster felt that localisms in America were less obvious than in Britain, but that without schooling and good textbooks, the common people would "fall into many inaccuracies which may . . . corrupt the national language". Meanwhile, however, "the intercourse among *the learned* of the different states . . . must gradually destroy the differences of dialect which our ancestors brought from their native countries". In considering Webster's calls in the 1780s to "establish a national language" for America and "to diffuse an authority and purity of language" we note that that uniformity was to be diffused, not created, since it already existed, in the standard English of educated Americans, though its degree of purity was at present more problematical, especially in respect of pronunciation, because of lack of access to appropriate models. For written English, and the grammar and vocabulary of spoken English, there were clear authorities, as was confirmed by the American Quaker businessman Lindley Murray, who moved to England and wrote textbooks. His *English Grammar*, first published in 1795, was hugely influential on both sides of the Atlantic and had sold a million copies by 1850. "The practice of the *best* and most correct *authors*, corroborated by general usage, forms, during its continuance, the standard of language, especially if, in particular instances, this practice *continue*, after objection and due consideration." Thus, particular innovative usages are acceptable if from certain prestigious authors, if validated by being accepted and copied by others, after a period of discussion. These were the elements and stages in the process whereby standardisation was achieved: the prestige of the author; durability of the forms used; validation by public discussion; then widespread acceptance.

But how did this process apply to the United States, with less direct contact with the approved forms of 'general usage'? Before Webster had published his dictionary which codified the use of distinctively American forms, the British lexicographer Herbert Croft discussed in a letter in 1797 the desirability of "making some grand attempt with regard to fixing the *standard* of our language in America" (his emphasis). Thirty years later the author of *The Last of the Mohicans*, the American James Fenimore Cooper, discussing the issue of linguistic standards in the two countries, wrote in 1828 that "an entirely different standard for the language must be established in the United States, from that which governs so absolutely in England".

We may summarise our findings so far by asserting that if by a standard dialect we mean one that is recognisably uniform, widely used and accepted everywhere as authoritative, then all these elements were perceived as being in place in discussions of the English language, on both sides of the Atlantic, at the time of American independence and in the first half-century thereafter. But we note also that the codification of standard English as a model at that time was perceived as not yet complete, and there were specific problems about the accessibility of the most acceptable model of pronunciation, especially accent. We also note that for pupils wishing to learn to read, write and speak the language, standard English had no rivals. All other varieties had difficulties with uniformity, and limitations of usage, and limited authority, and except in the case of the upper-class dialect ('hyperlect'), their speakers suffered specific disadvantages ranging from being perceived as uneducated or 'provincial' (unsophisticated, etc.) to being seen as vile, or vicious, or criminal.

Agents of change

Who was responsible for establishing this standard English from the fifteenth century onwards? The first agents* were around a hundred or more chancery clerks, i.e., mainly low-level civil servants, together with their young apprentices, who constituted a professional community in central London (one modern authority likens them to "the typing pool"). Then there were the printers who took up and popularised forms of standard English in all parts of the kingdom. Printing made possible their spread among all educated people, especially when they were taught to the young by school teachers. In London – the national centre for drama – actors popularised models of both dialect and accent. The burgeoning textbook industry, which we have sampled for the sixteenth century onwards, was a powerful mechanism of diffusion from then until the present century. Their writers were ordinary teachers or 'masters' in a great variety of schools, or headmasters, tutors, parish clergy, Quakers, nonconformist pastors, dames, tutors of children, sometimes married women. They were explicitly written for pupils in dame schools, private schools, public schools, academies, grammar schools, charity schools, Sunday schools, provincial schools, village schools, classical schools, religious seminaries, and writing schools; and for families, parents, adults, ladies and gentlemen, lads, infants, young people, foreigners, tradesmen, artificers, artisans and mechanics, private families, young readers of both sexes, and for 'private study'.

It is true that before the advent of compulsory mass education around 1880, the very uneven provision of schools between the sixteenth and the later nineteenth centuries made for a patchy

* The historian Thomas Cable identifies ten individuals who especially shaped the evolution of a standard written English: Wyclif, Chaucer, Henry V, Caxton, Tyndale, Elyot, Mulcaster, Shakespeare, Dr Johnson, Lowth. Only one of these (Henry V) was born into the ruling classes.

availability of formal access to standard English, but the hundreds
of thousands of copies of textbooks in each of these centuries
providing basic literacy, and often something much more than
that, are evidence of the spread of the standard. Between the 1750s
and 1850s primers of English grammar and spelling, originally
published for middle-class children, became so cheap and widely
published that they were within reach of all: for example, William
Mavor's *English Spelling Book*, *c.* 1801, which sold on bookstalls
everywhere, was said to be in its 322nd edition by 1826. Outside
the endowed grammar schools there was, growing up over that
period, a mass of dame schools, private schools, charity schools,
Sunday schools, often of indifferent quality but all assuming that
their pupils expected to be taught to read, write and speak standard English, though not necessarily with anything very close to a
standard accent.

But you did not even need formal schooling to have access to
standard English. Indeed you did not even have to possess any
degree of literacy: a great deal of traditional lore, in the form of
ballad and narrative in standard English, was handed down orally
to the children and grandchildren of the labouring poor, so that it
was possible for an almost illiterate nineteenth-century father, a
merchant seaman, to tell "wonderful stories in choice English,
never using a word of dialect . . ." For millions of working-class
children it was the churches and chapels which furnished their
access to standard English: in the historic language of the Authorised Version of the Bible from 1611 onwards and the already
archaic formularies of the Book of Common Prayer, in the great
treasury of English hymnody shared by Methodists (from the
eighteenth century), Anglicans, and virtually all denominations
(though probably less so by Roman Catholics), and in the sermons
of an ordained ministry for which education in standard English
was always an important qualification. The language of scripture
was an especially important influence, yet the only acknowledgment of it by Dr Crowley is made in order to belittle Prime Minister Baldwin's reference in 1928 to the unconscious moral effect of

hearing, Sunday after Sunday, the "superb rhythm of the English Prayer Book . . . and the language of the English Bible" to which children were exposed when, "fifty years ago [*c.* 1880] all children went to church". As late as the 1920s, a dialect-speaking Gloucestershire boy born into a poor family in a decaying rural cottage absorbed the standard English offered at his humble elementary school and at the parish church whose "confident bell rang out each Sunday": the whole village heard it, and "filed into the pews". On one day of the week "the discipline was Sunday school, learning the Collect, and worship both morning and evening". This was the background to the writer Laurie Lee's magnificent deployment of the resources of standard English in *Cider with Rosie* and other autobiographical works.

And it was not only the Authorised Version of the Bible and the 1662 Prayer Book (and its predecessors from the 1540s onwards), since, together with them, at least two other religious classics – Foxe's *Martyrs* from the 1560s and Bunyan's *Pilgrim's Progress* from around 1680 – exercised a profound linguistic influence, in a nation deeply penetrated by religious belief and observance, on every household in that overwhelming majority that would have been regarded as 'protestant' in religion. It was an influence that extended the currency of a standard English which perpetuated a limited range of already somewhat archaic forms like *thee* and *thy*, *-eth* for *-(e)s*, *spake* ('spoke') and *holpen* ('helped'), etc. Many historians of the period 1750–1850 have portrayed Methodism as a powerful channel of working-class radicalism, and here we must refer again to the pervasive influence on the working masses of hymnody, which was a hallmark of Methodist worship: Charles Wesley (1707–88) alone is credited, by some reckonings, with the composition of several thousand hymns, many of them widely used by other denominations, and all serving to extend the currency of the standard English in which they were written.

Well before the 1860s, the period when – according to Dr Crowley's account (and indeed also Professor Harris's) – a group of philologists was busy conspiring to manufacture the concept of standard English as a way of foisting this divisive new product on an unwary populace, we know that working-class people could already experience standard English through a mass of agencies which promoted popular literacy. Sixty per cent of children were attending private schools in 1833. By 1851, three-quarters of working-class children were attending Sunday schools, either in addition to day-schooling or as an alternative to it. By the very modest criterion of signatures in marriage registers (implying no more than very basic literacy), fewer than 60 per cent of grooms had been able to sign during the period from the 1750s to around 1800, but the figure rose rapidly and by the end of the nineteenth century was as high as 88 per cent in some counties, even if women lagged behind until the end of the period. Towards the end of the nineteenth century it was not uncommon among the more backward sections of the community for levels of literacy which had taken centuries to achieve, and which had remained unchanged since the mid-eighteenth century, to double in a single generation. Symbolic of the new scale of literacy is the expansion of letter-writing after the dramatic reduction from an average sixpence postage per letter to a penny in 1840. In 75 years, postage rose 55 times in volume, from 76 million items in 1839 to 3,500 million in 1914.

Professor David Vincent, from whose work many of these examples are taken, has extensively documented the extension of literacy in the period 1750–1914 and its consequences and uses. In the course of the nineteenth century, the increased provision of formal schooling, as well as the extent of popular churchgoing, were complemented by libraries and debating societies; many homes possessed religious books, though of course they were not always read. Costly three-volume novels were out of reach of most working-class readers, except second-hand or to those in neighbourhood groups of readers. But the first half of the century nevertheless saw the creation of a popular reading public whose growth was nurtured by shilling editions of Shakespeare, cheap editions of Pope, Defoe and Bunyan, a torrent of penny fiction and innumerable religious tracts.

The swan-song of regional dialect

These publications were overwhelmingly written in standard English, though there was also at first a vigorous dialect literature, including dialect books, tracts, verses, songs, and dialect columns in what were otherwise standard English newspapers, but all these publications declined sharply after the end of the century as dialect was felt to be inappropriate for some functions. Around the middle of the century many 'Olmenacs' (Almanacs) were published in northern dialects, parodying *Old Moore* – giving local folklore, the dates of traditional fairs, etc., and prophecies of great convulsions: "but whether it bee all Europe, or Ruth Puddleputty's youngest bairn, it izant clearly depicktad; haivver, it al be wisdom to be prepared for awthur [either]". These almanacks may have served to confirm the connexion between dialect uses and folk wisdom, local superstition, and folk remedies which were slowly being challenged by scientific medicine. And of course the decline of such dialect publications after the turn of the century mirrored the decline of dialect usage under the impact of education, communications, and greatly increased geographical and social mobility.

This distinctive dialect literature included poems, ballads, stories, published individually or in almanacks or monthly journals and annuals. They flourished especially in Yorkshire, Lancashire and the North East (but surprisingly little in other places such as Birmingham). While in the 1850s and 1860s every town of any size gained its local newspaper (written, of course, in standard English), many of these newspapers regularly published dialect sketches, poems or dialogues, sometimes by local authors, sometimes by well-established regional writers. Most of these dialect items were on a limited range of topics relating to the family, work, religion, leisure and the natural world, much of it nostalgic in character, looking backward to a romanticised past, a lost world of traditional village life.

Unlike modern urban dialects, characterised mainly by accent and a limited number of grammatical forms and sitting

uncomfortably alongside the Latinate vocabulary of standard
English, the writings of men like the famous Samuel Laycock,
between 1863 and 1893, readily incorporated the more 'literate'
vocabulary of standard English and indeed he himself (a York-
shireman writing in Lancashire dialect) used relatively little non-
standard vocabulary, reflecting the general nineteenth-century
tendency across the nation for specific dialect vocabulary to
decline. Many of these writers were, like Laycock, autodidacts,
deeply respectful of the linguistic forms which constituted their
hard-won education, often achieved in the face of grinding
poverty and unemployment – Laycock, indeed, also published
poems in standard English. Some of their most enthusiastic
admirers were from the upper classes and the intelligentsia, and
there were employers who encouraged dialect literature which
they saw as a way of advertising the economic strength of particular regions. A further characteristic of this literary movement must
be noted: the persistent themes of Northern chauvinism and of
anti-metropolitanism, expressed as a resentment of London and
specifically a disparagement of its lower-class citizens – the
'chirping' and untrustworthy Cockneys. This whole episode of
dialect-in-print, petering out around 1914, must be seen as the
swan-song of the historic dialects of England.

This final efflorescence of dialect was made possible because this
was also the period of the birth of the popular press, especially
the sporting press. Other types of newspaper, such as Cobbett's
Political Register and *The Northern Star* (to 1852), had a wide sale
aimed at the working class; from the 1840s on, Sunday papers like
Reynolds', *Lloyd's* (which cost only a penny from 1855) and *News of
the World* were all aimed at a mass readership, and *Reynolds'* was
financed essentially by its sales to "the literate and labouring
poor". *Reynolds'* in particular was a "consistent advocate of the
rights of the working man" – its founder, G. W. M. Reynolds, had
himself been an active Chartist, and the paper was a fierce critic of
what it perceived as the working man's enemies, including the
upper-class press (such as *The Times*). But the language in which

they were written was exactly the same standard English as was used by *The Times* and other more privileged papers, as when (for example) *Reynolds'* congratulated striking workers in January 1852 for the "noble demeanour which they have hitherto maintained", which had earned them widespread respect "despite the unscrupulous recourse which has been had to misrepresentation the most flagrant, and scurrility the most vile . . ." The Chartist *Northern Star* was written in self-consciously literary language and roundly rebuked any 'illiteracy' in its working-class contributors, yet it was "voraciously consumed" by its enormous popular audience. So far from identifying standard English as a 'class dialect' unavailable to them, working-class radicals read newspapers written in it, corresponded in it, conducted political debates in it, and organised strikes in it.

The socialist historian E. P. Thompson acknowledges this in his account of the 'making of the English working class', which he dates essentially to the period from the 1790s to the 1830s. Writing of the working-class radicals who passed from the peasantry to the new industrial towns, he writes: "They suffered from the experience of the Industrial Revolution as articulate, free-born Englishmen. Those who were sent to gaol might know the Bible better than those on the Bench, and those who were transported to Van Diemen's Land might ask their relatives to send Cobbett's *Register* after them." Thompson goes on to claim that "everything, from their schools to their shops, their chapels and their amusements, was turned into a battleground of class." What he does not tell us, but what was true and remarkable, was that the use of standard English rather than local dialect was not among these class battlegrounds, and indeed, as an obvious source of proletarian empowerment, never became a matter of working-class contestation.

The gateway to liberty

The magical world of the mind which could be opened up by the use of standard English was illustrated by the life of William

Cobbett, ploughboy and gardener, and later, radical agitator, born in Surrey in 1766. His father taught him to read and write in winter evenings, though his limited knowledge made it difficult to teach the boy grammar. Running away at eleven to seek work at Kew Gardens, he spent the three pence he had saved for his supper on a copy of Swift's *Tale of a Tub*, which delighted him "beyond description", producing "what I have always considered a sort of birth of intellect". Enlisting in the army, he used his leisure to exhaust the bookstock of a local circulating library, then set himself to remedy his "want of knowledge" of what he considered "the most essential, the grammar of my native tongue". "The pains I took cannot be described" – writing out the rules of Lowth's *Grammar* several times, and learning them by heart, repeating them morning and evening when on guard duty. Such was his faith in the power which he believed this gave him that in 1818 he produced his own *Grammar of the English Language* "for schools and young persons in general, but more especially for the use of soldiers, apprentices and ploughboys". The grammar of standard English which he thus attempted to codify "teaches us how to make use of words . . . in a proper manner"; the book was dedicated, in a democratic flourish, to the embattled Queen Caroline, whose only "efficient supporters [were] The People".

The *Grammar* sold 100,000 copies in the first fifteen years alone, and Cobbett received thousands of letters of thanks "from young men, and men advanced in years also", for the "great benefits" they derived from it. It continued to exercise a fascination for working-class readers throughout the century, and was later to be cited by the pioneering leader of the Labour Party, Jimmy Clynes, as one of the formative influences on his career. Not surprisingly, Cobbett receives no mention in Dr Crowley's book, but Cobbett's presuppositions about popular attitudes to the notion of prescription, and about the relationship between standard English and dialect forms, make his work a highly relevant source. The relationship between knowledge and power was one of Cobbett's most explicit assumptions, and he saw the acquisition of the grammatical forms of standard English as a "gateway" enabling the weak to assert their "rights and liberties" under the law: he proclaimed, in fact, that *language is power*.

Crowley argues that "the discourse of the 'history of the language' produced a new object whose study was to dominate much nineteenth-century linguistic work in Britain". The way in which the scholars he studies, because of their social and political agenda, imposed their own slant on the history of English led to what Crowley regards as a further exercise of bias: "the new science [of linguistics] wanted to *totalise* the English language by *synthesising* it as a whole and thus began by analysing component parts in order to fit them back with more understanding into the historical reality". If the reader is not certain what this means, we note that Crowley goes on to offer what he calls an explanation of the process which led to to the production of "a text whose central concern was the history of the standard literary language". By text, Crowley appears here to refer to the labours of the compilers of the *OED*. Writing of the 1880s, Crowley says that "it is clear that at this stage the 'standard' literary language has become equitable with [*sc.* equal to?] the English language 'pure and simple'".

To make the standard literary language the main focus of attention, as these nineteenth-century scholars undoubtedly did, is claimed by Crowley to be "in sharp contrast with the prevailing linguistic thought in the mid-century". After all, he can again quote the Oxford professor Max Müller, who had stressed in 1862 that "the real life of language is in its dialects", not in its literary forms. How far this one Oxford professor, or indeed his opponents, could be taken as representative of linguistic thought in England in the mid-nineteenth century, is never demonstrated, and it is proper to ask whether at this period anyone could define the 'mainstream' attitude to the issue of standard vs. dialect among academics who had a special professional concern with language matters, many of whom were in any case working in classical studies. Crowley never describes the individuals who are deemed to qualify as 'linguists' or to represent 'linguistic thought': in one case the 'linguist' cited turns out to be a journalist on the *Leeds Mercury* in 1863, in another case to be the writer of an 1890s school textbook. The assumptions and practices of textbook writers are highly informative in all periods, especially earlier ones when no body of professional linguistic scholars has emerged, but whether individual textbook writers can be taken as representative of the supposed dogma of academic linguists is a different matter altogether. By such questionable methods does Crowley 'construct' a discipline or 'discourse' of linguistics to which he imputes a particular ideological stance.

This failure to identify the membership of what he takes as the community of linguists in this period is part of a wider problem he has of neglecting to offer any indication, in respect of large numbers of the writers he quotes, of where they stood in relation to the politics of the day, to the education system, to the class system, to the power structure of nineteenth-century Britain, or even to the audience they were addressing. This is strange, given the importance he attaches to their "social and political concerns". Often identified only by surname and initial, without any clue as to their regional origin or their job, they flit through his pages as ghostly figures: it is as if such people are, in Marxist terms, just stooges of impersonal social forces in the unstoppable dialectic process of the class struggle.

But to represent the compilers of the *OED* as having done something peculiar, because of their alleged ideological preoccupations, in choosing to identify standard English with the standard literary language, is an absurdity. The close connexion between standard English and the forms used by the most admired writers is a fact dating from the sixteenth century at the latest: as we have seen, for three centuries or more, that connexion was cited time and again by writers who tried to find words to describe the concept of standard English. (An ordinary dictionary definition of that sense of 'literary' which is relevant here is 'having the characteristics of that kind of written expression which is regarded as having value on account of its qualities of linguistic form'.)

Moreover, what were the main sources for all the words whose history the new dictionary was planning to trace? Essentially they were written sources, which inevitably gave a weighting to standard over dialect uses, and in any case, what sources were available, a hundred years before the development of the tape-recorder, for the spoken English of past centuries? In fact, though they tried also to observe their own self-denying ordinance which disregarded scientific words and provincial dialects – partly in the struggle to contain within manageable limits what Crowley admits was their 'gargantuan' task – the compilers did include vast numbers of 'dialect' and 'obsolete' and regional forms. This was one of the reasons why the dictionary took more than sixty years to complete, by which time they needed to work on a supplement to catch up on all the changes during those sixty years.

Constructing a canon

The *OED* compilers' reliance on literary language as the basis for their conception of standard English had, for Crowley, yet another result: "The reason for the marked appearance of the canon of English literature at this period [the 1870s] was quite simply *its previous non-existence* and the need for it that had been produced by the work of the linguistic historians." Again, we have the implication that these scholars fabricated, and then filled, a new and artificial need, without historical basis, in order to feed their own preconceptions. By the 'canon' of English literature we understand, not the vast range of written sources which were eventually sifted to illustrate the *OED*'s histories of words, but the range of authors and the list of their specific works which in any given period are widely read by students (a range which has in recent years become a battlefield in the USA and Britain because women, minority groups, and authors from former colonial states writing in English have hitherto been under-represented in it, and old favourites like Shakespeare, Milton and Dickens have arguably been over-represented). According to Crowley, there was no such canon before the mid-nineteenth century, but again he is quite wrong.

We know that schoolchildren in their millions had from the sixteenth century onwards been exposed to samples of English literature in their school textbooks, and that from 1700 secular recreational reading was beginning to be provided for schools on a new and enlarged scale, and around this date anthologies for school use began to appear. By the 1770s the assumption that English literature would be taught in schools had become a normal feature of educational discussion. Such passages from literature were primarily "to create a taste for composition", and their use for this purpose, and the common practice of learning passages by heart, could only serve to confirm the prevalence of the grammar, vocabulary and idiom of standard English, just as recitation would extend the idea of a standard pronunciation. These anthologies often indicated their criteria for inclusion: for example "the most celebrated authors" (1783); "the latest and most celebrated poets" – there were 29 of them (1789); "works of distinguished writers" (1807); "the most eminent", the "most admired" or "approved" authors (1803, 1818, 1823); "the most approved standard writers" (1834).

Not only were schoolchildren widely exposed to English literature and literary language, but we have a good idea of exactly which authors constituted the canon for the periods 1771–1801 and 1802–75. Professor Ian Michael has reconstructed the main outlines of this canon, and indicated the rankings of favourite authors: Pope tops the list for the first period, with Shakespeare running fourth, and Addison and Milton equal fifth. For the second period several new authors have become available, including Wordsworth (equal third), Scott, Byron and Southey, but first place goes to Cowper, and Shakespeare is second; and whereas we saw that in 1747 a textbook had commended the reading of "some good author (the *Spectator*, for example) that is a Standard of good Style", Addison had dropped out of the top ten in the later period. It is fair to conclude from this that Dr Crowley's idea that, by their citations from a much wider range of authors, the *OED* compilers, or indeed anybody else in the later nineteenth century, somehow established a canon where none had previously existed, is simply a fantasy.

Because of his resolute neglect of comparisons with the history of other European countries, Dr Crowley loses the opportunity to learn from often exact parallels in the the case of the emergence of a standard form of the French language, which confirm the importance of literature as a determinant of such a standard variety. Professor Anthony Lodge has documented the ways in which the grammar and sentence structure of French were elaborated and transformed between the thirteenth and the fifteenth centuries, as the dialect of Paris – the capital and the site of the King's court – developed a number of important new functions. A few years after Shakespeare's death, a French commentator could define the best kind of French as associated with politicial power, education, and good literature (the first being subject to the second two): "it is the way of speaking of the most sensible part [*la plus saine partie*] of the Court, when that accords with the way of writing of the most sensible part of the authors of the day" – and this extended to women as well as men, and to 'refined' speakers who mixed socially with the Court. A century later, the Encyclopedists again defined it as "the way of *speaking* of the majority of the court when this accords with the way of *writing* of the majority of *the most highly esteemed authors* of the day".

A spoken standard

The main theme of the second part of Crowley's book is his attempt to demonstrate his contention that British linguists invented a concept of a standard *spoken* English, which was nothing more or less than a class *accent* – this process he calls "the cultural project of *imposing* a particular form of speech as the 'standard' to which others had to rise". Here his account is weakened by his persistent confusion between (a) those who spoke the forms of standard English in a 'standard', i.e., non-

regional, accent (which became known as received pronunciation, RP) and (b) those who used standard English (in its
grammar, vocabulary and idiom) but spoke it with an accent
which ranged from something close to broad dialect, to something a hair's breadth away from RP. His confusion is not entirely
surprising, since some of the main linguistic figures he concen-
trates on, including Daniel Jones and Henry Wyld, occasionally
blur the lines on this as well. (He also follows Wyld in disregard-
ing an important distinction between the 'mainstream' and the
'aristocratic' forms of RP.) Crowley's difficulty in distinguishing
between (a) and (b) is the more acute in that he does not
acknowledge, as those scholars did, the existence of a standard
English anyway. The first of these two groups of speakers, those
who used RP, was of course a relatively small and (usually)
socially privileged group; the second group was large and increasing, as more and more people experienced education, adapted
their grammar and vocabulary, and in many cases adapted, at
least in some degree, their accent.

All the commentators whom Crowley cites confirm that the
standard accent was non-local except insofar as it represented a
South of England provenance, and was mainly associated in a
general way with more educated people in the metropolis; and
they are likewise in complete agreement in using terms like *vulgar*,
rustic, *cockney*, *provincial*, *simple*, *rough*, *coarse*, to describe
dialects, which, for one observer, ranged "from the lowest vulgarity to mere provinciality". But all these are exactly, word for word,
the kinds of description which had consistently been applied
respectively to standard English and to dialect since 1600 and even
before, and very much the same prescriptions and proscriptions of
usage were being enforced over that period as were being enforced
in the nineteenth century.

Moreover, contemporary commentators were also in essential
agreement on the forces which were driving out dialect forms in
the nineteenth century: the spread of education, especially the new
board schools after 1870; urbanisation and geographical mobility;

the spread of railways, the day-trips and holidays that these enabled, and travel to more distant markets and fairs; communications, and the press.

Dr Crowley's case is that it was the efforts of linguists like the grammarian R. G. Latham and the compilers of the *OED* which caused the standard spoken form of English "to be taken as the primary or central spoken form according to which other spoken forms can be evaluated" and thus to become "the culturally hegemonic spoken form". But, as we have seen, and as contemporaries had long recognised, this had already happened – up to four centuries before. Their references to educational criteria like "well-bred and well-informed", "civilised persons", "the best speakers", "the people of best education" cause Dr Crowley to state that the crux of the definition of good English does not lie in any linguistic features, but that it lies rather with the delimitation of the class of its speakers. "All other English is, by means of a simple binary definition, bad English since it is not the English of the good and the careful [speakers]". This, he claims, makes the definition of standard spoken English socially specific : such a definition of usage, says Crowley, does not mean common usage, uniform usage, or the usage of the majority, but rather, the use of 'civilised persons'. (We note that while standard English was, and still is, not totally uniform, it was then, and is, more uniform than any one dialect.)

Crowley represents the majority of the linguists he studies as seeing standard English as deriving value from the *social status* of its users – the literate and educated – but we note that this is, of course, not a social-class criterion but essentially a *functional* criterion. Yet Dr Crowley states baldly that the 'educated' and the 'civilised' *came, of course, from the ruling class.* But in respect of the ability to read and write standard English, or to use its grammar and vocabulary in speech, this was just not true, and it was only partly true of the ability to use the correct 'pronunciation' or accent with which any person of education spoke that standard grammar and vocabulary. (Both the upper-class 'hyperlect', spoken by some members of the aristocracy and gentry, and all the local rural and urban dialects, were exclusive, in the sense that they were not formally taught, whereas standard English was 'mainstream' and inclusive.) William Cobbett in his *Grammar* insisted that learners should not worry too much about a correct accent – "the business of using the proper sound" – since "the differences are of very little real consequence". Instead, as he made clear, the essence of the empowering form of English lay in its grammatical usages, for "grammar, properly understood, enables us, not only to express our meaning fully and clearly, but so to express it as to enable us to defy the ingenuity of man to give our words any other meaning than that which we ourselves intend them to express".

For the particular spoken form belonging to a specific group (the educated, the civilised, the best speakers) to be taken as a standard for emulation is proof, for Dr Crowley, that their language is a *crucial signifier of their social status.* But again this is not true: the use of standard English – in writing or (with or without the standard accent) in speech – was a necessary but not a sufficient condition for higher social status. To take but one example: elementary school teachers, recruited overwhelmingly from the lower classes, were expected to use standard English, yet nobody thought this put them among the ruling class. Dr Crowley ought indeed to be arguing the case the other way round – that those with pretensions to high social status could not achieve this without being able to handle standard English.

He is clearly delighted to be able to quote Henry Alford, Dean of Canterbury and author of the widely quoted manual of usage, *The Queen's English* (1864), who referred to those features, mainly of grammar and vocabulary, which, "in matters of speech and style", constituted "the sure mark of good taste and good breeding". But in this passage Alford is specifically saying that what was involved is not social class of origin, but the ability to *acquire* standard English. The passage begins by insisting that not all standard English speakers are gentlemen by birth, so Alford is obviously (since he disqualifies the birth criterion) using 'breeding' (or 'good breeding') in an older sense. In present-day

English, 'breeding' is used essentially to represent physical reproduction, but a widely used earlier sense was cultural reproduction,
i.e., education – Milton wrote in 1653, "they have had the most of
their breeding, both at school and university, by scholarships",
and Sheridan wrote in 1777 of a girl who had her musical education
at home: "she has had her breeding within doors: the parson
teaches her to play upon the dulcimer". Then, by extension of
this sense, the term 'good breeding' was often used to indicate
the results of such education as shown in good manners and
acceptable ways of speaking.

Dr Crowley refers to an undated (later nineteenth-century)
teachers' union pamphlet which expressed the expectation that
working-class children in elementary schools would themselves
be England's workers a few years hence, and he uses this truism
in order to support his claim that "in linguistic terms this means
that the public elementary schools would *produce* vulgar-
speaking illiterates (as they were perceived) and the private fee-
paying schools would produce educated speakers of 'good
English' (as it was perceived)". But he is, again, doubly wrong.
The newly established state system of elementary schools after
1870 was highly effective in combating illiteracy, and, as observers
commented within a few years of their establishment, in introducing large numbers of children to standard English, thus
continuing to do – but now more effectively because of wider
coverage of the population, and by 1880 with the addition of compulsory attendance – what all schools had tried to do since before
1600, i.e., to teach the grammar, vocabulary and literary usages of
standard English.

Yet we know that there were also well-meaning dialect enthusi-
asts – some of them clergymen – who attempted to keep the old
local forms alive by having these taught in the new school system.
In Rochdale, an interesting preservationist inspector of schools
(HMI Mr Wylie) caused controversy in the local press in 1890 by
his attempts to foster the use of local dialect in school. The
response of some parents is illuminating: "Keep the old Lancashire

dialect out of the schools, Mr Wylie, for I want my children to talk smart when they're grown up."

It is this matter of access to a standard English accent that complicates the extent to which we can speak of a 'standard' spoken English in the nineteenth century, other than in respect of the other main features, grammar and vocabulary. It was widely claimed by contemporary observers that there was such a standard, but its currency was among a limited number – mainly among those of a certain degree of education, who lived in and around London, although it undoubtedly influenced educated speakers in other parts of the British Isles, including Scotland and Ireland, though they were developing their own variety of educated standard. The antiquarian F. T. Elworthy, born in 1830, commented in the 1870s on his experience of encountering "the very marked provincialisms in the pronunciation of educated men and women in the Northern and Midland counties". As we have seen, it was also common for the aristocracy and gentry in the provinces to speak standard English with traces of the local accent.

What was lacking to the establishment of a standard accent beyond the sixty-mile triangle of London, Cambridge and Oxford around 1800 was the absence of a system of education, whether for the higher or for the lower classes, in which such a 'unified' form of pronunciation was the norm. As the philologist A. J. Ellis wrote in 1869, it is difficult to speak of a standard form of pronunciation in the context of a varied experience of "superior education". For the upper and middle classes this opportunity did not come until the second half of the century, essentially by around 1870, with the coming into being of a 'public-school system' in the new sense of an *interacting* community of boys' schools, typically mainly or partly boarding, with an infrastructure of preparatory schools modelled on them, together providing up to ten (or more) years of intensive social and linguistic processing to produce the new-style 'public school man'. (Similar schools for girls, closely modelled on them, soon followed, though they seldom achieved the same importance as those for their brothers; nevertheless the role of women within their families was to be of great significance in the diffusion of a standard accent.)

In respect of the rest of the population, it was again A. J. Ellis who emphasised in 1869 how "anxious and willing" the "social inferior [was] to adopt the pronunciation of the superiorly educated, if he can but learn it". But (Ellis demanded to know), given the limited access available to models of it, "how can he?" Yet within a few years, observers were already commenting on the effectiveness of the newly established elementary schools in giving greater access for dialect-speakers to the forms of standard English, and they also offered, though to a more limited extent, access to a standard English accent, especially after the 1880s when inspectors and training-college staffs became much more prescriptive in matters of accent.

Crowley claims that, far from there being any kind of uniform linguistic practice, the standard pronunciation that had become available in the school system, and especially secondary schools and universities, by the early decades of the twentieth century was "*precisely* [his emphasis] the preserve of those of a certain gender, class and region: the men educated at the private, fee-paying schools in the south of England". The most obvious fault of this claim is that all these criteria were the opposite of precise. Women spoke RP as readily as men and possibly more so, but because they were in that period treated as subordinate and perceived as partly 'invisible', we can understand how it would have been an anachronism to have made them the basis of any definition, though it would be unwise for us to disregard their crucial contribution ourselves. Though the region involved was the south of England, in fact the northern schools* of that public-schools

---

* If he really believes that the standard English accent was an essentially 'class' phenomenon, Dr Crowley ought logically to be able to show that RP was under threat from northern English by the end of the nineteenth century, because of the vast economic power of the north by that time. Interestingly, some linguists were indeed arguing, around 1900, for the superiority of Northern English.

community which is referred to in definitions of RP also gave access to this form of accent – as did a mass of lesser schools which, by popular demand, imitated them in this. The class involved was the educated class, and this did not by any means involve exclusively upper-class *origins*, since the group of fee-paying schools he mentions always included at least a small proportion of pupils, more frequently lower middle-class pupils but also even working-class pupils, so it was never an exclusive *preserve* (as Crowley calls it). Nor was the accent which was diffused by those schools an exclusive preserve, since one of the bizarre characteristics of the new-style public school system after *c.* 1870 was that most of the advantages, in terms of social privilege, which were conferred by the ability to style oneself a 'public school man' were also available to anyone who could speak with an RP accent. Thus, for example, in World War I, when the number of public-school candidates as officer recruits ran out, it was, among other candidates to be considered, men with RP accents who had the best chance of the dubious privilege of being chosen for this lethal promotion.

And of course great numbers of pupils outside the "private, fee-paying" system (Crowley's term: in fact all private schools were fee-paying) had access to RP. He suggests that if, as Professor Wyld held, the ultimate models for RP around 1934 were public-school-educated speakers and thus members of 'a tiny minority', then it must follow that they would constantly have been misunderstood, since their accent would have been unfamiliar to the majority of the people around them. This implication, too, is a fantasy, since RP was much more widely diffused by 1934 than it had ever been in the nineteenth century. Not only had it extensively penetrated the education system – now educating children up to older ages – at all levels, but working-class children had heard it on the lips of clergy as well as teachers, and even more widely, on the BBC, which from its foundation in 1922 took over from the public-school system the role as the main agency for the diffusion of RP – and now into every home in the land.

The crux of Crowley's critique of commentators like Jones and Wyld is that in their attempts to define standard English, especially in respect of accent, they saw themselves as neutral scientists, but "their self-images were false" since they "constructed" their theories concerning standard English "along the lines of the preferences and prejudices that had been present in the nineteenth century and earlier"; their work was not 'purely scientific' in that it was "influenced by certain cultural presuppositions", in a field of linguistics that was in any case "dominated by social and rhetorical concerns", and influenced by "certain cultural presuppositions, and thus became part of a larger formation whose task was to set out the politics of discourse". Our response to this must be, first, that by ascribing the operation of different social judgments on the character of standard and non-standard English essentially to events in the nineteenth century, with a brief reference to the eighteenth century, and above all by failing to note that all these judgments had been made on standard English at every stage of its life since its emergence in the fifteenth century, Dr Crowley has grossly misrepresented the situation.

Secondly, it is entirely proper to examine and criticise the social and political assumptions which may influence a scholar's analysis, provided only that one performs one's examination accurately and fairly, and it is further entirely proper that one sets out one's own social and political assumptions for inspection. Several aspects of Crowley's own presuppositions have emerged during the above examination, and in a moment we must we try to explore these further. But first let us look again at the "preferences and prejudices" of the nineteenth- and early-twentieth-century commentators on these matters. Their basic cultural presupposition was that a variety of English which reflected the uses of the educated was more to be admired than any variety which represented the uneducated, the unsophisticated, the ignorant. Given the inevitable tendency of language, as it is actually used, to encode a system of values, how could it be otherwise?

Established by whom? For whom?

Roy Harris touches on a similar issue when he points to what he alleges is "the paradox of what was, sociolinguistically, a very restricted form of English being *passed off*, under the label 'standard', as an optimal form of English transcending mere class, geographical, individual or other differences: that is to say, as a single national norm, an 'English par excellence'". The *OED* compilers' references to "established linguistic practice", he says, beg the important questions: established by whom? For whom? We must be able to answer Harris's questions: they had already been established, by educated users of English, in ways which were accepted by everybody who read a simple book or newspaper, or went to church. The attempt to codify the forms of that 'established', 'standard' English, by methods which included the propagation of a doctrine of 'correctness', which was used in teaching, had the effect of making them available to all. As soon as a language is taught, you must have standards, regularities, and you must involve pedants, whose reference-point will always be those who are widely perceived as the 'best users'.

Roy Harris quotes the views of the French social theorist Pierre Bourdieu (1982), who claimed that any form of linguistic theoris-ing which constantly refers to a monolithic abstraction called something vague like 'English' is *already on the side of officialdom* in promoting a *socio-political idealisation*. "What is thus reinforced is the view that there is only one legitimate form of language for any given community. It is no mitigation THEN to talk of 'dialects', 'sub-dialects', 'varieties', etc, for these have already been marginalised at a single official stroke".

But, unlike Harris and Bourdieu, we can recognise that this 'official stroke' had been preceded by another, and more crucial, event: the coming of literacy. This is because we can recognise that a standard language is created the moment a written language is created, because the process of teaching pupils to read and write it requires standardisation, and this process is intensified as soon as there are admired writers, and then teachers who want to share that admiration with pupils. Yet for Harris, "part and parcel of the myth [of a 'standard English' which in reality was created by nineteenth-century scholars] was the patronising assumption that although the children of the working classes could already speak some kind of English without the benefit of going to school, it was only a very inferior kind of English. It needed to be 'improved'." But everybody from the sixteenth century onwards assumed that all children, especially those of dialect backgrounds, needed schooling to equip them in standard English: that is why the whole industry of English teaching, and the writing of textbooks, came into being, and why people like ploughman Cobbett wrote to extend the opportunities of the underprivileged to do so.

We have already seen (page 71) how later editors of the *OED*, writing some seventy years after the first discussions on the *OED* proposal, recorded in their *Supplement* that the earliest citation for the term 'standard English' that could be found was its use by their predecessors, those original planners of their dictionary in 1858. For Roy Harris, "there can hardly be a more be a more remarkable example in intellectual history of quoting one's own claim as evidence in order to establish the validity of what was [being] claimed". We now know, however, that the use of the term 'standard English' in the discussions which preceded the launching of the huge *OED* project was by no means the earliest use, nor even the earliest written use – we know of others earlier in the nineteenth century and perhaps even a century before.

When Raymond Williams discovered earlier uses of words like *class* and *culture* which his books had claimed dated from a later period, he added a footnote that these amendments should be noted, but that the *effective social history* of a meaning must always be in terms of its passing into normal usage. I would suggest that the case could be put the other way round. What we need to note is not the date when a particular word or term is first used, but rather when the *concept* it now stands for was first widely discussed and accepted. The 'effective social meaning' of the concept of standard English was there in the sixteenth century.

We note on the cover of Crowley's book the generous puff from Professor Roy Harris: "a great work of demythologization . . . a book which every teacher of English in the country should read". In interpreting this commendation, it is helpful to know that Professor Harris was research supervisor for the doctoral thesis which was the essential basis of Crowley's book, and that its external examiner was Raymond Williams, and further that the doctorate was awarded for it. This calls to mind the striking words of Professor Harris about there being hardly a more remarkable example in intellectual history of quoting one's own claim as evidence, in order to establish the validity of what was being claimed.

In my own account I have tried to distinguish – in a way Crowley fails to do clearly – three issues. First, was there, at any period before the mid-nineteenth century (the period crucial to these three re-writers of history), a variety of language which could be identified in any 'objective' sense – i.e., with a recognisable regularity of form, with a generality of use, and with a degree of authority – as a form of standard English? Secondly, did people in any earlier period perceive that such a standard existed? Thirdly, did they attach to it the label 'standard English' for the period in which it existed? Our answer to the first two questions must be a resounding yes, in respect of the period from at least the mid-sixteenth century onwards, and in respect of the form of English which was written, but its generality of use for speaking was in one respect limited before the mid-nineteenth century, insofar as only a fairly small section of the population, essentially those with access to education, and especially those who lived within easy reach of the London area, spoke its fairly uniform grammar and vocabulary with what could be regarded as a uniform accent. To the third question we must answer that the label 'standard English' only achieved wide currency in the nineteenth century, but that an assortment of other terms was used for it before that time. (After all, the term 'literacy' seems to have been first used in the USA in the 1880s and in Britain in the 1890s, but that does not mean that this condition did not exist in Britain many centuries before that, nor that its prevalence in any earlier period cannot be estimated by historians.)

The new 'received wisdom'

If we were dealing with some inconsequential academic figures, the startling differences between (on the one hand) Raymond Williams's and Roy Harris's brief accounts, now supported and elaborated in great detail by Dr Crowley's book, and (on the other hand) the more traditional picture I have set out to reaffirm, would be, in all senses of the term, 'merely academic', a minor storm in a teacup. But their conclusions have passed rapidly into the received wisdom of linguistics, and Crowley's book is now widely and approvingly cited, and has the potential to make a significant difference to the way children are educated. The proposition which his book seeks to support was already, for some linguists, firmly established: that standard English is merely a 'class dialect'; Crowley's signal service is to have documented the recent and arbitrary historical process whereby this is said to have come about. In tune with many linguists who disparage the notion of a 'standard English', Adrian Pennycook, for one, is very clear (in his much-cited 1994 book) that, "as Crowley and Harris have convincingly argued, standard English was itself *the creation of the nineteenth century*".

Even one of the most admiring critics of Crowley's book, however, has conceded that "one fears that readers without much background in this area may be led to think that the emergence of Standard English took place in the nineteenth century, about five centuries too late", and suggested that Crowley "can be taken mildly [*sic*] to task for 'forgetting' at least to outline the previous 500 years of activity at engineering the emergence of Standard English". Yet even so, Professor Joseph assures his readers, Crowley's "strongly held political opinions do not compromise his historical judgment".

But why would anyone go to such lengths of fantasy in order to concoct a story about a group of linguistic scholars who 'invented' a 'new' concept of standard English in the 1860s? The whole idea, and all the language in which it is discussed, are instantly recognisable to anyone who has read Foucault, the guru whom (as we saw) Dr Crowley acknowledges at the outset. Along with his fellow-Frenchman Jean-Paul Sartre, Michel Foucault (1926–1984) was among the most influential intellectuals in the West in the second half of the twentieth century. Tortured by his homosexual nature and the hostile attitude of society to this condition, Foucault spent his life re-examining the ways in which society came to categorise the normal and the abnormal, the 'standard' and 'non-standard' ways of behaving and thinking. Believing, like many French social philosophers of his period, that there is no 'absolute' truth, he claimed that what passes for 'knowledge' is simply what a particular group of people in a certain period get together to decide is true. The mental force exercised by a minority who possess power by virtue of the expertise they claim, induces others to accept their version of the 'truth', and especially their categorisation of what is 'normal' or 'abnormal'. This applies also to the way these élite groups cause academic knowledge to be parcelled out into the various professional 'disciplines' in which it is studied in educational institutions such as universities, and to the boundaries between subject areas.

All this led Foucault to explore the history of madness, of illness, of criminality, and of what society labelled as sexual 'perversion', in a series of difficult and densely written books and articles which established his academic reputation and his credentials as the leading French radical of his generation. Partly perhaps because his own sexuality involved bizarre forms of sado-masochism, he was intensely interested in the ideas of discipline and punishment, domination, subjection and subjugation, power and oppression, and his fascination with violence led to his endorsement of its indiscriminate use by the IRA. He recognised that knowledge, too, is power – power exercised in a certain way.

In Foucault's system madness, for example, had, in modern times, come to be defined in ways which enabled middle-class people to label as 'mad' lower-class people who in certain ways did not conform to a middle-class standard. It was thus a concept which served to exclude some people, a tendency which was reinforced by the assumption by middle-class experts of a high moral authority.

Discourse, which is a favourite term for Foucault – and features in the title of the British edition of Dr Crowley's book – carries connotations of the way knowledge tends to be discussed, and the way all forms of communication are defined and manipulated in order to serve the purposes of élite groups and to propagate their totally arbitrary notion of what is 'standard' or 'normal'. On this principle, it follows that – as Dr Crowley set out to show – there can be no 'rational' or 'innocent' explanation for why one version of a language should have emerged as standard: the whole thing must instead be a purely social construct – invented, like all those other concepts, by self-interested specialists bent on carving out a particular area of knowledge for their own ends.

Of course, this brief and necessarily bald summary cannot do justice to a wide-ranging philosophical system characterised by frequent flashes of brilliant insight which are worked out with considerable finesse in the mass of Foucault's writings. Like the Marxism in which it is rooted, it appears to offer an intellectually satisfying explanation of a whole range of human conduct, appealing – like many irrational belief-systems – especially to those whom it endows with superior knowledge and to whom it provides a key to the way human life is *determined* by powerful dark forces. And it touches reality at just enough points to give it a kind of credence, particularly for those who crave the kinds of certainty it offers, which now supersedes all previous explanations and systems, especially those which assume that events may have a 'natural' or 'innocent' cause. And where the pattern does not appear to fit, then the facts can be adjusted, the story re-written, to make it work – there is, after all, no 'objective' truth. Perhaps it is only to be expected that Foucault's philosophy, which arose out of restless and radical questioning of all established systems of thought, should now be applied imitatively but unquestioningly by his disciples in areas where it does not really fit.*

The other clues to Dr Crowley's political motivation lie not just in the manufacture of his perverse conclusions, but in his use of certain terms which are key words in the contemporary discussion of Marxist and neo-Marxist ideas: *hegemony* and *hegemonic*, as in his 'culturally hegemonic'. These derive from ideas developed by the Italian Marxist Antonio Gramsci, whose views on the rise of a standard Italian language have already been referred to.† Stated crudely, 'hegemonic beliefs' are, for present-day Marxists, typically 'common-sense', but ideologically incorrect, ideas which the lower classes – supposedly because they are amazingly stupid and easily misled by the ruling classes – readily accept. The concept is necessary to explain why the project of proletarian revolution has everywhere run out of steam.

But lest my own reservations about such theories should disqualify me from giving a fair account of them, let me refer the reader to a standard book, *Hegemony* (1986), by Dr Robert Bocock, a leading exponent of modern Marxist thought at the Open University. Bocock compares the popular understanding of the term 'socialism' with the terms 'freedom', 'justice', 'liberty',

---

* There is now, especially among Continental scholars, a body of scholarship which is highly critical of Foucault's writings in such fields as literary criticism, linguistics, and history, and which demonstrates the flimsy and incoherent basis of the evidence cited in his writings.

† Gramsci's very explicit views on dialect are not, however, quoted by Dr Crowley. Gramsci wrote: "Someone who only speaks dialect, or understands the standard language incompletely, necessarily has an intuition of the world which is more or less limited and provincial, which is fossilised and anachronistic in relaton to the major currents of thought which dominate world history. His interest will be limited, not universal; it is at least necessary to learn the national language properly. A great culture can be translated into any language with historic richness and complexity, and it can translate any other great culture, and can be a world-wide means of expression. But a dialect cannot do this."

and even 'equality', and he admits that for many people 'socialism' is regarded as the opposite of the others, connoting an oppressive state system (if not actually a police state), a lack of personal freedoms, a politically and culturally repressive atmosphere, and a low standard of living. Based on the actual workings of professed socialist regimes all over the world – Eastern Europe, the former USSR, Asia and Africa – "socialism sometimes means little more than that a country is ruled despotically and that no political opposition is allowed". His admission is surely confirmed by the fact that in countries across the globe (including Britain, Australia and New Zealand, as well as large tracts of Europe) where socialist parties have sought to regain power, it has only been by abandoning central principles of socialism, and embracing free-market economics and human rights that they have succeeded.

Against this background, Marxists have had to attempt a reformulation of their theories. The two most basic planks in the platform of Marxist theory are the central principles expressed in the statement that "The history of all hitherto existing societies is the history of class struggles", and in the notion of the primacy of the working class. (The first of these "may look like an empirically testable proposition but, in fact," says Dr Bocock, "no evidence is ever allowed to count against it" by Marxist theorists.) Both of these fundamental dogmas are threatened by the emergence of liberal-capitalist societies which encourage and make possible a high level of mobility between classes and provide far higher levels of material satisfaction, and a greater absence of repression and coercion, than have been characteristic of all Marxist regimes that have so far existed. If Marxism is to be regenerated, new ways must be found for stimulating the class-consciousness without which class conflict cannot be realised. Thus, "classes have to be produced" – that is, artificially generated – "by political activities": members of economic classes (like the working class) simply do not 'know' their material interests. They derive their knowledge of them from the culture of the world around them, which, if it is a liberal-capitalist state, may be inimical to producing the 'correct' forms of working-class consciousness. But they can be persuaded to form the right conceptions of their 'class' interests by political propaganda. Here the reinterpretation of history – as well as of literature, sociology, political science and linguistics – is a valuable tool, and the education system (schools and universities) is the obvious mechanism for this important work of re-indoctrination.

Not all Marxists accept this: there is in fact a long-running debate about the fundamental basis of classes, and whether they can be so 'manufactured' by cultural propaganda. So there are those who accept the above analysis – that "modern capitalist society maintains and reproduces itself through the effects of a dominant ideology which successfully incorporates the working class into the existing society, thus perpetuating its subordination", and those fundamentalist Marxists who cling to economism – the old belief that the crucial element in the subordination of one class to another is always to be found in the organisation of production. The otherwise puzzling approach of the book with which this chapter has been mostly concerned, Crowley's *The Politics of Discourse*, can only be understood in terms of these internal debates among Marxists.

It is not difficult to see where Dr Crowley stands in these debates, nor to understand the rationale of a book whose central argument obediently provides vindication for an already well-established ideological stance, articulated by Raymond Williams and Roy Harris, on the 'class' nature of standard English. ('*That it might be fulfilled as was written . . .*') The same admiring critic who commented on the liberties that Dr Crowley, in his book, has taken with historical fact, described the author's standpoint as "(post-) post-structuralist, post-Marxist, and quintessentially post-modern" – a position which, as we can see, incorporates some of the most radical, but also some of the most disputable, theories about society, language and literature, in the modern academic world. At any rate, if it can be shown – or at least loudly proclaimed – that "Standard English *is, and always has been, a class variety*" (Deborah Cameron, 1995), then a case can be made for resisting the process of exposing working-class children to it.

The Newbolt Committee on the Teaching of English called in 1921 for "systematic training in the use of standard English" for all pupils in schools, and Conservative governments in the 1980s and 1990s tried, if often clumsily, to decree its availability. But for Janet Batsleer and her socialist co-authors (1985), "'Systematic training in the use of standard English' has proved one of the most effective ways in which the exploited classes, children and adult, have been *induced to consent* to the conditions of their own *cultural subordination*." Standard English is always being represented, she claims, as the language itself, the "neutral and unchanging norm" by which the linguistic practices of all other varieties are judged as non-standard and inferior ("for what else does 'standard' mean?"), whereas standard English is, in reality, merely "*a particular historical practice* of language with its own appropriate occasions and *limitations of usefulness*". In the same paragraph she writes that it is "one of the illusions of the epoch" that the school system can "bring into harmony, single-handed, the *antagonistic forces of capitalist society*". That is an illusion which socialist teachers, "whether as socialists or as teachers, can ill afford to share", so "it is the contradictions that need, at this stage, to be stressed" – the contradictions in capitalist society, and the contradictions that socialists can cause people to perceive in the idea of working-class children having to learn standard English. She is right, of course, that standard English is not a 'neutral' norm: it is the badge of literacy and educatedness, and it is true that some form of cultural 'subordination', or at least *adaptation*, may be inevitable if working-class children are to have access to the forms of knowledge of the modern world.

Class loyalty

As we saw at the end of Chapter 4, the Marxist notion of social class entails for many socialists the implication that non-standard English is part of the integrity and solidarity of the working class. It follows that to allow some working-class children to adopt the speech-forms of the more educated classes crucially weakens that solidarity and political power – according to Professor Arthur Brakel's picture of the power élite's self-interested device of 'skimming-off' the most dynamic members of the lower classes, and British linguists' attempts to represent as jealous opportunists those among the lower classes who have become socially mobile through their use of standard English. The whole idea of moving between social classes – or at least of *other people*'s doing so – is therefore deeply suspect. It is interesting to see this notion at work in the writings of the three main writers we have considered in this chapter.

So we have Roy Harris ridiculing those who, when nowadays urging the case for "standard English" (a term which he puts in quotation marks) use the argument that "it is the [kind of] English to learn for better job opportunities and improved social status" – and the reference he cites at this point is my own 1983 monograph on standard English (see below, Chapter 9). It is easy for someone who has himself moved upwards socially from lesser beginnings to a university professorship (as he has done, and as I have also done) to belittle the ambition of others who would like to do the same.

For an old-fashioned Marxist like Raymond Williams, "the supposed new phenomenon of classlessness" was simply a "failure" of class-consciousness: "the traditional definitions [of the social classes] have broken down, and . . . the resulting confusion is a serious diminution of [class-] consciousness". Of course (he insisted) he was not interested in social mobility for himself – yet it was known that he made a point of sending his own children to private schools, a matter of some comment among his political friends. Despite its sometimes sloppy scholarship and its amateurish sociology, his book dealing with standard English is charged with the warm good nature of an old-fashioned socialist, though even this may to be some extent misleading. Critics have pointed out that from his emotionally frigid home background (he came from a poor family, and won his way to grammar school and Cambridge) Williams learned to love 'the People' rather than actual people. It is not unfair to note as a measure of his *practical* humanity that as a Cambridge don he is said to have neglected his students so flagrantly that they were forced to demonstrate against him: they found he was just "never there" for them.

Dr Crowley's view of the the vexed question of social mobility can be judged by his comments on the account by the nineteenth-century Dorset poet and dialect grammarian William Barnes of a Dorset lad who began work as a servant in the house of a lady who strove to correct his very non-standard grammar. This the boy resisted, threatening to leave, on the grounds (expressed in his own words) that adapting to standard English would expose him to ridicule at home – the use there of such "fine talking" would clearly not be regarded as congruent. Crowley applauds the boy's resistance to the idea of bilectalism, and to adopting what he calls "the language of the educated", which he suggests is rightly regarded as a social handicap among uneducated people.

Despite the assertions of this re-written version of history, standard English was not "the authoritarian creation of a small and self-serving élite" (as Deborah Cameron says the revisionists have claimed; see Chapter 4, pages 52–3); nor, as Leith implies, of government functionaries and élite groups of literati: in fact many of them were just clerks (the "typing pool") and teachers. From the sixteenth to the nineteenth century (with a great boom in the eighteenth century) the majority of those who tried to instruct the uninitiated in standard English and to codify its forms were clergy – both Anglican and nonconformist, often with conspicuous social consciences – and political radicals, and ordinary teachers trying to compensate for the inadequacies of the then school system in giving access for the underprivileged to the forms whose 'correctness' was overwhelmingly attributed, not to their being aristocratic – which of course they were not – but to their being associated with educatedness: the 'learned', the 'literate', 'the generality of scholars'. Professors Howard Giles and Peter Trudgill, in describing their widely quoted 'imposed norm hypothesis' which is used to explain the way ordinary people consistently give the highest evaluations to speech forms perceived as associated with educated people, cite the fact that the emergence of one dialect as standard in the fifteenth century was arbitrary at that time, in order to imply that the prevalence of this norm in the twentieth century is somehow imposed as arbitrary – whereas it is of course a reflection of present-day realities arising out of five hundred years of history. It is, in fact, a widely *accepted* norm, and should be termed such. To use the jargon of modern sociolinguistics, it is a set of norms which are inherent in, or intrinsic to, the sociolinguistic situation of any language or variety in any literate community.

I have made no attempt in this chapter to conceal my considered conclusion that Dr Crowley's book is a disreputable work and, what is more serious, a dangerously mischievous one. But if any should imagine that I misrepresent the book, I beg them to read it, and read it carefully, noting the way it uses evidence, taking account of its gross historical howlers (some of which I have listed on page 277 below), and savouring its use of language – the often dense passages of jargon, the linguistic usages which might almost have been chosen as a challenge to present-day notions of standard English. One of the more valuable insights of Marxism is its notion of *mystification*, a standard and effective device for subordinating and controlling other people.

To be fair to Dr Crowley, it must also be said that he has located and brought together an interesting range of sources relating to attitudes to the English language in the nineteenth and early twentieth centuries, and his bibliography will in this respect be valuable to future scholars, despite its startling gaps in some fields. The problem comes with the way he uses those sources, the perverse conclusions he draws, and the ideological straitjacket into which he feels impelled to fit that evidence.

CHAPTER SIX

Authority in Language:
Anagogy and Prescription

Vigilance in language is worth preserving, lest, in slipping,
others should think you careless in larger matters.

Lord Chesterfield

In this chapter we explore the nature of authority in language –
essentially the question of who or what determines when a particular use of language is judged to be right or wrong, correct
or incorrect. Three closely related elements are at work in determining that kind of authority: standardisation, codification (i.e.,
the setting out of explicit rules), and prescription/prescriptivism
(the actual imposing of those rules on language users).

Prescription and prescriptivism are overlapping terms; they are
sometimes used interchangeably, having the same sort of relationship to each other as authority and authoritarianism, one being a
force, the other the operation of that force. I hope the context will
make it clear in what sense I am using either word. (Incidentally,
the first edition of the usually authoritative *Collins English
Dictionary*, 1979, lists none of these specific linguistic senses of
prescription or prescriptivism.)

For at least three decades now, prescription has been something
of a dirty word in academic linguistics: the task of linguists is never
to prescribe how words should be used, only to describe how they
can be seen to be used in actual practice. "First, and most important, linguistics is descriptive, not prescriptive," wrote Jean
Aitchison (now a linguistics professor at Oxford) in 1978, and this
has been the dominant view in this discipline from the 1950s on,
with just a few bold dissenters. As Professor David Crystal's *First
Dictionary of Linguistics* correctly puts it, "On the whole, the term
prescriptivism is pejorative in linguistic contexts."

The standard work in this field since the mid-1980s has been a book called *Authority in Language* by the husband-and-wife team of James and Lesley Milroy, two established British scholars in the field of sociolinguistics – some of Lesley Milroy's work has already been referred to in my Chapter 3. Their highly influential book, which is now widely cited as authoritative by the linguistics establishment, was deferred to in the Cox Report on English Teaching and is compulsory reading for most British students doing any form of linguistics; it was first published in 1985 and came out again in a slightly revised edition in 1991.

The Milroys begin by disputing the assumption accompanying the proposition about 'description not prescription', which is that we do not need to study what goes into the prevalence of prescriptive attitudes to language. Their book sets out to analyse the whole phenomemon of prescription and standardisation, especially in terms of its social ingredients, for they claim that the study of 'linguistic authoritarianism' is an important part of linguistics. Unfortunately they bring to this task a particular set of assumptions about the elements which went into the standardisation of English from the fifteenth century onwards which other scholars might want to question.

For the Milroys, the early diffusion of standard English was as a result not only of the writing system, the educational system, etc. (no dispute there), but also of various kinds of direct and indirect forms of 'discrimination' *against* non-standard speakers – never, of course, a process of voluntary discrimination by such speakers *in favour of* a variety which opened up what they saw as educational and intellectual opportunities for them. Or if there were such people, this was because of the wider functions available through the use of the standard and, again, involved a somewhat discreditable kind of exploitation: the operation of self-serving, utilitarian motives in those who sought upward social mobility, hoping that they might profit from the prestige associated with standard English – they had "noticed that the *most successful people* used it in writing and, to a great extent, in speech". The Milroys thus echo that emphasis among linguists on the processes of discrimination against non-standard speakers which we have already met in socio-linguists like Howard Giles and Peter Trudgill, who treat respect for, or adaptation to, the standard as involving 'imposed norms' rather than as freely accepted norms. The extent to which these norms derive crucially from respect for a wide range of literature, including popular literature and the literature of religious belief and observance, finds little place in the Milroys' account. Scattered throughout the book are several glimmerings of an awareness of a connexion between standard English and the language of literacy, but nowhere do they show that they discern this as a defining criterion.

Indeed, as we shall see, the fact that norms of 'correctness' reflected the written word rather than vernacular speech is made a matter of criticism. It is represented as incongruous, even absurd, that for hundreds of years people have taken note of the prescrip-tive rules embodied in books, rather than simply following the spontaneous rules enshrined in "the linguistic and communicative competence of the millions who use the language every day". Here again we encounter the assumption, now made famous by Steven Pinker, that everyone automatically speaks their own dialect correctly and therefore has no need to learn the rules of a standard variety which cannot in any sense be regarded as 'better' for any purposes. The Milroys tell us that the need for uniformity in the way language was used was, especially from the eight-eenth century onwards, "felt by influential portions of society" – that appears to be, for them (as for many linguists), enough to damn it.

We are not allowed to know how widely this view was shared by ordinary people. The Milroys admit that ordinary people are con-scious of the existence of a standard form of the language – "People *believe* that there is a right way of using English", although they do not necessarily use the 'correct' forms in their own speech – but these authors do not explain why this is so, apart from the operation of crude self-interest, nor do they show how that consciousness operates. They use the example of a standard

British accent (RP) to claim, following Trudgill, that as few as 3 per cent of the population speak with such an accent, despite a century of mass schooling which has tried to promote its use, and seven decades of radio and four of mass television, both likewise dominated by the use of RP. Two points need to be made here: that the figure of only 3 per cent of RP speakers is a highly speculative, not a scientific, one, and that much more significance attaches to the power that RP has exercised, over that period, in causing speakers to adapt their accents in the *direction* of RP, even though most do not make the adaptation complete, but retain in their accent at least some trace of their regional origins.

A crucial ingredient in the formation of a popular consciousness of 'correct English' was what the Milroys label "the complaint tradition", which they suggest started in the eighteenth century which was "largely, but not wholly, a century of authoritarianism and prescription". But the new eighteenth-century emphasis on such correctness which, as we saw in Chapter 5, led to a spate of dictionaries and manuals attempting to legislate on points of usage was, as we also saw, a continuation of tendencies which had made themselves very obvious in the sixteenth and seventeeth centuries. The Milroys attribute this eighteenth-century emphasis to "the need of a developing nation and developing power" which required, among other things, reliable communication in writing. They do not emphasise two no less crucial eighteenth-century factors – an unprecedented scale of social and geographical mobility, and the lack of an adequate system of popular education. Despite the scorn with which they (and many other linguists) treat later manifestations of "the complaint tradition", they nevertheless recognise the successful achievements of the eighteenth century in establishing, through codification, a much more widespread consciousness of a relatively uniform and 'correct' English than had been possible before.

They find fault with that popular consciousness because of its tendency to "legitimise the norms of the formal registers of standard English rather than the norms of everyday spoken English", but they show little understanding of why the more formal English of the written mode is held in higher respect as a model of 'correctness' than is everyday, informal, conversational speech – which, as was explored in Chapter 3 and has just been confirmed, has to do with the special regard felt at all levels of society for higher forms of literacy. For this reason they cannot explain, and treat as totally arbitrary, the prescriptions (and proscriptions) of particular usages which have been common among textbook writers since the eighteenth century. The fact that a textbook treats the particular usage as 'obviously unacceptable' (when the reader would expect some reference to logic, etymology or clarity) is claimed by the Milroys to be an example of the existence of a 'transcendental' norm of correct English – i.e., one which does not require precise definition in terms of statable rules, but which relies on assumptions about an inherent kind of correctness. We must return later to that 'transcendental' element, with its further associations with morality and the 'rightness' of 'correct' usages.

So their lack of understanding of the basis of popular respect for literate forms is due to their failure to recognise the popular association of standard English with educatedness and competence, and with the ability of that standard variety to perform a range of functions in relation to a complex society which non-standard varieties are not equally well equipped to handle. For the Milroys, particular usages in standard English are valued or disparaged in various periods, not for any 'linguistic' values, but only for 'purely social ones', which they imply have to do with *social status, social class, social snobbery*. Moreover, particular commentators on language 'correctness' are wrong, say the Milroys, to assume that "the model of spoken language lies in the written channel" and to further assume that all reasonable readers will agree. For this, they claim, is not true: "the structure and function of written language is *altogether different* from that of spoken language".

This is not the place to debate, in fine detail, that latter proposition. It is important, though, to emphasise here that many educated people, including some respectable linguists, and also huge numbers of ordinary and not particularly educated people, act as though they believed that those forms of spoken language which are the most acceptable for a number of functions, especially functions associated with formality, are the forms which most closely reflect written forms. Much of the spoken language which is expected of pupils in schools and universities is of a fairly highly structured kind which has been memorably described by Professor Gillian Brown as "*parasitic* upon written language", and she has pointed out that it is extremely hard to develop it in the absence of written language skills. This persistent general respect for the written form helps to account for 'spelling pronunciations' (like *often* with a 't', *fore-head* for 'forrid', *waistcoat* for 'weskit' and a hundred others) and for sometimes incongruous grammatical forms like 'It is I'. What is clearly at work here is the operation of a value-system which admires the literate forms of educated speakers of English and tries to emulate them in speech. As an example of an absurd case of the ignorant comment – a typical present-day manifestation of the complaint tradition – to which these (mistaken) popular views give rise, the Milroys quote from a reader's letter to a newspaper citing a secretary's use in an interview of the phrase "I seen two men . . ." and questioning whether such forms were appropiate in a secretary who had been trained for office work.

Only one correct way?

Underlying this type of comment, say the Milroys, is a set of 'universal' assumptions among all such people who complain about these types of usage: that there is "one, and only one correct way" of speaking or writing, that non-standard usages are illiteracies and barbarisms, signs of an ignorance which justifies adverse comments on – and other forms of discrimination against – those who use them. Yet in fact, they claim, the choice of 'I saw' rather than 'I seen' is *ultimately arbitrary*: the latter is stigmatised for reasons which have nothing to do with *linguistic* values, but rather with purely *social* ones, and which are based on unconscious assumptions about the 'superiority' of one language system over another.

It is of course true that the 'rule' prescribing *I saw* rather than *I seen* is arbitrary, but then so is all language: I say *dog*, a Frenchman says *chien*. But the 'social' values which make it inappropriate for an Englishman to go round talking of his 'chien' to his British neighbours extend to an assumption that a person speaking in a formal interview will know that it is more appropriate to use 'I saw' than 'I seen', unless they are illiterate or ignorant, in which case their usage will be an efficient marker of that ignorance. That judgment about the extent of their educatedness will indeed be closely associated with an assumption – conscious or unconscious – that the language system of standard English, with the greater functional efficiency of its wide range of vocabulary, grammar and styles, is more appropriate to use in such a context than the informal non-standard variety spoken among friends. That assumption is not an absurd one – every one of us, including the Milroys, makes it every day of our lives – and there is a case for saying it is part of the language *system* which we call English.

The Milroys are wrong when, following the sociolinguists Dick Leith and Einar Haugen, they claim that standardisation involves intolerance of variation, "the suppression of optional variability", "a strong compulsion to select one, *and only one*, from a set of equivalent usages". You have only to glance at a dictionary, a text-book of English grammar or indeed the leader columns of a literate newspaper to encounter a wide range of equivalent forms in everyday use within standard English. *Dreamed* and *dreamt*, *among* and *amongst*, *learned* and *learnt*, *though* and *although*, *toward* and *towards* (each of the latter pair capable of being said as one or as two syllables) are only a handful from among thousands of examples of sets of options available. In pronunciation, standard English is full of shibboleths, but a glance at a pronouncing dictionary such as the famous one by Daniel Jones (and its updated editions), or the very good new one by J. C. Wells, reveals the huge number of variants among which to choose with little fear of incurring invidious social judgments – including common words like *again*, *graph*, *lather*, *finance*, *tenet*, *either* and *neither*, *project* (pro- or prod-), *Pakistan* (pack-, park-; -stan, -stahn), *glacier*, *cervical*, *genus*, *primarily*, *trait*, *garage*, *sure*, *tissue*, *lichen*, *issue*, *deity*, *usual*, *privacy*, *envelope*, *poor*, *transit*, *appreciate*, *demonstrable*, the first syllable of *ideology* (ide- or id-), of *economics* and of *electricity*. In fact, standard English abounds in permissible alternatives.

In the grammar of standard English, there are several different (and acceptable) ways of expressing a *future* event, including '*he goes* to London next Tuesday' and *he is going to go, he will go, he'll go*, the use of the last being limited only in certain highly formal contexts. Most educated people would nowadays allow a choice of singular or plural verb after *neither* and *none*. There are at least four permissible options involved in making a statement like *I would have had to be very angry before I would do a thing like that*, substituting either (or both) of *would have to be* and *would have done*. As to word-order, I have freedom to say either *The patient is thought not to be in danger* or *The patient is not thought to be in danger*.

The fact is that Leith, the Milroys and Haugen have all exaggerated the degree of intolerance of variation which is involved in the evolution of a standard language. The tendency at work is not the *suppression* or *elimination* of optional variation, but its *reduction*. There are at least four reasons for that tendency. First, communicational efficiency (even the Milroys recognise this): standardisation is essential for communication outside a local area. Secondly, ordinary people – as opposed to the most learned specialists in English – feel more comfortable with the idea that one particular variant is 'correct'. Thirdly, the reduction of options in grammar and pronunciation which standardisation tends to produce is accompanied by a vast expansion in the range of meanings of words – what linguists call 'polysemy'. Look, in any good dictionary, at the proliferation of different senses of common words. My dictionary lists at least 17 senses for *settle* and 20 for *bolt*; *touch* has more than 40. How many different senses can one think of for words like *appreciate* ('his investment has appreciated', 'I appreciated your kind act', etc.)? Most dictionaries list at least five senses of *surgery*: a branch of medical science, a medical procedure usually involving cutting, a place where a doctor sees patients, a session for doctors to see patients, and nowadays also – a fairly new use – a session for an MP to see constituents. In many instances (as with 'appreciate' and 'surgery') these different senses can only be distinguished by the context in which the word appears. It is as if the standardisation of English worked on the principle that the reduction of variation in grammar and pronunciation operated as a kind of trade-off for the expansion of variation in the meanings of words. Leith appears to be referring to this possibility when he claims, quoting Haugen, that a standard language has minimal variation of *form*, but maximal variation of *meaning*. When we actually inspect the amount of variation which persists – indeed flourishes – in standard English, the first part of that definition is exposed as a gross exaggeration, but if we re-define it is a *reduction* of variation in form, and an *expansion* in the meanings available, we can accept that the first tendency may help to make it easier for the second to occur. So much for what the Milroys describe as *"the total uniformity* that is required by the ideology of standardisation".

A very significant fourth factor seems to be at work, but is in danger of being overlooked in the analysis of standardisation – though the Milroys do finally confront it at a late stage of their analysis. Those who find 'incorrectness' in *I seen* or in (another Milroy example) *them houses is nice* are not merely acting on an impulse to reduce the number of options available to a speaker of acceptable English in the interests of communicative efficiency. Their judgment is the result of the social symbolism carried by these particular non-standard forms, which appear to announce that the speaker or writer is uneducated, or lacking in awareness of the contexts in which such forms might be appropriate. There is, after all, a demonstrable tendency for such non-standard forms to be used by people of least education. And because educatedness is, in many contexts, a highly valued variable, its absence makes the users of its characteristic forms of speech – as well as those forms themselves – open to disparagement.

The Milroys devote space to showing that many of the stigmatised forms around in non-standard English today were used by
some of the great writers in English of past time. It is perfectly true
that English took hundreds of years to standardise certain features
such as its system of negatives (multiple negatives like Bacon's *he
was never no violent man* were still common among educated
people in Shakespeare's day and for some time later), its double
comparatives (*most unkindest cut*) and the distinction between
simple past and perfect tense forms of verbs (many writers around
1800 still used 'have wrote', and Jane Austen had many examples of
uses like 'they *sprung*' for 'sprang'). But it is the conventions of
standard English in one's own lifetime that operate as the decisive
ones.

The Milroys claim that many complaints about specific usages
are actually claims about the 'superiority' of standard English over
other varieties, but without the complainants being explicit or
even aware about this, and that "the function of such complaints is
to maintain public acceptance of one variety as superior to others"
– a superiority which, of course, they (in accordance with the 'linguistic equality' ideology) cannot accept. But they have already
admitted that standard English is the one variety which possesses
the resources of a vastly elaborated and precise vocabulary and
other features which are necessary for the fulfilment of a whole
range of crucial functions in a modernised society, so it is hard to
see why the complainants' assumptions are held to be so perverse
or unjustified, or why the supposition of the superiority of that
standard when used for these functions is held to be reprehensible.

Non-standard speakers may also be subjected to judgments
which relate to 'morality' – the Milroys make a distinction
between what they call Type 1 complaints, which are broadly 'legalistic', and Type 2 complaints (broadly 'moralistic'), while admitting that many forms stigmatised as 'incorrect' involve a mixture
of both elements. The 'moral' factor in prescriptivism would seem
to have two dimensions, though the Milroys do not make this
distinction clear. One is at the level of society in general: the

'correctness tradition', they claim, always involves the idea that the English language is in decline, and this "usually carries with it the notion that general standards of conduct and morality in society are also in decline". The other is at the level of the individual: the use of *I seen* or *them houses is nice* is taken as "a sign of stupidity, ignorance, perversity, moral degeneracy, etc." in its speaker. It seems hard to avoid the probability that judgments about the speaker's degree of educatedness will be made in such cases; where 'moral degeneracy' is assumed it must relate to the idea of carelessness (the speaker has learned, in school, the 'correct' form but is 'carelessly' using the non-standard form in an inappropriate context) – though, as we have already seen, many linguists have dismissed the idea that any speaker uses their language carelessly, or even slurs their speech, and the Milroys themselves insist that "it is simply not possible to distinguish reliably between 'a local accent' and 'careless speech'."

We must return later to this general notion of a kind of morality which is bound up with the use of certain kinds of language. But at this point we need to look more closely at the reasons why people – not just teachers and specialists, but ordinary people – find fault with the use of non-standard forms in contexts where they feel standard English is more appropriate. If we move on from grammatical examples like *I seen* and *them houses is nice* to instances of pronunciation (which is an area peculiarly sensitive to value-judgments of various kinds) we can find many words in which variation is perfectly tolerable and 'innocent' (like *graph*, *lather*, *ideology*, *electricity*, etc.) but alongside these are vowel or consonant alternations which are value-laden. If I say *muvver* for mother, or *barra* for barrow, my pronunciation may be disparaged as Cockney – in other words, it is judged to be non-standard or incorrect, and the option to use it is closed off, for the reason that it calls into play a value-judgment about the educatedness (and perhaps other aspects) of the speaker. Standard English allows me to say *financial* with the first syllable as either *fine* or *fin*, but if I stray into a third option, with the first syllable as *foyn*, it is judged 'non-standard' or 'incorrect' because of its associations with the least educated speakers.

And let us look beyond the changed sounds of single vowels or consonants to what happens if we drop parts of words. I, and many people of a similar educational background, systematically drop (or 'elide') the *k* in the past-tense form *asked*. Test yourself in a recording of your speech: giving the full value to the *k* sounds very fussy and we usually say 'ast' (with, in my case, a long *a*), even when we are speaking deliberately and formally. I likewise drop the central *n* in *government*. Speakers of non-standard varieties who drop part of a word – which may happen systematically in their variety, even when speaking confidently and clearly – will neverthe-less be judged 'incorrect' because it is a feature (however regular) of what is deemed to be less educated speech. It is not the act of dropping (elision) which is judged 'incorrect', it is the whole system of which it is a part, and whether it is perceived to be compatible with educatedness or not.

Not only does standard English drop particular sounds, it drops whole syllables. I seldom say 'library' (three syllables), I normally say 'libry' (two), and I systematically drop a syllable which the spelling suggests is present in words like *interest, chocolate, medi-cine, arbitrary, history, business* (never three syllables, unless I mean a state of being busy), *geography, corporal, suppose, different* and *usual*. *Veterinary*, theoretically five syllables, becomes three for many educated speakers of English – vet-'n-ri. I have met high-ly educated speakers who make one syllable of *police* and I have often heard *balloon* as one syllable. Not content with dropping the central *n* in *government*, many educated speakers drop the whole of the second syllable: guv-m'nt. *Particularly* is often heard, from educated people, as four syllables rather than five. But *Italy* with-out its second syllable, and *ridiculous* or *particular* without the third, and *deteriorate* as 'deteriate' are likely to be regarded as non-standard, 'incorrect', 'uneducated', unless the rest of the accent in which it is spoken is that of an educated person. To change the first *t* to hard *c* in *etcetera* ('ecsetra') is regarded as a non-standardism, and the opposite change, from *c* to *t*, which makes *picture* sound like *pitcher*, carries the same 'non-standard' label. The point I repeatedly emphasise is that 'standardness' in pronunciation is a function of the way educated people tend to pronounce, which has its own set of arbitrary rules, just as standardness in grammar involves excluding the grammatical forms of dialects not associated with the educated. Alongside the four options involving (in my example) *I would have had to be very angry to have done that*, a fifth or sixth option involving either 'would *of* had' or 'to *of* done' is closed off by judgments about educatedness.

Because they reject the possibility that any 'deficit' – of the kind implicit in Basil Bernstein's theory of elaborated and restricted 'codes' – could be involved in speaking a non-standard form of English, the Milroys set out to offer a "better" explanation for working-class children's underachievement in school by developing their theory of 'standardisation', which claims to take proper account of the historical, social and cultural factors which were actually involved in the development of standard English. They deserve credit for their clear recognition that linguistic behaviour is rooted in the social, but the question that must be asked is whether their particular explanation of the social mechanisms that they claim are at work is the right one.

Status and solidarity

Like several other sociolinguists, the Milroys address the paradox that large numbers of people continue to use low-status varieties when they know it may well be in their economic and social interests to acquire a prestige variety. Their answer, as we have seen in the references to Lesley Milroy's analysis (Chapter 3), lies in the pressures exerted by informal ties of kin and friendship in close-knit working-class communities, which generate a strong (even fierce) form of *solidarity* based on social class and locality. Against this, standard English, the prestige form, is held to represent 'status'. As they point out, it is "quite rare" in these working-class groups for a person to prefer status to solidarity. In both varieties of language, specific usages are maintained and enforced by pressures to conformity. As the sociologist A. H. Halsey confirms, "solidarity can have the unacceptable face of exclusiveness".

The idea that a sense of *solidarity* involving groups bound together by social class and locality (and in the Belfast of the Milroys' researches, also by sectarianism) is a crucial factor on one side of the equation, is a readily acceptable explanation. But as to *status*, we have to ask again – as we asked in Chapter 3 – whether what speakers of standard English are choosing when they opt for this variety is essentially status, in the sense of higher social position relative to others: "non-standard usages of certain kinds [they claim] are simply not *socially* acceptable in formal and *high status* contexts. They are stereotyped markers of social class . . ." It is perfectly true that a higher social position is often, though by no means always, available to users of standard English, but, independently of that, a whole range of benefits may accrue to those who can handle standard English – access to a vast literature, the ability to handle complex technology, the ability to exploit the resources of an educational system – which are not automatically of relevance to the user's social status. The defining quality symbolised by the use of standard English is not social rank as such, but instead *educatedness*, of a kind which usually leads to a degree of respect even from those who do not themselves possess it, and often *but not necessarily* leads to an improvement in economic and social position.

These authors rightly point out several differences between spoken and written English. Because speech can rely on a number of situational factors, including shared knowledge among speakers, tone of voice, emphasis, gestures, etc., much more ambiguity and ellipsis in the words actually used can be tolerated, since potential misunderstandings will be reduced by these devices, and speech is usually spontaneous, whereas writing typically involves planning. This leads the Milroys to claim that it is a 'disease' or malfunctioning of the ideology of standardisation that the prescriptive rules derived from written English should be applied to the way spoken English is used. What they fail to address is the problem of how linguists or educationists can persuade the great British public to abandon their longstanding and deeply held respect for the widely available forms of a highly standardised written English, and to treat the spontaneous and context-dependent forms of a much less standardised and codified spoken English with the same deference they give to forms enshrined in centuries of admired literature.*

In any case these two genres (spoken and written English) have in recent years been growing closer together. Many highly literate writers nowadays use contractions and other constructions which are closer to everyday speech (I was*n't that* keen, etc.), and the conventions of writing often invade conversational speech, as when people say 'i.e.' for *that is* (Latin *id est*), or 'conservative with a small *c*' or flap their forefingers to indicate inverted commas round a spoken phrase used in a special sense. The excellent work of the Plain English Campaign has succeeded in reducing the use of the pompous and unintelligible kinds of extremely formal language used on government forms and notices, and bringing it closer to speech. Many (though not all) students become aware, often with minimal explicit guidance from teachers, of the contexts in which the more formal or the more colloquial uses of language are appropriate. There may be a case for advising students that in conversation *To whom were you speaking?* sounds pedantic and *Who were you speaking to?* is much more appropriate, but the same would be true in any piece of writing, since *Who . . . to?* is now the more acceptable form for this 'interrogative' use in standard English, written as well as spoken. The 'rule', however, is more complicated, since in the 'relative' use, written English is happier with *the man to whom I spoke* or *the man whom I spoke to*, where spoken English would prefer the forms involving 'who'

* We noted, in Chapter 5, Lindley Murray's highly influential definition (1795) of standard English as the practice of the best authors, as corroborated by general usage.

rather than 'whom', *the man who I spoke to* or simply *the man I spoke to*. The Milroys are completely right to argue for schools (and examination boards) to offer clearer guidance on where the norms of spoken and written English may differ, but it must be emphasised that in both cases the norms that students will expect to be taught will be the realistic norms of educated speakers of standard English.

And they do need to receive explicit teaching on this. The Milroys fall into the same trap as Chomsky, Pinker and many others when they insist that "all native speakers have implicit knowledge of the grammar of English: it is this knowledge that enables speakers to use and understand their language". Such knowledge is of the usages of their native dialect, and if that is a non-standard variety of English with a host of grammatical, vocabulary and stylistic differences from standard English, they will need prolonged exposure to standard English, and, almost certainly, also some specific guidance and practice on its rules. It is perfectly true that, far from being merely debased and simplified versions of standard English, "non-standard varieties are grammatical and rule-governed forms of English", but the fact that those rules are *different* from the ones required to use standard English correctly, means that the rules of standard English will have to be learnt. It is also true that speakers of non-standard varieties should not automatically be judged to be speaking sloppily or carelessly; and true, too, that sometimes they indeed may be, just as standard English can on occasions be spoken sloppily and carelessly – or even just casually – even by the most educated.

The Milroys point out that in some industrial contexts such as coal-mining areas in Yorkshire, using the 'literary' grammar of standard English is regarded as "hardly appropriate or functional, and non-standard grammar is preferred – or even enforced". The challenge for schools in such areas must surely be to find ways to convince pupils of the potential value to them of standard English, and methods to break through the resistances and the forms of 'enforcement' of the local dialect. These efforts will not be greatly helped by the constant reiteration of the linguists' doctrine of linguistic equality, nor by their warnings against the implications for social class divisions if schools do succeed in breaking through. What they call "the development of a linguistic value system [i.e., the prestige attaching to standard English] which both reflects and reinforces *social class* and *power* distinctions" has the effect that non-standard speakers "are very resistant to attempts to change their language patterns". But should schools never attempt to transform the options of their students, or to do things which might change their students' class loyalties? The Milroys claim that 'Type 1 complaints', i.e., the insistence on legalistic rules of correctness of the *those things* (for *them things*) type, "amounts to a rejection of the social values of the speaker" and by inducing feelings of guilt must be "counterproductive". But any offer of forms of education which can take the student out of an immediate environment which may be very limiting, represents choices among conflicting social values – and inevitably the possibility of rejection of those values which represent part of those limitations. We must return, in a later chapter, to the general educational and social implications of offering school students access to standard English.

In short, from all the points we have just been discussing, it must be concluded that the Milroys' *Authority in Language* cannot be regarded as a satisfactory account of the three closely related factors – standardisation, codification, and prescription – which constitute the main elements of the concept of authority in language. It is suggested here that they have wrongly identified the key element which is symbolised by the use respectively of standard or non-standard English, which is a quality of perceived educatedness rather than specifically social class, rank or status. They are generous in their strictures on "extreme and illiberal" forms of prescription and their sparse examples of these rely heavily on one or two specific textbooks which happen to be easy targets, but they themselves give no clear indication of what they would regard as *acceptable* forms of prescription. Though full of protestations of their own 'dispassionate' approach (which they contrast favourably with nearly all other writers on the subject), they show an insistent need to misrepresent the ideas of people with whom they disagree (see especially Chapter 9, below).

The transcendental aspect

There is another ingredient which is almost entirely missing from the Milroys' detailed analysis, though they deserve credit for at least their brief mention of it. As we have seen, they use the useful term 'transcendental' to describe the tendency amongst very ordinary people to regard certain uses of languages as 'correct' or 'incorrect' without being able to give any reason – and certainly no reason which the Milroys would accept as 'linguistic' – in support of its alleged correctness or otherwise. Here is a paradox, for this tendency prevails even among people whose resistance to education strengthens their own determination to stick to the non-standard forms of their immediate local community, yet who recognise that the usages of standard English are, as Professor Richard Hudson has put it, "in some absolute sense, 'right'". The question is, why do so many ordinary people – including people who do not themselves have a high standard of education – nevertheless go along with all these judgments about 'correct' English, showing great respect for the standard, stigmatising 'incorrect' spoken or written forms, even condemning their own speech as faulty or substandard, and often deceiving themselves as to the extent to which they themselves use standard forms? One obvious reason is, as we have seen, the generalised connexion between standard English and educatedness – people who do not themselves have a high level of education nevertheless defer to this quality in others, indeed they rely on it in the professionals with whom they come in contact (teachers, clergy, doctors, lawyers, accountants, scientists etc.). But there is more than this at work. What we must try to account for is that 'transcendental' quality which the Milroys ascribe to people who demand 'correctness' of language, but for which they offer no explanation beyond an assumption of popular ignorance or perversity about this.

Of the many strands involved in the process of language standardisation, it is this one which hard-nosed empirical linguists find it especially difficult to handle – the set of values which are commonly and popularly attached to the standard dialect and are an important part of its prestige, and by which the sanctity of the rules of correctness in spoken or written language are treated as comparable with a set of moral precepts: for a language user to break these rules is to be treated almost as 'immoral'. Thus we have the American language maven John Simon: "There is, I believe, a morality of language: an obligation to preserve and nurture the niceties, the fine distinctions, that have been handed down to us." To claim a connexion between 'correct' language and morality is, of course, easy to ridicule – as if it implies that the acquisition of correct grammar will cure a man of wife-beating or cheating on his income tax – but the persistence of this 'moral' element forces us to explore the whole notion more deeply.

Around 1750, the coal-miners of Kingswood in Gloucestershire were notorious for their barbarous and savage behaviour, especially when they invaded the nearby city of Bristol; and their dialect was described as "the roughest and rudest in the nation". But, half a century later, an observer could comment that thanks to the efforts of the Methodist pioneers George Whitefield and John Wesley in establishing among them a church, meetings houses, Sunday schools and day schools, they were now "much more civilised and improved in principles, morals *and pronunciation*".

I learned this lesson, as a very green young teacher around 1960, in my first teaching post in a grammar school in the north of England, when I found I had got off on the wrong foot with one rather difficult class I had been given temporarily to teach English to, and their behaviour and written work were careless and sloppy. The following term their respected regular teacher returned, and the care given to their written work – and its resultant 'correctness' and general quality – was transformed, suggesting a connexion between pupils' carefulness in speech and writing and their respect for their teacher and general sense of discipline.

The extreme form of this set of values and attitudes is that which attaches to religious language – the linguistic expressions of religious revelation, knowledge, ritual, or observance – and often gives rise to extravagant veneration for old-established codes of religious language. Consider the following comments, the first of which comes from a Baptist minister, Rev. Leslie Stokes, in BBC Radio 4's *Prayer for the Day* (4 January 1984):

> It shouldn't be possible to hear the majestic truths of the Gospel as if they were commonplace.

When, later in that same year, the Conservative minister Alan Clark (Eton and Oxford) visited a favourite parish church and found that a modern version of the Bible and Prayer Book were in use, he confided his rage to his (now famous) diary: "But no proper Bible, or King James's Prayer Book". And he continued:

> I am completely certain that this degradation of the ancient form and language is a calculated act, a deliberate subversion by a hard core whose secret purpose is to distort the beliefs and practices of the Church of England.

And more recently, from another of Margaret Thatcher's former ministers, the Earl of Gowrie (Eton and Oxford), in a letter to *The Times* (19 August 1996):

> Our church's abandoning of the Book of Common Prayer and the Authorised Version is the biggest single act of cultural vandalism in my adult lifetime; an equivalent of Cromwell's men hacking off the noses of carved saints in Ely cathedral in their iconoclastic frenzy almost 250 years ago. Indeed, the Church's good intentions only highlight the horror of the deed.

Clearly not everybody responds to changes in religious language in this way, and I can cite my own reaction, in the 1960s,

to the new translations of the Bible and the new versions of the
Prayer Book in everyday English, which was very different: I was
exhilarated – thrilled, sometimes – by the new immediacy of the
language and felt I understood its message with a new clarity,
though I also venerated the older versions, and was happy to alter-
nate between the two. Yet we need to recognise that many people
are profoundly disconcerted and disoriented by changes in
religious language – the words in which God is approached and
heard. It is not surprising that in past ages popular riots were
provoked by translations or other changes in the wording of Scripture or liturgy. 'In the beginning was the Word' – and the Word is
not to be messed about with, because it is *sacred*.

But in a much less extreme form, this kind of respect can be seen
to attach also to the standard languages of modern states, among
many ordinary people who regard the 'correct' forms, which they
tend to perceive as unchanging, as having a species of sanctity.
Linguists give short shrift to this sort of attitude, which they tend
to deride as typical of the irrationality and ignorance of what they
call 'folk-linguistics'. One aspect is its assumed connexion with
'morality'; but it also goes beyond the moral and shows itself as an
almost mystical quality of respect for forms of language as, among
other things, the embodiment of nationhood, or national identity
or unity. Another of its characteristics is the assumption that language change is inappropriate, even in some contexts an act of
sacrilege, and as we will see, there is a strong tendency to exagger-
ate the unchanging character of language and to disregard the fact
that any language except a dead one is changing, at least to some
small extent, all the time.

The anagogical sense

This complex of many attitudes involving a sort of veneration
for certain – usually the most conservative – forms of language
can usefully be given a name: I have called it *anagogy*. This is
a convenient word for what the dictionary describes as 'the

interpretation of a word, passage or text (as of Scripture or poetry) that finds beyond the literal, allegorical or moral senses a fourth and ultimate spiritual and mystical sense'. (The *OED* definition refers to "the hidden spiritual sense of words".) Thus the attitude to a language as somehow – in some mystical or intangible sense – embodying aspects of the value system of a society or group, may usefully be described as anagogical.

This is not a new notion: linguists already know (though in their common hostility to the notion of prescriptivism often forget) that – as the American linguist Bloomfield showed for the native American Menomini – even simple preliterate societies have strong notions of 'correct' and 'good' (as opposed to 'wrong' and 'bad') forms of speech. And, as we have seen, linguists are aware, too, that languages, and particular varieties, encode value-systems, though they are often in dispute over what particular values are at issue in any one such language or variety.

Our understanding of this concept of anagogy is helped by the work of British and American anthropologists and sociologists like Mary Douglas, Clifford Geertz, Kenneth Burke and Bernice Martin, all of whom have tried to illuminate aspects of the cultures of both preliterate and modernised societies. These scholars were not primarily, or in any detailed way, concerned with language as such, in their discussions of the mechanisms, and especially the symbols, by which aspects of culture are sustained, and social cohesiveness made possible. But I think their discussions have important implications for linguists.

As each of these scholars emphasises, human beings cannot be understood except as symbol-using animals. Through symbolic activity humans create sense and order in their world, employing words, objects, images, gestures, and so on "both to pin down and to point beyond". This enterprise of culture is (for Burke) "the indispensable condition of human-ness", and for Geertz the creation of order out of chaos and meaning out of flux is the crucial defining function of this activity. This drive to make sense of experience, to give it form and order, is evidently as real and as insistent as the more familiar biological needs of eating, sleeping and sex.

The 'mainstream' forms of language of a given society – whether primitive or advanced – are thus invested with weighty symbolism. Together they provide a kind of social cement; they also provide boundaries which are essential to the framing of the symmetry and hierarchy of that somewhat idealised concept of society in which system has been imposed on what Mary Douglas points out is "an inherently untidy experience", and a semblance of order created. The 'fiction' of an entirely stable language may be seen as part of that pattern-making tendency which enables each human being, in a chaos of shifting impressions, to construct "a stable world in which objects have recognizable shapes, are located in depth, and have permanence". As already mentioned, these forms of language also symbolise, in large modern states, the idea of national unity, one which may have varying degrees of reality but which is in all cases important to a proportion of its speakers.

The work of Mary Douglas can also show us powerful reasons for popular unease about, and resistance to, the kinds of unconcern about linguistic correctness which are so characteristic of present-day linguistic theorists. In her account, culture is seen as the public and necessarily *standardised* values of a community, providing basic categories of thought and behaviour, "a positive pattern in which ideas and values are tidily ordered". Above all, it has authority, since each individual is induced to assent because others do, and its public character makes its categories more rigid. True, those rigidities are often confronted by exceptions and anomalies, which force the culture to devise strategies to cope with change. Such change must, however, take place in an orderly way. Because, as these and many other thinkers have made clear, our selfhood is tied securely to the sacred boundaries and categories that define who and where we are, we must not be surprised if ordinary people are profoundly disconcerted by notions of linguistic relativism or anarchy or the 'let it all hang out' approach. As Bernice Martin (1981) has pointed out, the counter-culture of the

1960s and 1970s, with its attack on established values and institutions, was experienced by a great many people as a conspiracy to take away their defining landmarks. The argument for the exercise of prescription as a mechanism of rudimentary social cohesion through control of both written and spoken English seems to be strengthened by such an analysis. To offer strength and stability – and a sense of reassurance – in a situation of potential disorder is a not inconsiderable benefit, even if we always have to stretch the facts about how firm and unchanging the rules really are.

Mary Douglas has claimed that speakers of what Bernstein called the 'elaborated code' (see above, page 22: roughly equivalent to the more complex type of standard English) are more challenged than are speakers of the more restricted non-standard varieties to stand outside their immediate culture and to inspect – if necessary to reject – their values. We observe, too, that since every distinct cultural group is likely to have rituals and symbols which serve to celebrate specific aspects of its culture, it may be significant that while plenty of ways exist in which to celebrate (in poetry, music, etc.) feelings of regard for the language of the wider group – the national language, or a well-established regional dialect – it is noticeable that the residual social dialects of contemporary Britain – what I have called the 'ghost' dialects – seem to have few opportunities to be celebrated by their speakers. However, the recent proliferation of various television series whose main characters use the non-standard forms characteristic of the vernacular speech of several different regions, now offers one form of celebration.

Bernice Martin is particularly illuminating in her analysis of aspects of English north-country working-class culture, which she is able to make both from her own personal experience and as documented by other sociologists' studies. She draws attention to "the persistent association of respectability with symmetry" in the way the traditional working-class home is decorated and furnished and even in its very lay-out, claiming that this association is deeply embedded in working-class culture. In 'respectable' households it is important that things should have their proper and appointed place, and a whole host of domestic activities – the rota of chores, laundry, personal cleanliness, eating, courtship and even the disposition of items of furniture used by particular family members – are all subjected to the organising principles of ritual and repetition. Margaret Forster's autobiographical *Hidden Lives* shows the same for the rituals of shopping. All these "ritualisations" in working-class culture are crucial elements in "the basis of order", a deeply felt sense of the 'rightness' of structure, order, pattern, repetition, which is a manifestation of "the common predicament of the urban industrial working classes" – the need to create order and meaning in conditions of scarcity, which is also part of the need of the factory system for a disciplined and orderly workforce. But this is not all it was for, since (as Martin emphasises) human beings are never *only* ciphers of the needs of a system, they are conscious moral agents too. Historically, this working-class subculture, rooted in "the sanctity of *boundary and order*", offered the only hope of creating human dignity and a modicum of self-determination against all the odds. Until very recent decades, the price of relaxing any of the boundaries and controls was very high:

> It made the difference between respectability and degradation, between coping and debt, between survival and starvation, independence and the workhouse. The crucial difference between the rough and the respectable was that the rough refused the disciplines of boundary and control. Consequently their homes were hovels in which chaos was signified by literal as well as symbolic dirt, their work was casual and irregular, their budgeting was a seesaw of excess followed by inevitable destitution. The rituals in the working-class culture of control were the foundations of such dignity as they were able to wrest from a hard environment. The *control* was not merely external societal coercion; it was the control which the individual could actively exercise over his own conditions of life. Those who would not or could not exercise this control were infinitely more coerced by

circumstances than were those who embodied controls in
their own lifestyle.

In Bernice Martin's view, this "distinctive proletarian culture of
control" was, paradoxically perhaps, the prerequisite of the organised Labour movement in Britain and of the perhaps uniquely
British tradition of the inherent dignity of manual labour.

If, with the evidence of all these scholars, we try to see how this
pattern of attitudes might influence popular beliefs about language, we can accept that it is likely that – however non-standard
the language of the home and local community – the most
respected forms of language will be those seen to exemplify most
clearly these characteristics of order, stability and control. Those
who are persuaded by this analysis will go on to stress that this
widespread and deep-seated concern with orderliness among sections of the traditional working class is not hostility to change as
such – it would have little respect from modern social theorists if it
were simply that. But change, to be accepted, must be seen as
controlled and orderly change.

A very similar concern about the implications of 'disordered'
language was voiced as long ago as 1599, in the treatise on the
polished rhetoric of "the best English" by Shakespeare's contemporary, the lawyer and writer John Hoskyns: "disordered
speech is not so much injury to the lips which give it forth as to the
right proportion and coherence of things in themselves so wrong-
fully expressed". He also made it clear that his strictures applied
not just to written but also to the spoken English of conversation,
to "the shame of speaking unskilfully", since "careless speech" not
only reflects badly on the importance of the speaker but also dis-
credits his reason and judgment, and the "truth, force and uniformity" of what he is talking about.

Making authority work

Our examination so far of the nature of authority in language has
confirmed that a substantial proportion of the population, includ-

ing both educated and less educated people, share the long-held view that here is such a thing as correct English and that certain uses are wrong or incorrect and may bring some kind of discredit on their users. To quote the late Professor Sidney Greenbaum, they subscribe to the notion that "correct performance marks the user as a responsible member of society", whereas "incorrect performance is viewed as contributing to the decay of the language". They believe this despite the fact that there is, of course, no absolute or plainly obvious authority for that 'correct' English. In France there is an official Academy which regulates the French language in an authoritative way, proclaiming permissible changes in spelling and many other aspects of French. In Germany, the standing conference of the Ministries of Culture of the various länder appoints, from time to time, a commission responsible for proposing changes in German usage, and after consultation with Switzerland and Austria and with ordinary citizens, changes in spelling, punctuation etc. become official. But Britain has always resisted the idea of language management by an official body, especially an Academy: various seventeenth-century projects which might have led to the establishment of one came to nothing, and in 1712 Jonathan Swift proposed the creation of such a body designed "for correcting, improving, and ascertaining [i.e., fixing] the English tongue", but this project also fell through and nothing has come of later efforts in that direction. The task has been left to unofficial groups – like the Society for Pure English (1913–46) founded by the poet laureate Robert Bridges, and more recently the Queen's English Society, or semi-official agencies like the BBC's Advisory Committee on Spoken English which operated in the 1920s and 1930s.

In default of any formal bodies charged with this responsibility, the main agency for prescription (the observance of rules) and codification (the formal setting out of the rules) is teachers, textbooks and reference books, especially dictionaries and manuals which give advice on usage. Because newspapers and magazines have the potential to exercise a strong influence through their wide readership, the printed guides to the 'house style' of particular publications, together with the blue-pencillings of editors and subeditors, are also important. The *Oxford English Dictionary*, though now only one of several respected dictionaries, is widely believed to have special authority, and in the USA *Webster's* has traditionally had pride of place. The definitions in the great Dr Johnson's dictionary, published in 1755, gave free rein to his personal opinions, but the way modern dictionaries label words as slang, taboo, or in other ways limited in acceptability, often causes controversy. Nevertheless such indications of acceptability (which are inevitably 'prescriptive') are essential, since, as is claimed in this chapter, *prescription is part of description*, and it would be extremely unhelpful not to inform the reader that particular words are used in particular ways – that *corpse* and *dead body* are not simply interchangeable in use – and that others (like, for example, *shit*, *fuck* and even *ain't*) need to be used with care in certain contexts.

Many commentators in the past have thought that the meanings of words could be 'fixed' (as Jonathan Swift wanted) for all time. Dr Johnson knew that this was a vain hope, since a living language is undergoing small-scale change all the time. Many words like *wit*, *candid*, *place*, *very* and *lovely* have substantially changed, and gone on changing, in the ways they were used, in the past five centuries. The main sense of *office* used to be a job, now it is a place. In the present day the meaning of *intelligence* which hearers first expect is to do with IQ; in default of that meaning, they might deduce from the context that in fact it has to do with spying. But in Jane Austen's books the primary meaning of 'intelligence' was *news* (though she also used it occasionally in the 'IQ' sense), so we can say that the 'primary' meaning of that word has changed since 1800, and the best kind of dictionary will try to indicate that kind of expectation. *Prestigious* used to mean 'deceitful; given to using sleight of hand', but nobody can nowadays use it in that sense, and any modern dictionary that is any good will point this out to its readers, using a label like 'rare' or 'archaic' for that meaning. If I say that being an MP is a *prestigious* occupation I am not referring to the 'sleaze' (another new word, popularised by the mass media in the 1990s, a noun derived by them from the adjective 'sleazy': it is not in many dictionaries before 1990) which is associated with some politicians, but to their usually high prestige (status or reputation). *Promiscuous* has also undergone radical change of meaning over the centuries.

Many other words have experienced changes, over the years, in the way they can be used, for examples nouns as verbs, and vice versa. *Freeze* is a verb, but we can also have a wage freeze, or remember the big freeze of the winter of 1962–3. Where once I would have had to *make contact with* somebody, I can now simply *contact* someone, a good example of the flexibility of our language. I remember that it was in 1971 that I first heard the word 'diarise', another useful addition to the resources of English. But it is just not true that *any* word can change its form class (i.e., function as a different part of speech): not all nouns can automatically be used as verbs, or vice versa. I can *inch* forward, but not *yard* forward. I can *rail* my goods to London, but cannot (yet) *railway* them there, though MPs can *railroad* the new regulations through Parliament.

Every year some hundreds of new words enter the English language – I am old enough to remember the arrival of *bikini* and *sputnik* – and every year some existing words may be put to new uses. Not all of the new words or uses will stick, and the longer dictionaries contain a proportion of words that are dead or dying. Seventeenth-century scholars who used words like *abstertive*, *caliginous*, *glumosity*, *inscious*, *prolation*, in the hope that they would pass into general use, failed to achieve this. The fact that more than a billion people are now speaking or learning English across the globe means that the number of potentially acceptable forms of English is increasing exponentially. This great acceleration of change, compared with the past centuries of gradual modification, offers considerable possibilities for disquiet and disorientation among native speakers of English. But traditionally, any new use, whether by some scholar, or, more commonly, by groups of less educated people, must pass through the filter of approval by educated people generally. It is the task of the dictionary-makers to monitor that approval, and with the grammarians to describe the extent to which new uses are widely acceptable among educated people.

That filter, and that criterion – acceptability to the educated – constitute for English the mechanism of authority, and embody the notion of prescription which is then codified by dictionary-makers and grammarians. Because they do it unofficially (and because few authoritative grammars are read by mother-tongue speakers) there may be a wide gap between what these codifiers write about the way rules actually operate, and the tradition of prescriptive English – the body of what is regarded as 'correct' English by many ordinary educated people, as well as by many teachers and those who mark for public examination boards. That prescriptive tradition is, as we have seen, dominated by highly conservative notions of grammar and meaning, often showing resistance to any kind of change, always ready to quote highly restrictive rules and other taboos – on split infinitives, on beginning or ending sentences with prepositions, etc.

Yet we know that standardisation, together with its attendant prescription, is "an intrinsic feature of the use of language", and that prescriptivism is universal: in most societies it constitutes "an integral part of people's attitude to language". Even in small aboriginal tribes in Australia, older persons perform the role of pedants, policing the 'correctness' of young people's use of language. In this chapter we have explored reasons why, in the British context, this should be the case. The general contempt of contemporary linguists for prescription is mistaken, and some linguists are beginning to admit this – note especially Deborah Cameron's important book *Verbal Hygiene* (1995). It is the aim of this chapter to argue that the function of prescription is not the prevention of change but rather the *management* of change – a process of control which allows change to be seen as an orderly process.

The fault with much of what passes for prescription in Britain is not in being prescriptive but in being wrongly prescriptive – in quoting rules which are derived from Latin models which may be inappropriate for English, and most of all in failing to represent the real consensus of educated usage in the present day. The application of rules of written language to spoken language is especially inappropriate when those differing rules of English are not codified and made available to teachers and students. The layperson's lack of appreciation of the continuity of change in the English language is only possible because of widespread ignorance, strenuously cultivated by our school system, of the history of the language and of the way English actually works in the present day.

Public opinion may be mistaken about the way language change operates, but not necessarily about the need to control it. The 1996 Reith Lectures were a classic example of the linguist's contempt for popular concerns about language, dismissed as "a cobweb of ideas" which "must be swept away", and ridiculing the assumption that "someone, somewhere, knows what 'correct English' is". For Professor Aitchison, there is no such thing as lazy speech (except by drunks), since "humans naturally adjust their speech to suit the situation". Explicitly dismissing any criteria of educatedness or logic, her verdict – "we need to understand language, not to control it" – disregards all the deep-rooted anagogic concerns that I have tried to outline in this chapter.

CHAPTER SEVEN

Safeguarding English

When the language in common use in any country becomes
irregular and depraved, it is followed by their ruin and
their degradation.

John Milton (1638)

If, as the previous chapter maintained, prescription involves not opposition to all change, but instead the management or control of change, it would be useful to look at the kinds of control which it might be beneficial to the language to exercise.

Newspaper letter columns and talk-back programmes on the radio are full of complaints about particular usages in English which readers and listeners feel are 'incorrect' or 'bad' English. In fact, very much the same uses continue to crop up as exercised the minds of our ancestors, and with increasing emphasis from the eighteenth century onwards. Many shibboleths, like the rejection of 'different to'* (in favour of 'different from') date back to the eighteenth-century grammarians, but the split infinitive ('to boldly go') was a nineteenth-century taboo, and the dangling participle ('walking along the street, the car ran into me') is a relatively recent concern. In many of these cases, like that split infinitive, and the ban on prepositions at the end of sentences, what is wrong is not the giving of a rule, but rather the attempt to enforce an inappropriate rule.

Let us examine some of the ways in which English is changing around us, to see how the activities of prescription and codification could usefully operate to encourage certain uses and discourage others.

---

* A. L. Rowse, distinguished man of letters (born 1903), reports that the sole fault he could find in his long-time friend the novelist-musician Lord Berners was the latter's use of 'different *to*'.

Consider first an example from grammar, very basic grammar indeed: the way we follow a plural noun (or a pair of nouns) with a verb that is also marked for the plural: one bird sings, two birds sing, the boy and the bird sing. We call this 'number concord'. But look at the following sentences:

A1: The government are planning to increase taxes.
A2: The transport workers' union are threatening to strike.
A3: The company have dismissed seven of their staff.

This form is now so common for speakers of British English (some other varieties of English are slower to accept it) that I have not bothered to quote real-life examples from newspapers. The rule is that when a noun is thought of as a collective, it may take a plural verb. A surprising number of words are now thought of as collectives, like police, majority, etc., and the plural verb may follow.

Unlike A1–3, The next four examples have been noted down by me from actual use during the past fifteen years:

A4: Poverty and suffering is, of course, no stranger to Mother Theresa. (BBC Radio 4, religious programme)
A5: The condition of our car and its reliability was terrible. (*Which* magazine report on new cars)
A6: Food and drink has been sent in. (BBC Radio 4, news item on terrorist attack on London embassy)
A7: The cold weather and snow that has hit Britain in the last few days could continue. (BBC Radio 4, weather forecast)
A8: It'll be a long time before peace and harmony is restored. (BBC Radio 4, Labour correspondent of *Guardian* newspaper, discussing a major strike)

Obviously there is a different principle at work here: two nouns (or noun phrases) are joined together to govern a singular verb. Because this form is widely used by educated people (I have scores of examples, indeed the form is so common that I have stopped recording them), we can say that we need to codify a rule of concord for what is regarded as a 'conjoint' subject governing a singular verb.

> A9: More than forty years of Social Democratic rule in Sweden was ended by the defeat of Mr Palme. (BBC Radio 4, news bulletin)
>
> A10: Twenty miles is a long way to walk.

Are these two incorrect – a plural noun with a singular verb? No, because they express a measurement: a period of forty years, a distance of twenty miles. Like all the examples so far, this particular rule of concord has been around for a long time in English. The rule for the conjoint subject (as in A4–8) is now heard in use more than ever, but the A9 and A10 examples are just as commonly found as they always were.

> A11: In England, one in four of the poor today are children. (Canon Eric James, *Thought for the Day*, BBC Radio 4)
>
> A12: One in ten academics are women. (Representative of Association of University Teachers, in *Times Higher Education Supplement*)
>
> A13: Usually, more than one egg are fertilised. (Channel 4 TV, introduction to debate on test-tube babies)

Usages of the type A11 and A12 ('one in four are . . .') are increasingly common among the educated, and avoidance requires what some speakers feel an even more awkward singular, so we may have to get to used to this type, and adjust our concord rules accordingly. A13 may be more of a problem, since 'more than one egg' implies the plural. Here there would be an advantage in some public discussion of which form to prefer.

> A14: The wording of the directions *have* to be checked carefully. (BBC Radio 4, industrial correspondent)
>
> A15: The government have formally announced that the wearing of seat-belts *are* to become compulsory in Northern Ireland. (BBC Radio 4, news bulletin)

Most readers will feel that these two examples are simply incorrect: they do not conform to any of the above rules of number concord, and are examples of a speaker or writer fixing the concord of the verb to the wrong noun – the one nearest to the verb instead of the one which actually governs the verb.

All these refinements of the basic rule for subject-verb concord are to be found in a good grammar book, like the ones produced by Randolph Quirk and his associates, though A13 deserves further discussion. It is true, however, that a large proportion of the population feels (or feel) very uncertain about the reasons why most of the above variations on the normal rule for number concord (especially A1–3 and A9–10) are acceptable. But we also need to be reminded that it is not only this type of concord that is, in specific ways, under pressure of change, as in the increasing frequency of types A4–8 and the expanded number of words which are treated as 'collectives', as in A1–3. Confusions involving the very form of the plural may be causing change: this is happening with many words of foreign origin which have been expected to take plural endings of a foreign form which is not widely understood in English. People, even educated ones, say or write 'a new phenomena', 'different stratas of society', 'a useful criteria'. In the original Latin: one stratum, two strata; one datum, two data; one medium, two media. In the Greek: one criterion, two criteria; one phenomenon, two phenomena. But neither Latin nor (classical) Greek is nowadays an essential accomplishment in an educated person, as it was earlier this century. Especially in cases where the singular form was never firmly established in use, it is now common to hear the plural form treated as singular: *bacteria* is a good example of this. When it became necessary to devise a new term to cover, not just 'the press' but also radio and TV, a phrase 'the media of mass communication' was available, but because few people had ever heard of one 'medium' of mass communication, and most did not know Latin anyway, they treated 'media' as singular – 'people believe that the media is at fault' – and media as a singular with this meaning is now common. The singular *datum* never enjoyed much currency, so the plural form which entered general use then came to be written or spoken as if it were singular – this has the result that *data* can now, in practice, be used as either, without (apparently) doing any harm.

Likewise *graffiti*: the singular Italian word *graffito* ('a scratching') achieved currency in English only in its plural form, which then tended to be used as the singular, since knowledge of Italian (beyond the terminology of music) is not common even among more educated people in Britain. The point of all these examples of plurals is that what many people think are simple rules for forming a plural noun, and when to use a plural verb after a noun, are in fact more complex, and the codification of the relevant rules needs periodic updating in order to reflect actual (authoritative) usage.

Because we remember the history of hundreds of words (like *wit*, *candid*, *prestigious*, *lovely*) which have changed their meanings or their functions over the centuries, we must turn our attention to the ways in which certain words have been changing their meanings in very recent years. *Fulsome* has long been on the slide: it used to carry connotations of excessive generosity, so that 'fulsome praise' meant praise heaped on to the point of insincerity, but this sense is being lost and it usually simply means generous. Even so, when the BBC nowadays tells us that the *Daily Express* is "fulsome in its praise of the prime minister", or that the Home Secretary "is fulsome in his praise of the police", we may have to stop and think whether that useful 'over-generous' sense (which is in danger of being lost) could have been intended. In Canada the confusion may be even worse, since the premier of Ontario, David Peterson, was (at least until 1990) given to using 'fulsome' in a positive sense, e.g. describing his relations with other Canadian premiers as "very fulsome", and saying that debate in his Cabinet was "free, open and fulsome", whereas in the rest of Canada fulsome is certainly understood to mean insincere or excessive.

Decimate has suffered a similar fate. From its Latin root involving 'ten' (compare *decimal*), it was used for many centuries to indicate the taking of one in ten. The ancient Romans could deal with mutiny by decimation – taking (we could nowadays say 'taking *out*') every tenth man; in seventeenth-century England a decimation was a tax which took ten per cent of some people's money. In the nineteenth century the famous Irish Roman Catholic seminary at Maynooth dealt with demonstrations against its severe rules by the young priests-in-training, not by mass expulsion – that would be too wasteful of future manpower – but by decimation, expelling ('culling') an arbitrary one in ten (*pour encourager les autres*).

With the decline in a widespread knowledge of Latin among the educated of the late twentieth century, the one-in-ten meaning of decimate was lost, and people who heard or read the word judged from its context simply that it meant that something drastic had happened, so commentators on the BBC told us that a long dispute with the unions "would decimate the railways" (i.e., severely damage), or that "the manufacturers don't like being decimated by the media" (i.e., severely criticised), and a spokesman for the Nature Conservancy claimed on the BBC that our natural woodlands had, "in a word, been decimated" – which he followed up with the explanation that since 1945 there had been a loss of 40 per cent of woodland. The sportsman who expressed sympathy on BBC TV for a colleague's misfortune, "I feel absolutely decimated for Steven", presumably meant something like 'heartbroken'. Describing the effect of the Stalinist purges in the USSR in the 1930s, a former KGB agent (or, more properly, his English translator) wrote in 1994: "The Bolshevik old guard had been annihilated, the Central Committee *decimated*". Does he really mean 'reduced by 10 per cent'? Does he intend a contrast with 'annihilated'? In fact, what does he mean? A worse problem arises from the kind of use by the *Daily Mirror* to describe the rout of the England rugby team in the World Cup at the hands of New Zealand, and one of their players in particular: "Jonah Lomu destroyed, then decimated England."

Whenever this process overtakes a word, we are entitled to ask whether the change involves a loss or a gain to the language. In this case it clearly does involve loss: the useful one-in-ten meaning, usable for centuries in a number of contexts, is now virtually lost since it impossible to keep apart the old sense from the modern ignorant sense, which is simply yet another variant for *damage* or ('completely decimated') *destroy* (or, for the *Mirror*, presumably worse). It is worth asking the question whether it is still too late to take action on decimate, or on some other words which will be discussed in this chapter.

The reticent cohorts

Among further examples of words which are undergoing a similar process of change in the way they are used even by apparently educated people, let us look first at *reticent*, which for centuries has meant 'taciturn', 'reserved', 'tending to remain silent'. We now have a generation of writers, and speakers on radio and TV, who use it in a different sense: doctors are *reticent to commit themselves* (BBC commentator on the Queen Mother's operation); the BBC's Balkans correspondent speaks of various nations' *reticence to break the arms embargo*; a Black American civil rights activist speaks of being *reticent to believe*; the presenter of a BBC profile of Alan Bennett says that the writer is notoriously *reticent to try to analyse* his craft; the biographer of novelist Sylvia Townsend Warner writes of Sylvia's *reticence to interfere*; a Tom Clancy novel claims that terrorists have never been *reticent about breaking the rules*, and the linguistics professor John E. Joseph writes of dialect speakers' *reticence to talk* into the microphone. An American writer on China has two such uses in the same book, *reticent to talk* and *reticent to show*; and an Oxford professor of politics compares one theorist's refusal to join in some movement with another theorist's lack of any such *reticence*. Even while I was writing this paragraph, an American interviewee on BBC radio was talking of the American press's *reticence to get involved* in some argument.

Clearly, those who use reticent in this way are confusing it with *reluctant*, a word which already overlaps the more limited and specific meaning of reticent (reluctant to speak). It is interesting to note that this same confusion is now also apparent in French, and *reticent à* (or *de*) is now used for 'reluctant'. A doctor explained, in a French TV item on the incidence of AIDS, that many countries of the world *sont très réticent de publier les chiffres*; and a news item on French TV, looking back at the reign of Belgium's late King Baudouin, referred to the way he resigned himself to taking on the burden of kingship: *le roi accepta avec réticence*. Does this confusion matter? It does, because it makes it more difficult to use *reticent* in its original and more specific sense, and this involves a loss to the language. In this case it is an avoidable and unnecessary loss, the result of ignorance and careless use.

Another example is *cohort*. This useful term was originally the name of a group – a military formation in ancient Greece and Rome, strictly speaking a unit of 300–600 men, or, more loosely, just a band of warriors. Then it came to be applied to a group used for statistical and other comparisons, e.g. the cohorts of subjects born respectively in the 1930s, 1940s, 1950s, etc. Thus the writer of a book on AIDS in Uganda correctly quotes a medical expert on how, "on the evidence of *cohorts* of infected people who had been studied for up to four years, about 15–20 per cent seemed to get AIDS, 30–40 per cent developed minor forms of illness . . .", and a writer on French intellectuals of Sartre's generation uses the traditional sense when referring to "that remarkable *cohort* of French thinkers born in the early years of the century".

In recent years, however, this valuable sense has been overshadowed by an ignorant use which equates cohort not with a group but with a single person, a colleague or associate, by a false analogy with co-pilot, co-worker, etc. – 'co-hort'. So BBC presenter Max Pearson announces the radio news headline that "Sir Geoffrey Howe, a Thatcherite *cohort* for eleven years, has bitterly criticised her"; a writer in the *Independent* tells us of a crash after a plane carrying "General Zia and his *cohorts* mysteriously exploded"; another BBC news presenter, Oliver Scott, announces that "the acting President of Bangladesh rounds on Ershad *cohorts*"; and the *Economist* refers to the Conservative minister "Mr Baker and his *cohorts*".

Writer Hilary Mantel, formerly literary editor of the *Spectator*, describes in her novel of Saudi Arabia an exchange on a plane between an Englishwoman and a businessman: " 'We,' he indicated his *cohorts*, 'are stopping at the Marriott hotel.' " John Le Carré – an Oxford graduate with a first in German who once taught at Eton – has two of these ignorant uses in the same book, *The Russia House*: "Clive and Bob were mounted on either side of him like *cohorts*"; and "Brock and Emma had one wall [of the room], Bob, Johnny and their *cohorts* the other wall and centre aisle". Bestselling American author Scott Turow has a similar use, and perhaps the most surprising lapse of all is from Alistair Cooke, a 1930 Cambridge graduate who uses the English language carefully and with admired authority, in one of his weekly radio 'Letters from America' on the BBC, when he told listeners that *Tom Brown's Schooldays* had produced in the USA a horrified reaction at the stories of bullying "by Flashman and his sneaky cohorts".

The loss to the English language is very serious here, since an AIDS expert, for example, can no longer talk of 'the cohorts of infected people' and be sure of being understood to mean the different *groups* of such people, rather than the associates or *colleagues* of the infected people. Trying to protect this distinctive meaning is not just a case of the etymological fallacy – the supposition that a word must mean today what its origins show it used to mean in the past. On that misguided principle, the term 'dual carriageway' must only be used for carriages, not cars; I must not 'dial' a number on a modern telephone which has buttons but no dial; 'pallbearers' must never be used for the people who carry the *coffin*, since the term derives from the pall, the large black *cloth* which covers the coffin; and it is claimed to be wrong to offer three different 'alternatives', since the Latin *alter* meant one of two, so instead I must refer to three or more 'options'. Trying to restrict the use of 'cohort' to *group* rather than *colleague* follows the different principle of protecting a distinctive and valuable use. If there were any important distinction of meaning involved in the difference between (two) *alternatives* and (more than two) *options*, then it would be worth taking action to preserve it, but so far no one has shown any such distinction. By the same token, though the distinction between *can* and *may* was once a battlefield, we no longer fight this one now, because experience has shown that no significant confusion is involved, and the once fairly clear distinctions surrounding *shall* and *will* have mostly dissolved without serious effect, to the advantage of *will*. There is a reduced use, and a declining understanding of the use, of the subjunctive – the distinctive form employed for some verbs in certain contexts to express certain kinds of uncertainty, as in the hypothetical 'if I *were* rich' or 'he insists that it *be* (or should be) done'. In this latter case there may be a loss of a useful distinction. A British professor describes her trip as guest lecturer to a foreign university, where she is summoned to an audience with the pro-rector "who insists I am paid at the appropriate professional grade". Is her host ordering that she *be* paid a fee, or insisting that the fee she is *being* paid is the appropriate one? Again, there may be a crucial difference between 'I am concerned that drugs *are* available' and 'I am concerned that drugs *be* (or *should be*) available'.

May have been confused

This principle of protecting an important distinction is at work in resistance to another tendency which is now widespread in both British and American English, a confusion between *may have* and *might have*, when the first expresses an unfulfilled condition. (A very crude rule-of-thumb is: *might have been* could have happened but didn't, *may have been* could have happened but we don't know yet.) Thus, commenting on the death of a teenager (Leah Betts) from drugs, the BBC TV reporter claimed that the "she *may well have* survived if she had not combined taking Ecstasy with drinking large quantities of water". Hitherto 'may well have' would only be used if there were a possibility that Leah had in fact survived, but the reporter has already told viewers that she was dead, so *might well have* is the appropriate form. Another reporter, said (of a tragedy in which youngsters drowned for lack of life-saving equipment) that "four others perished, but the prosecution says they *may have* survived if the equipment had been available". To say that they may have survived means that there is a possibility that they have in fact survived.

Novelist and politician Jeffrey Archer, interviewed on the radio about being awarded a peerage on the nomination of John Major, said, "If someone else had won the leadership, or if the Conservatives had lost the election, my life *may have* taken a totally different course" – but we know that it did not take that different course. Commenting on the currency crisis taking place in Italy, an ITV reporter said that "if a central European-bank had existed, a crisis *may have* been avoided" (but it had not been avoided!). When a totally blameless and admirable teenage exchange student from Japan was shot by a trigger-happy American householder after knocking on the wrong door, CNN's presenter Bob Losure reported that "Peairs says that he thought Hattori *may have been* high on drugs." After the serial child-killer Robert Black was convicted of one murder, a BBC TV reporter suggested that without the use by the prosecution of the evidence of other murders, "Black *may never have been* convicted". Writers, too, use this misleading form. Reviewing a book on the KGB for the *Los Angeles Times*, Phillip Knightley wrote that the Czech agent Arnold Deutsch recruited many bright students at Cambridge "and *may well have* [i.e., might well have] done the same in American universities had not the Germans torpedoed his ship on its way there in 1942". The British scholar Catherine Phillips, in her 1992 biography of the poet Robert Bridges, wrote of Gerard Manley Hopkins's destruction of his original copy of the poem 'The Wreck of the Deutschland': "If Hopkins' work had met with a warmer reception during his lifetime, he *may have* felt it worth preserving."

In trying to defend the distinctive uses of particular words, we note that it is not true, of course, that two or more very different senses of a word cannot exist at the same time – indeed even completely opposite senses. Consider *curious*: if I say 'he is a curious man' I may mean that he shows curiosity about other people and things, or that I am showing curiosity about him. Here the different senses (expressing curiosity, attracting curiosity) are kept apart by the context, and there is seldom room for confusion. On different pages, Jane Austen used *grateful* to mean expressing gratitude and deserving gratitude, though the latter sense is no longer available to us. Other words with apparently conflicting senses are *dubious, suspicious, sympathetic* and for some speakers (so my dictionary tells me) *dazzle*. *Quite* has two incompatible meanings ('fairly', or 'very') which are usually kept apart by intonation (i.e., emphasis and 'tune'): 'I was quite content'. Until I say it, it is difficult to know whether I was reasonably or perfectly happy. But in some words the senses are potentially so close that it is a struggle to keep them apart, except by providing a lot of very specific context.

The point we return to is this. Most of the changes and new ways in which English is used reflect an enrichment of the language. But in several specific instances, such as the new uses of *reticent, cohort* and *may have*, change involves loss or potential confusion, and we must ask whether something can be done to reverse these particular undesirable tendencies.

Just in case

Now let us examine what appears to another recent development, affecting the 'case' of the pronoun. Some languages have elaborate 'case' systems which change the ending of a noun according to whether it is the subject of a sentence, or the object, or to express possession, and many other relationships. Just as, over the centuries, standard English lost the second person singular pronoun *thou*, so also the language lost most of its noun cases over the centuries – except insofar as the possessive ('genitive') case is represented by *'s* (plural *s'*). But pronouns are one of the last bastions of case, and first person singular *I* (subject case) becomes *me* in the object case and *my* in the possessive; likewise *we, us, our, he, him, his*, etc. When a pronoun is in co-ordination with (i.e., joined to) a noun or another pronoun, that noun or other pronoun goes into the appropriate case: '*I* went home', so 'my wife *and I* went home'; but 'she gave the book to me', so 'she gave the book to my wife and me (or to *her and me*)'; '*we* British expect this', but 'it is expected by *us* British'.

That, at least, is the rule, and people who disregard it are regarded as 'incorrect' – it is the subject of the strongest complaints from listeners to the BBC about unacceptable English, and for one American commentator it represents "an unsurpassable grossness". But in October 1995 I published in the journal *English Today* evidence drawn from more than fifteen years of recording examples of educated people who use the supposedly 'incorrect' forms – 'to my wife and I', 'between you and I', 'for we British', etc. My fifty examples came from prominent literary figures, from university professors (including well-known professors of English), distinguished Oxbridge theologians ('for we who are in chapel today'), politicians (including several party leaders, and three education ministers) like Paddy Ashdown, Lord (David) Owen, George Walden ('the likes of you or I'), Sir Rhodes Boyson, Alan Clark, Paul Channon and Mrs Thatcher ('for we who remain'), and in 1996 we had an example from John Major. Shakespeare himself used this form, Queen Mary II used it in 1689, and King George VI used 'for you or I' in 1945.

It is difficult (indeed, I think, impossible) to show that any confusion can result from these uses, despite the claim by that American commentator that they lead inevitably to "every type of deleterious misunderstanding". Moreover, such a volume of consistent present-day use by people who satisfy every normal criterion of 'educatedness' – graduation from (often famous) universities, or literary reputation, or the ability in all other respects to use the language in highly acceptable ways – or who are in some other way high-status figures (like royalty), means that we must question whether there is now only one rule for pronoun case, or whether, as I have suggested, we should now recognise that there is an alternative rule. But, to be an effective rule, recognised *by whom*?

Many people express irritation – even rage – at particular usages, often without any reason, simply dislike of the new. I know a retired, Cambridge-educated, professor who cannot stand any reference to *Oxbridge*, although this term has been in common use for several decades, serves a useful purpose as a shorthand term for the two ancient universities (especially in comparison with the newer ones), and involves no loss of meaning. Alan Bennett's diary for 1995 mentions some of his particular hates: he dislikes 'grounded' (for *gated*), 'Brits', 'for starters' and, when used intransitively, 'hurting'. Readers contributing their own hate-words or phrases to a Sunday newspaper nominate executive (as in 'business executive'), heist, male chauvinism, marginalisation, post-modern, sassy, sexuality, sisterhood, spirituality, gobsmacked, gutted, feisty, parameters, Brits, dodgy, iffy, guy, gay, basically, concept, prioritise, totally, synergy, whatever, seriously, stuff, hardline, die-hard, ex-pat (*sic!*), in terms of, I guess, user-friendly, fayre, driveway, gale-force winds, weather conditions, in excess of, meet up with, head-butt, cutback, price-tag, scoreline, after (for 'afterwards'). Obviously, many of these are purely personal foibles and would be regarded by most people as useful contributions to effective communication. A reader who hates *actually* claims that "It is difficult to construct a sentence containing the word 'actually' that changes its meaning if the 'A' word is removed", but grammarians can show a very definite apologetic function for this useful word. For many years people resisted the use of the adverb *hopefully*, arguing that it could not be used as a 'sentence adverb' indicating the speaker's attitude to the main verb ('hopefully, the train will now arrive early'), whereas such sentence-adverb uses were already well-established with plenty of other words like *sadly* ('sadly, he died young'). Their resistance was due to the fact that this was a relatively new example, and they were suspicious of new uses; also, for British people, the resistance was because the new use was observed to be common in America. In America there had been resistance because this usage was thought to be an echo of German. So what the English language needs is a form of authority that can easily be appealed to for guidance as to the uses which are acceptable compared with those which are not – an authority based not on an individual's irrational likes and dislikes but on the genuine consensus of educated opinion.

As we saw in Chapter 6, attempts to create an official 'Academy' to fulfil this function for English, on the lines of the one in France, have consistently proved unsuccessful, and the nearest we have to this is appeal to the most respected dictionaries, especially the *Oxford English Dictionary*, and a number of grammar books and manuals of usage, among which the works of H. W. Fowler and Sir Ernest Gowers are the best known, though neither is regarded as totally definitive.

The fact that English has no official regulatory body like an Academy has many disadvantages for speakers of the language. It matters little to people like me, since I have made a special study of the history and present character of English and I use it with a certain confidence – though even in my case there will be people who hunt through this book and gleefully seize on 'mistakes'. But the vast majority of speakers of English in this country have not had that privilege. Their ability to use English with confidence is compromised by two different types of 'linguistic insecurity'. One form of insecurity is the fear of making mistakes and being thought incorrect; the other is the lack of any clear guidance about what *is* considered correct. In our concern to reduce the effects of the first type of insecurity we have simply increased the disadvantages of the second. Linguistic theorists thought that by pouring scorn on prescriptivism and the power of rules of correctness they would abolish the first type of insecurity – speakers and writers living in dread of saying or writing the wrong thing – but, as we saw in Chapter 6, the notion of correctness cannot be dismissed simply by wishing it away or declaring it dead. Not only do very ordinary people feel unhappy when they encounter what they believe to be 'wrong' uses, but judgments about correct and incorrect – acceptable and unacceptable – English matter very much in day-to-day encounters where the user's authority or credibility are at issue, and in courts of law, in interviews for jobs, and in public examinations where candidates may officially or unofficially be penalised for their faults in using standard English.

This is why I have come to the conclusion that the time has again arrived to agitate for the creation of an authoritative body to issue advice on the 'correct' use of English – i.e., the most acceptable usages, those which find most favour among educated people. As has been suggested for particular linguistic points in this chapter, some common forms will be condemned, others welcomed, and others admitted as permissible alternative usages. These judgments must be codified as 'rules' of guidance and must be made available to everybody, taught to children in schools and made accessible through reference books available in public libraries. Any disadvantages from the existence of what some will doubtless reject as 'dictatorship' will be more than compensated for by the confidence which it will give to ordinary people that they now know clearly which forms carry the most respect, so that the arbitrary privilege enjoyed by professional linguistic scholars like me is extended to the ordinary citizen.

There are two ways of doing this: by creating an *official* Academy on the French model, or by encouraging the formation of an *unofficial* group of respected users of the language who will offer guidance on a whole range of specific points, updating their judgments at regular intervals – but always bearing in mind that their codified 'rules' of usage will only have as much credibility as the wider community of the educated is prepared to give them. The underlying principle is the democratic one of creating greater equality of access to the forms of language which, in a thousand ways, have the greatest power to improve the lives of ordinary people.

Engineering the language

One of the responsibilities of such a body would be in relation to 'language engineering' – the deliberate attempt, for social reasons, to alter the way people use certain forms of language. The informal pressures of public opinion, led by high-minded individuals including linguistic scholars, editors, teachers and others, have already had considerable success in making speakers and writers conscious of the undesirable use of certain words on grounds of racial offensiveness or the disparagement of women. In my boyhood I heard people readily using verbs like 'to jew' or 'to welsh', or the hate-filled word 'nigger', in ways which must have been deeply offensive to Jewish, Welsh or Black people, and it is largely thanks to these efforts that the vast majority of people – and most notably the younger generation – now find such words totally unacceptable. The pressures, from feminists and others, to replace the use of gender-specific words like waiter and fireman by wait-person and firefighter, have had a degree of success, though extremists who insist on *herstory* for history and *ovular* for seminar have put an unreasonable strain on the public's general sympathy – as have the excesses of the 'politically correct', with their insistence on *visually challenged* for blind, *differently abled* (for disabled), *differently hirsute* (for bald), etc. The most effective alterations are likely to come when not insisted on, but as recommendations subjected to the test of voluntary use, but it would help if there were a recognised body of agreed rules into which these improvements could be formally incorporated. We note that it is only standard forms of language which are likely to be subject to control by 'language engineering' of this kind, helping to discourage sexism, racism and other undesirable forms of prejudice.

From the 1980s on, it has been common to substitute *their* for *his* (or *his or her*) in constructions like 'Everybody must clear up their own mess', and this option has good historical precedents. The problem is that *they*, *them* and *their* for *he*, *him*, and *his* have gained ready acceptance but the combinations involved are harder to swallow. Professor Laurie Taylor's column in a university teachers' newspaper imagines a notice in a university department which advises what students should do if "the member of staff the students wish to see is *themselves* out". An important task of any regulatory body would be to establish the use of a unisex pronoun to replace the cumbersome *he or she*, *his or her* and all their combinations – many candidates for such a set of pronouns have been suggested over the years,* but the lack of any authority has prevented the taking of any action.

Another aspect of English which cries out for some form of regulation is spelling. The arguments for radical reform are, for me, much less convincing than the case for piecemeal change in instances which give rise to constant confusion. This is obviously the case with a handful of words like *read*, *lead*, *live* and *row*, and it ought not to be difficult to create a contrast between *to read* and *have redd*, *to lead / led / ledd* (with *ledd* being used for the metal Pb), *to live* but a *lyve* (i.e., not recorded) performance. A choice would have to be made to change to either 'rau' for row (noise, fight) or 'rho' (or 'roh'?) for a *row* of beans, or to *row* in a boat race. It is odd to have a University of Reading (rather than Redding), since all universities are supposed to be about reading.

Estuary's missing consonants

One major development in the way English is used – specifically its pronunciation – has been labelled 'Estuary English'. This term was coined by the British scholar David Rosewarne in the early 1980s and has been taken up by many others since then (sometimes without attribution to Rosewarne), and in 1995 Estuary English was specifically named and condemned by the Secretary of State for Education as a form of English to be discouraged by schools. Rosewarne drew attention to the fact that many people in the

---

* Among the suggestions are: ne, en, thon, hi, le, ip, ir, ons, e, hesh, se, co, ve, tey, ze, na, po, em.

South East of England, especially the wide general area adjacent to the Thames Estuary, were tending to use an accent close to RP (the standard 'BBC' accent) but characterised by certain features of what some linguists call 'popular London speech', such as the distinctive treatment of 't' and 'l' in certain words. In my own book on accents in 1989, I drew attention to the invasion of RP by these features of 'popular London speech', but without using Rosewarne's convenient term. As an example of what we can now usefully call the Estuary treatment of 't', I used the phrase 'there's a lo*t* of i*t* abou*t*', to show how the 't' at the end of a word is now tending not to be sounded – linguistics specialists call this 'word-final t-glottalling'. Cockney (of which 'popular London speech' is a modified form) has long had not only this tendency but also the dropping of the 't' in the middle of the word, as in Cockney's *a better bit of butter*, in which the 't' sound at the end of *bit*, and also in the middle of *better* and *butter*, is strangled. The ordinary citizens of Glasgow also tend to do this in their local accent, i.e., with the 't' both in the middle and at the end of the word. So far, only the end-of-word 't' strangulation has become general in Estuary English (and indeed far beyond South-East England), and it will be interesting to see whether the middle-of-word tendency will follow. Together with this end-of-word treatment of 't' is the other 'popular London' (and originally Cockney) feature, the making of 'l' in certain words into a vowel, so Walter becomes 'water', milk 'miwk' and St Paul's 'St Paws'.

It remains to be seen how far this treatment of 'l' will become general among speakers of standard English, but the end-of-word treatment of 't' has reached epidemic proportions in England, and it is now common to hear it among school teachers and other professional people, including university professors, especially among the younger age-groups. Oxford's Professor Aitchison, whose scorn for all forms of prescriptivism has already been noted, has ridiculed the idea that anyone should be concerned about tendencies such as this, pointing to the example of the French language which cuts off the endings of many words which end in consonants. That example is indeed relevant, though she under-estimates the feeling of deep unease which this development in our language causes to speakers of what are now centuries-old forms, partly because they do not know what possibly far-reaching impli-cations there might be for the ability of English to function clearly and efficiently as a means of communication (including inter-national communication). Until we can think these out, and be sure that there is no real loss to the language, we must seek ways of trying to bring this new tendency in spoken standard English under control. This might be the first task of a newly founded Academy or its unofficial equivalent.

CHAPTER EIGHT

Language in School:
The Lost Generation

*No serious damage is done to national tradition if a boy is taught
to say 'I'll hit him' instead of 'Us'll hit he'.*

George Sampson (1925)

English has been taught as a school subject in England since the
sixteenth century. In the nineteenth century, with the beginnings
of mass education, it became dominated by the teaching of grammatical rules, mainly based on Latin models. That influence of
Latin was entirely understandable, given the fact that English had
by then incorporated up to a quarter of the entire vocabulary of
the Latin language, and that all educated people had had a training
in Latin, so change awaited the work of a new generation of
grammarians – essentially after 1950 – with a model of grammar,
independent of Latin, which actually reflected educated English
usage. Old-style teaching of English, emphasising parts of speech,
spelling, punctuation, the sequence of tenses, the ability to change
singular words into plurals (*scarf* into *scarves*), and for older pupils
leading on to précis skills and to exercises breaking down sentences into clauses and naming their respective functions, was
often taught in highly abstract ways, unrelated to real-life use of
the language, and though abler pupils often derived great benefit
(sometimes felt only in retrospect), many teachers doubted the
effectiveness for the average pupil.

Around 1960 this emphasis on the explicit teaching of grammatical and other rules gave way, within a short period, to a totally
new emphasis in which many of these elements were not specifically taught: the assumption was that these basic skills would
develop by a process of osmosis – from exposure to appropriate
literature – and by the processes of their own creative writing.
Sheffield's Professor Norman Blake describes the situation thus:

"Grammar, taught through rules, was deemed prescriptive and thus inhibiting for schoolchildren who were to express themselves as well as they could. Expression was considered by many teachers to be more important than its correct formulation and packaging." As a result, he says, many pupils left school with "very little understanding of how English as a language worked and what its component parts were. Parsing and other grammatical exercises were abandoned in favour of creative writing."

Yet the new emphasis was not merely the drastic reduction, in classrooms and in public examinations, of these elements of explicit language study, but their replacement by activities deemed to further the pupils' 'personal development'. In this respect they ran parallel with contemporary tendencies in schools in North America and in Australia. An American educationist characterised the typical programme of English teaching in his country as "an amalgam of journalism, play-production, business letters, research techniques, use of the library, career counselling, use of the telephone, and advice on 'dating'." Many British pupils did not even receive all those arguably useful elements, but in all these educational systems the school subject 'English' had come to be regarded by many teachers as a "free-wheeling vehicle for the child's emotional and social development" rather than a rigorous academic discipline to be learned.

These changes chimed with a number of trends on both sides of the Atlantic. First, there was the emphasis on linguistic equality which, as we saw in Chapter 2, became common in this period, effectively disparaging both standard English and notions of correctness: "all English is standard in its appropriate domain", which is fine provided that the respective domains appropriate to standard and non-standard varieties are spelled out. With what some linguists now concede was insufficient regard to the need for qualification or the dangers of overstatement, leading scholars made pronouncements which made them seem to be 'language libertarians' – since "if there were no single standard English, then all varieties were standard, thus *anything goes*". The notion that, in any case, research had 'proved' that the teaching of grammar did not improve pupils' skills in written English lent powerful support to the abandonment of its formal teaching, and we must return to this topic later. Labov's famous demonstration that there was no such thing as language 'deficit' was widely publicised in the United States and Britain from 1972 onwards, and in 1975 Professor Peter Trudgill of Reading University published his book *Accent, Dialect and the School*, which confirmed the message of linguistic equality: standard English is "simply one dialect among many" and any prestige it has is *only* because of its association with "higher status speakers in our community"; any advantage for a pupil in using standard English on an application form is a "purely social one". Trudgill argued that it only required that teachers' attitudes towards non-standard English become more positive, and this would be sufficient to remove the educational disadvantages experienced by non-standard speakers, especially if everyone could be persuaded that "judgments about 'good' and 'bad' language are, from a linguistic point of view, completely arbitrary, and *without foundation*". The reception of Trudgill's book by the educational press as a valuable corrective to the 'obsession', on the part of schools, with standard English has already been noted (page 25). Many teachers now came to accept what they were being told on all sides by linguists: that to 'correct' their pupils' 'mistakes' in English was the imposition of an *alien* dialect, and thus constituted an *act of oppression*. It was not long before these ideas began to penetrate the pupils' own textbooks, encouraging schoolchildren to believe that standard English is only "just as correct as any other dialect".

The 'anything goes' principle came into its own in the 1960s when, according to Professor Brian Cox, "children were encouraged to write freely without the discipline of craft, and without bothering about spelling, punctuation and grammar" – and were so taught by what the poet Ted Hughes called "ill-trained and sometimes politically motivated teachers" who for the next three decades "simply stole the term 'creative writing' to dignify their travesty". The 'personal development' case was advanced by an influential book by the school teacher (and later Cambridge don) David Holbrook: its title, *English for Maturity* (1961), appeared to imply that it would be left to the teachers of other subjects, like history and foreign languages, to teach for literacy. In 1967, for example, graduates training at Cambridge University to become specialist teachers of English were told not to teach grammar, and especially not parsing or clause analysis, because Chomsky's 'transformational grammar' had changed everything, but was too hard for pupils to understand. (Since then, the Chomskyan model has lost its predominance, in Britain if not in the United States, in favour of an updated and more credible version of traditional grammar.) The hostility to the explicit teaching of grammar was reflected in the journal of NATE, Britain's National Association of Teachers of English, which in three decades from 1964 published a total of only two articles on grammar teaching, both of them critical of the teaching of this element, and official thinking in the association is echoed in the title of an article on lesson content by its editor in 1978, an influential teacher-trainer: "When in doubt, write a poem".

Enough public concern about these developments had begun to be expressed by the early 1970s for Margaret Thatcher, who was Secretary of State for Education and Science in the Heath government (1970–74), to establish a Committee on reading and other uses of English, under the historian Sir Alan (Lord) Bullock, which sat from 1972 to 1974 and reported in 1975. It is no secret that she had hoped that it would come down firmly in favour of an emphasis on standard English and on the teaching of grammar, but in this she was bitterly disappointed. In the voluminous report there is hardly a mention of standard English, but there are remarks critical of old-style prescription, and it reiterated what was by now a widely repeated truism that "it has been shown that the teaching of traditional analytical grammar does not improve performance in writing". However, it stated firmly that "standards of writing, speaking and reading can and should be raised", and its main recommendations required schools to have concerted policies on reading and on general language development, especially on what it called "language across the curriculum". In its battery of tabular evidence it exposed the gross mismatch between the qualifications of teachers and the needs of the school subject 'English': barely a third of those involved in teaching English had any discernible qualification directly relevant to the task (in the sense of having, for example, a degree or a teacher-training certificate in which English was a major subject). Indeed, the picture may have been even worse than that given by the Bullock Report, since the subject 'English' studied by most university graduates in that field, and by many who in that period trained in colleges of education, might consist entirely of the study of English *literature*, and bear no direct relation to the needs of the secondary school pupil in the 11–16 age-range, where English language rather than literature was a compulsory subject.

In this respect the Bullock report confirmed what many observers had already begun to lament: that, as a result of these large gaps in teachers' knowledge and in what was required of pupils, Britain was the only country in Western Europe in which school pupils were not given a systematic knowledge of how their language worked. It is not uncommon to meet (for example) products of the German educational system who can discuss aspects of English grammar and usage, as well as comparable aspects of German, more readily than products of British education can discuss English. Any project to restore the systematic teaching of English grammar would have to confront the limitations of knowledge of that 'lost generation' of teachers no longer confident about describing to children how English works.

Disappointed at the outcome of the Bullock enquiry, and convinced (rightly or wrongly) that standards of English usage among school-leavers had fallen, Mrs Thatcher when she became Prime Minister made another attempt, and the Kingman Committee appointed by her Education Secretary Kenneth Baker early in 1987 produced their report, to a "very tight deadline", in March 1988. Necessarily much briefer than Bullock, it began by emphasising that for uses beyond the immediate community, "the standard language [is] indispensable" – standard English is a "great social bank" – and that the ability to move with facility between a home dialect and standard English should be open to all. At the same time it displayed the now routine deference to the principle that "all languages are rule-governed systems of communication, and none is linguistically superior", leaving it unclear, certainly to any lay person, what *linguistically* superior might mean. It argued against a return to traditional grammar teaching, which "over-emphasised parts of speech, sentence structure and punctuation", partly because it was based on a model derived from Latin, and the Committee proposed its alternative model of simple, non-Latinate grammar which was to be the basis of a new emphasis on 'knowledge about language' for pupils in primary and secondary schools and for intending teachers.

Professor Cox's Report

In 1988 the Conservative government imposed a national curriculum, for the first time in British history, making English one of three core subjects for all pupils aged 5–16, and in the same year a working group was set up under Professor Brian Cox to advise the government on appropriate attainment targets and programmes of study for the four key age levels at which all children would in future be tested. Cox's credentials were impeccable: he and A. E. Dyson – two inspirational university teachers of English literature – had founded in 1959 the journal *Critical Quarterly* which, both by its contents and through the vacation courses for teachers which grew out of it, had an important influence on generations of teachers and students of literature. Both had won their way from underprivileged homes via grammar schools and scholarships to Cambridge, and their concern that headlong 'comprehensive' reorganisation of schools, and other aspects of the progressivism of the 1960s, appeared to be closing off the very opportunities which had led to their own intellectual liberation, inspired the series of Black Papers which they instigated between 1969 and 1977.

Professor Cox's working group produced its recommendations for the English curriculum in June 1989. They made important proposals about reading and the pupils' development of "knowledge about language" (in fact another name for grammar), and stated unequivocally that "competence in standard English is clearly a central aim of the English curriculum". There followed the usual ritual incantation that "On purely linguistic grounds [standard English] is not inherently superior to other non-standard dialects of English, but it clearly has social prestige", but this was immediately qualified by indicating the important educational, official and international functions which are available to standard English because of its elaborated vocabulary and syntax.

Professor Christopher Brumfit, an expert on language and education, has described the Cox Report as representing "the current liberal consensus on good classroom practice" in English teaching, and it is hard to quibble with that judgment. But it was also something else – the prelude to fierce controversy. The media created a storm of controversy around the Cox proposals, and especially over the apparent avoidance of any firm commitment to the teaching of what could readily be recognised as traditional grammar. This furore was described by the erstwhile Cambridge structuralist Colin MacCabe as "the most ignorant and the most viciously stupid public debate of the past twenty years", and that was in 1990; there were to be several more years of dissension over translating the Cox proposals into a national curriculum for English.

According to Cox's 1995 account, *The Battle for the English Curriculum*, a small group of right-wing extremists, including "elderly traditionalists, emotional about language", mounted a campaign, with other pressure groups, against the Cox Report and in favour of "old-fashioned grammar lessons" and "the imposition of what was called 'grammatically correct spoken Standard English' for all children from the age of 5", and this group took control of the National Curriculum in 1991. Throughout this time, criticisms were also coming from the political left. One consequence of the agitation from the right, and of the hostility of Conservative education ministers, was the cavalier treatment of Professor Ronald Carter. This widely respected expert in English language studies was commissioned by Kenneth Baker in 1989 to mount a £21 million project to produce materials on Language in the National Curriculum (LINC), but when presented with them in 1991, Baker's successor Kenneth Clarke not only suppressed the materials as, in conservative terms, politically incorrect but tried to prevent them from being made independently available to teachers. The official view was that the development of the materials had been excessively influenced by people who were against the systematic teaching of spelling and other basic skills, and in favour of the 'developmental' or 'emergent' approaches.

All this was being transacted against a background of media discussion which regularly oversimplified and trivialised the issues as a battle between two 'absolutes' – between patently obvious 'correct' English and all the 'loonies' who wanted to allow pupils, for example, to split infinitives or end sentences with prepositions. It must be doubted whether the British press has done any service to the cause of standard English by wild and indiscriminate defence of the most conservative and inflexible notions of correct English. Again, it did not help that a model of reasonable prescription reflecting the actual usage of educated people is not widely available in Britain.

It is possible to see these years of bitter controversy as involving a confusion of three interrelated but separable issues: beliefs about declining standards; beliefs about the efficacy or otherwise of the explicit teaching of grammar; and beliefs about the nature and functions of standard English itself.

Whether the general standard of education in Britain (or indeed America) has fallen in recent years is a vexed question. There are specific areas of concern, such as whether 'A' levels represent for

18-year-olds the same standard in certain subjects today as they once did; whether the replacement, after 1987, of 'O' levels by GCSE has represented a dilution of standards for 16-year-olds; how far the reading and mathematical skills of pupils at various ages compare with their counterparts in other countries. On the other hand, it is obvious to me that students in our best universities work harder, and to better effect, than did my generation more than thirty years ago, and they also have to work harder and achieve a higher standard in order to enter such universities. Yet alongside these positive signs of improved standards there is a mass of evidence suggesting that at the other end of the ability range there is much which should seriously concern us, and that there are well-founded worries, not so much about the level of knowledge or skill in specific disciplines, but about the general ability of the products of our educational system to handle the English language, especially in its written form.

Some observers have noted that whereas many young people demonstrate incisive speaking skills, their writing skills seem impoverished: their models seem to be the tabloid newspapers, whose staff consciously limit the complexity of their sentences and the level of sophistication of their vocabulary. To give a few examples: around 1990, Economics 'A' levels for some leading examination boards replaced longer exam questions by half-questions, which are less testing of the candidates' ability to develop and sustain an argument. Those responsible at the European Parliament in Luxembourg for recruiting British translators of written texts from foreign languages into English complain that strong candidates with a good command of the foreign language may be let down by serious weaknesses in written English, even in such basic skills as spelling and punctuation. The columns of the educational press regularly feature reports of the frustration and despair of university teachers at the inability of their students to handle the basic conventions of written English – this has long been true for North America but is now commonplace also for Britain, Australia and New Zealand. Teachers in British university departments of English Literature nowadays need to explain to their Honours students not only that Milton came before Shelley, but also that they should not refer in their essays to *Keat's* poetry or *Dicken's* novels.

A survey of standards of English among undergraduate students at a sample of Britain's 'traditional' universities (i.e., before the upgrading of polytechnics) was carried out in 1991 by Dr Bernard Lamb on behalf of the Queen's English Society. That body is widely regarded as committed to a very conservative notion of correct English, and this may be taken into account in evaluating the findings of the study. As a guide to the reliability of its scientific method, it should be noted that Dr Lamb is Reader in Genetics – a discipline rooted in statistics – at Imperial College in the University of London. The survey, for which the response rate was very satisfactory, was conducted across a range of subject departments, aiming to evaluate students' ability to communicate about their own academic discipline, but there was a slight preponderance of English departments, where it was assumed that standards might be higher.

A small proportion of the respondents (who were usually senior tutors) showed themselves unsympathetic to the body conducting the survey, and the "narrow prescriptive approach" which they associated with the Society. One of these, an economist, while admitting that "many of our students do have weak English", felt that "the best response is in much more reading and writing, rather than drilling in punctuation and grammar". Almost all respondents admitted a serious problem, which they felt arose mainly from the way English was taught at school.

The head of one English department considered the problem to be twofold: "trendy educational theories dreamt up by out-of-date mediocrities, and teachers who are themselves barely competent in English usage". A philosophy don called for an education which would give "a conscious, articulate knowledge of traditional grammar", including parts of speech and "how to diagram a sentence". But scientists were, if anything, even more scathing, and especially engineers, who pointed out that many of their graduates might expect to spend most of their working lives in generating persuasive arguments in written and spoken English, and urged the re-introduction of the teaching of formal grammar in school "as a matter of urgency". One biologist claimed that in the future, more sophisticated word-processors would automatically 'pickup' (*sic*) punctuation and grammar errors, but many more biologists expressed this sort of view: "Low English standards seriously affect the ability of many students to express scientific ideas or facts with any accuracy or coherence. And standards are dropping. Correction of their errors in English is often strongly resented and 'has never been done before', they say."

The annual reports of public examination boards tell the same story, year after year, of persistent spelling howlers, the inability to write in sentences or to punctuate. But at this point one important note of reservation must be made. A *small proportion* of these errors are errors only in the minds of the complainers. Amongst all these adverse comments on the use of English by examiners and university teachers, there lurks a highly conservative and in many respects inappropriate model of correctness, based on the model of good English usage which was available in the critic's youth. Thus, examiners in the 1970s and 1980s, for example, continued to deplore the use of newer vocabulary which some of them found personally uncongenial, such as *life-styles, syndrome, empirical, nuclear family,* or of colloquialisms like *met up with* or 'he *came up with* a new idea', or 'errors' like 'he ran *quicker*'. This inappropriate form of censoriousness is only possible because the codification of modern English – the real rules which operate among the educated – is insufficiently well-known among those who pass judgment on usage in these contexts. But it would be wrong to imagine that this caveat accounted for the great majority of complaints by examiners, who, for 'A' level English, for example, continue to deplore the distressingly poor quality of candidates' written English, referring to "a minimal number of scripts where the English could be described as genuinely accurate".

The study of university students was followed up by the

Society's national survey of the communication skills of young entrants to industry and commerce, carried out in 1992–3, again by Dr Lamb. Subjects were mostly aged 16–18, though some slightly older ones had degrees or professional qualifications. The response rate this time was much lower, but a massive 92 per cent of respondents stated that schools were not giving their pupils sufficient command of English – findings which were in line with similar surveys quoted in the report. Many firms wrote graphically of the shortcomings of their employees, and of the practical problems that these caused, which were confirmed by a Gallup study commissioned by the Adult Literacy and Basic Skills Unit, which in 1993 produced estimates of annual losses to industry of £4.8 billion from weaknesses in literacy and numeracy, from lost business and time spent rectifying errors. More than eight out of ten companies reported that staff failings in reading, writing, verbal communication or simple arithmetic reduced their efficiency, left the workforce unable to adapt fast enough to technological changes, and offered a poor – and commercially damaging – image of the company to customers. One firm in seven reported that these deficiencies affected the work not just of manual workers, but also of professional and managerial staff. In another national survey by that Unit of the reading and writing habits of people aged 16–20, 25 per cent reported difficulties in reading and writing, 35 per cent with spelling, and 45 per cent reported that they never read books. An officer of the Unit stated that research among the unemployed suggests that 25 per cent have illiteracy problems, which have increased in seriousness with technological change. Whereas in the past a security guard might have got away with not being able to read or write properly, he might now have to deal with sophisticated surveillance and alarm systems, and the written instructions for using them, and to be able to enter information through keyboards to VDU screens – all of this, of course, in standard English. The Unit's 1994 study which involved tests on 1,650 people born in 1970 confirmed that one in five of these 24-year-olds had serious problems with literacy and numeracy, and that one in four could not follow instructions written in clear English in a manual.

A similar study by the Society carried out in 1995 examined the opinions and practices of teachers of English to 11-to-18-year-olds across Britain. Its findings were even more depressing. There was widespread support for a return to more systematic teaching of grammar, spelling and punctuation, though many teachers claimed that a number of their colleagues "are themselves incapable of correcting English errors". One teacher wrote, "I have always been out of sympathy with the NATE philosophy of teaching English, itself reflecting the view of the Inspectorate and most heads of department ... I believe in direct teaching of punctuation, grammar, etc., and this is now required by the National Curriculum" – which represented "such a change from the demonisation of it which was characteristic of my present department when I joined eight years ago!" The saddest finding was that teachers in some comprehensive schools and further education colleges estimated that as many as 75–85 per cent of their leavers were still 'poor' at written English, compared with much lower figures from grammar and independent schools. Thus the system is failing the very pupils who most need help with these basic skills of literacy.

That's what they always say

Yet even if all this huge battery of complaints were proved to be justified, would it not simply be a case of *déjà vu*? Is it not always true that every generation has looked back with nostalgia to a golden age when you could reasonably expect that nearly everybody who had been to school knew how to use the language properly? The Bullock Committee in 1975 reported the views of employers that young school leavers "cannot write English grammatically, are poor spellers, and generally express themselves badly", and were able to quote exactly the same sorts of complaints made to the Newbolt Committee which reported on

English Teaching in 1921 – and Professor Brian Cox shows that similar complaints were being made in 1912. What the Bullock Committee did not mention, however, is that the young people involved in those early complaints had almost all left school at 13, whereas they now stay to 16 and in increasing proportions to 18. Educational expenditure in Britain this century has escalated, in real terms, and especially since mass secondary schooling was introduced after 1944. Not only did public spending on education treble (in real terms) between the 1920s and the 1950s, but the lengthening of school life meant that expenditure per school life was about a third greater. Since the 1950s it has risen steadily, and if we take only the sixteen years between 1979 and 1995, official figures show that spending per pupil in nursery and primary schools in that period increased in real terms by 55.1 per cent, and for secondary schools by 49 per cent. Compared to seventy years ago, when perhaps one in twenty could expect to attend university, the figure in the 1990s is nearer *one in three*, representing a massively greater investment in higher education. The scale of illiteracy among British school-leavers, and of sub-literacy among 18-year-olds and even graduates, must thus be measured against this vast expenditure of money and effort. It is this kind of squandered opportunity which causes old-fashioned socialists like Richard Hoggart to make the otherwise surprising claim regarding the establishment of state education for the masses that "the decades since the 1870 Education Act have been, overall, an educational failure".

That failure is most obvious in two respects. The first is the national condition of under-achievement in literacy, which means that even graduates display all kinds of weaknesses, and many school teachers are insecure about their written English – a greater emphasis, in the new National Curriculum, on how language works will slowly begin to remedy this, though it will take decades. The second is international comparisons, and especially in relation to the literacy skills of the weakest and most vulnerable members of society – the academically least able. Economics professor S. I.

Prais estimated in 1995 that the bottom 40 per cent of British 13-year-olds lag two years behind their German counterparts. Lacking a mastery of the 3 Rs, fewer than 30 per cent of Britain's workforce have vocational qualifications, compared with 60 per cent in Germany. He concluded that British teaching methods produce a pool of under-educated, frustrated and disaffected children incapable of learning the skills required in a technological world. Many other international comparisons – including some with, for example, Taiwanese schoolchildren – confirm this sort of picture, and recurrent tests of the literacy of British youngsters at various ages also show that the worst feature is the very long 'tail' of underperformers in basic skills, especially literacy.

The same comparisons show that North America, with a similar culture of low educational expectations, fares no better. On the one hand, the commentator Daniel Bell has shown that in the United States, the decade from 1975 to 1985 showed a doubling in the number of bookstores and an increase of 30 per cent in book sales. But a 1994 survey of the literacy skills of American college graduates found that they ranged from, at the top, "a lot less than impressive, to mediocre, to near alarming", with the majority of graduates performing at levels 3 or 4 (only the best got 5), indicating ability to write a brief letter explaining a wrong bill, or describing the argument of a long newspaper article. The widespread use of multiple choice tests bears some responsibility for much poverty of expression. And at the bottom of the pile, and especially among Blacks, there are very serious problems of literacy. In the twenty years to 1995, Black pupils showed a 24-point rise in SAT (Scholastic Aptitude Test) scores, but still trailed behind every other racial group. In 1995 it was reported that one in five of Americans surveyed did not understand the directions on an aspirin bottle, and almost one in four cannot work out a weather chart in a newspaper. In March 1996 the American Secretary for Education declared that the most pressing business of the American education system is to improve reading skills.

Traditional grammar teaching

The efficacy of teaching grammar explicitly to pupils was the second bone of contention in that bitter public controversy, and has long been the subject of much misunderstanding. The traditional methods of teaching what was often an inappropriately Latin-based English grammar had long been known to have serious limitations. Indeed, as long ago as 1845 one of Her Majesty's earliest Inspectors of elementary schools, Mr F. C. Cook, reported that "it appears very questionable whether grammar should be taught as a separate subject", and the poet-HMI Matthew Arnold expressed similar reservations in 1876. But until around 1960 teachers continued to find it convenient to teach (and public examiners to demand) a body of rather abstract knowledge, often by way of drilling pupils in firm rules, however remote from the children's lives much of it must have seemed. There were four main arguments raised against grammar teaching.

First, it was boring, which unimaginative methods often made inevitable for many pupils, though a proportion always claimed to find it stimulating. To be boring became a crime when pupil-centred education became the fashion, though it never stopped the teaching of mathematics which many pupils find unremittingly boring. Secondly, it took time from other more pressing concerns such as 'personal development', or literary criticism which was seen as a more effective way to sensitise pupils to the need to change society. Thirdly, linguistic theorists from the 1960s onwards preached the Chomskyan gospel (which we met in Pinker – see Chapter 4, above) that the child automatically speaks her or his own grammar correctly. It continues to be preached by the Milroys – "the grammar of a language is a complex system inherent in a language and not imposed by overt prescription: all native speakers have implicit knowledge of of the grammar of English" – whereas we know that the child requires prolonged tuition in order to be able to handle the sophisticated resources of standard English. A similar message came from Geoffrey Thornton, an inspector-adviser to teachers of English in the North and in London for eighteen years in the 1970s and 1980s, who used the linguists' definition to claim that 'grammar' is not something found in books, ridiculed the teaching of parts of speech or exercises in punctuation or irregular plurals, and belittled the notion that language development involves any "teachable content".

The fourth argument questioned its effectiveness. We noted the Bullock Committee's re-emphasis of the (by then) well-established view that the teaching of "traditional analytical grammar is ineffective in improving pupils' writing", and the Kingman Committee's rejection in 1988 of traditional grammar teaching in favour of "knowledge about language". A similar claim for a programme of such knowledge, especially among teachers, had been made in 1986 by Geoffrey Thornton, who went on to nominate the crucial kinds of information that such a programme would provide, including the unqualified assertion that "all dialects are linguistically equal", and that the status of standard English is entirely "a product of the class-structure"; and around the same time another of his teacher-adviser colleagues at the Inner London Education Authority, John Richmond, was making references to "the prestige dialect *misleadingly* referred to as Standard English". The Kingman Committee repeated the reference to "research evidence" which "suggests that old-fashioned formal teaching of grammar had a negligible, or, because it replaced some instruction and practice in composition, even a harmful, effect on the development of original writing".

The decline in the formal teaching of grammar both in the United States and, since around 1960, in Britain, is closely related to these claims about the definitive findings of rigorous research into its effectiveness. Yet, in fact, the research studies upon which this whole case has been built up "are so flawed that they should never have been taken seriously". That criticism comes from Professor David Tomlinson, who has devoted many years to the re-analysis of these studies, the earliest of which dates right back to

1906. The account which follows is heavily indebted to Professor Tomlinson's work.

The studies are basically of two kinds. The earlier ones, up to about 1960, aimed to compare pupils' scores on tests of grammar knowledge with their performance in essays, and the study usually quoted is Nora Robinson's 1959 master's degree thesis at Manchester University. Because the studies always found a negative correlation, researchers concluded that grammar teaching was pointless. In fact, there could never be a positive correlation anyway. Essay marks are a compromise assessing a bundle of different skills, and interference from other components subsumed under the 'total impression' mark means that the essay score can never correlate with the score for any single aspect of writing ability, no matter what you take. This basic error first appears in F. S. Hoyt's Columbia University MA thesis in 1906. The Hoyt study was replicated many times, with minor improvements, but the erroneous assumptions underlying it were also replicated over the next fifty years from study to study, without the researcher or the supervisor ever realising that the conclusions could not be sustained on the basis of the experiment described. The extent to which these studies have been approvingly cited is truly remarkable. Professor F. R. Palmer once wrote in the *Guardian* that supporters of grammar teaching were incorrigible – in the face of the overwhelming evidence, they were like 'flat-earthers' clinging to totally discredited beliefs. Yet this *overwhelming evidence* is largely a case of a set of highly suspect research conclusions which have been passed on uncritically by commentator after commentator who have not themselves actually studied the research on which they were based.

The research studies after 1960 typically compare the performance of a class which has been taught grammar, of one kind or another, with a 'control' class which has not, and conclude either that there is no difference at all, or that the class which has been taught no grammar performed better. One such widely cited study is R. J. Harris's 1962 PhD thesis at London University. This study has a basic confusion over the meaning of the term 'formal grammar teaching', an ambiguous phrase which turns out to mean, for Harris, not so much the teaching of formal grammar as the *formal teaching* of a classificatory *grammar* of a most dry-as-dust kind. Thus his 'control' classes, presented to us as supposedly non-grammar classes, were being taught grammatical usage *non-formally*, because that did not count as formal grammar teaching. As opportunity arose, they received informal instruction in usage, with simple non-technical explanations. This is quite a good way of teaching grammar to non-academic 12-year-olds, but the Harris study does not thereby prove – as its author claimed – that the teaching of grammar is useless. Quite the opposite. Contrary to its stated aims, the Harris study contrasts two ways of teaching grammar to non-academic classes. And it was this study which was cited by the Bullock Committee as the basis of its rejection of grammar teaching.

Indeed, every study from the beginning of the century to the 1960s is flawed additionally by semantic confusion over the meanings of 'grammar'. If one is trying to assess the benefits of teaching children the grammar of their language, it is important to be very clear about what exactly they will be taught under the name of 'grammar'. Even in common everyday use, 'grammar' has different basic meanings: three meanings, according to Nelson Francis in 1954, or five (Hartwell, 1985), or even seven or eight (Quirk, 1972). Simply teaching parts of speech is not in itself going to have much effect on students' knowledge of that part of grammar we call usage, though it may help the learner in the future to organise his thinking about how his language works. And if the researcher painstakingly discovers this limited effect in the present, it does not follow that all grammar teaching is therefore pointless, only that the experiment used the class time on the wrong meaning of grammar.

The study of this kind which is now most frequently cited is the one by W. B. Elley in New Zealand in the early 1970s. This was a carefully controlled experiment comparing, over a period of three years, three English classes which took a standard programme differing only in the grammar component. One class had one period a week of traditional grammar, the second had Chomskyan 'transformational' grammar, and the third used the time instead on reading and exercises in creative writing. Each pupil had ten essays awarded grades by experienced markers for content, mechanics, style and structure, but no significant differences were found to distinguish any of the three classes. This result is rather a mystery because, given what was taught as 'grammar' to the two grammar classes, and given what is reasonably claimed for enhanced reading programmes, it was the reading class which ought to have shown the greatest short-term improvement.

However, the Elley team used, as its basic yardstick of the pupils' development in English, a measure known as the Hunt T-unit, which is essentially a measure of clause length (words per clause), because this is said to increase as pupils grow older. The T-unit is a primitive and clumsy measure, too crude for the reliability expected of it by the Elley team. For example, while it counts a compound sentence as two clauses, co-ordination around the same subject is counted as only one. Clause ellipsis, which we expect pupils gradually to learn to use as a way of packing more information into sentences, is not counted at all because the verbs of abbreviated clauses are frequently only participles. The T-unit counts only finite verbs, a sign that it must derive from the despised 'clause analysis' of traditional grammar. Nor did the Elley team assess text cohesion, an aspect of writing little appreciated in those days. It seems they attempted to measure the development of pupils' writing skills, but failed to establish a base-line by assessing these at the very beginning. There are serious queries about the low levels of motivation among the students studied. As a result of all these problems, little reliance can be placed on the team's conclusions, and it is doubtful whether Dr Elley himself would today make the claims for it that are now often made for this study – by authorities including Professor Brian Cox, who, in his 1995 book on the curriculum, continues to commend the wide scale of this research and to treat its conclusions as decisive. Professor Tomlinson points out that, because of individual stylistic variation and differences in learning styles between pupils, it may be impossible to measure pupils' improvement in English language according to a formula – any formula at all.

No major research of this kind involving grammar teaching has been reported since Elley's. Because of the 'experimental paradox' (the closer the experiment comes to the real classroom situation, the more difficult it is to control the variables) it is probably impossible to design a watertight experiment to test the effect of teaching grammatical usage: certainly none has been produced so far. But Tomlinson points out that, while the educationists and teachers have been wrangling, an experiment of another kind has been quietly going on behind everyone's backs. Schools all over the country, for at least two decades until recently, abandoned all grammar teaching, and the volume of complaints from various sectors has become – as we saw – greater than ever, concerning cohorts (yes, cohorts) of students who have been exposed to a great amount of correct written English, yet who without positive instruction have apparently failed to absorb the necessary 'rules'.

It ought to be blindingly clear that, to write clearly and concisely, writers need to edit their own writing, and for most people this is only possible if you have been taught what to look out for. This means teaching the usage of the language, and in order to do this you may have to teach at least some basic 'meta-language' – the language in which we describe language (for example, verb, noun, passive, ellipsis, past tense, conditional, etc.); how much of this is necessary depends on the goals of the instruction programme. It is also important that the rules that are set out should reflect the realities of educated usage, not some nineteenth-century grammarian's idea of what is 'correct', and most people will agree that the Kingman and Cox proposals represent an appropriate advance in this regard.

What will also be crucial is the way in which students are taught: the Kingman Report rightly criticised the traditional methods of grammar teaching "through exercises unrelated to the child's real needs", and now that the rudiments of grammar have begun to be restored to the nation's schools, a great deal of help will be needed to prevent 'knowledge about language' from being reduced to an unimaginative grind by teachers from the 'lost generation' whose own knowledge in this field will require to be systematically extended.

Major developments in linguistics

Professor Cox has admitted that his proposals in the Cox Report reflect changes in his own views over the past twenty-five years, in the light of "major developments in linguistics, literary theory and the teaching of English which are accepted by most professional teachers, both in schools and in higher education". But that professional consensus concerning the inefficiency of grammar teaching always had its doubters and is arguably now discredited. Some of those who took control of the National Curriculum after 1991 were, Cox writes, "unsympathetic to almost all the research in linguistics of the last thirty years". But perhaps those misguided luminaries were not entirely wrong to be suspicious of what linguists have been saying about such crucial topics as the nature of standard English and its relation to other varieties encountered in schools.

Professor Peter Trudgill, the British professor of English Linguistics whose views we have already encountered in this chapter, wrote to the *Times Higher Education Supplement* in July 1993 to attack the defence of standard English offered in that journal the previous month by the man in charge of the National Curriculum:

> Standard English is not characterised by 'correct use of vocabulary and grammar'. There is no such thing as Standard English vocabulary. It is perfectly possible and indeed quite common for non-standard dialect speakers to employ technical and formal vocabulary without switching dialects. Nor is Standard English grammar more 'correct' or 'accurate'

than the grammar of other dialects, it is simply different. It has higher prestige, certainly, but this has no connection with its linguistic structure.

His letter went on to claim that "If we wish people to become articulate speakers of English, we can best do this by encouraging them to be confident and fluent speakers of their own dialect, rather than wasting time and undermining confidence by persuading them to become speakers of [standard English]."

Every sentence in Professor Trudgill's argument deserves specific comment. *Standard English is not characterised by 'correct use of vocabulary and grammar'*: to this I must point out that standard English has standards of correctness which are simply not available in non-standard dialects. *There is no such thing as Standard English vocabulary*: the word-stock of any normal English dictionary, shorn of all words marked as dialect words, constitutes the distinctive vocabulary of standard English, and a large number of the more commonly used of these words, especially the most literary and scientific words, are never normally used by non-standard dialect speakers. *It is perfectly possible and indeed quite common for non-standard dialect speakers to employ technical and formal vocabulary without switching dialects*: it is possible to do so, certainly, but common observation shows that for many dialects it is not usual, for the very good reason (explained in Chapter 3) that their use is not felt, by either speakers or hearers, to be congruent. *Nor is Standard English grammar more 'correct' or 'accurate' than the grammar of other dialects, it is simply different*: not true: the 'correctness' and 'accuracy' of the grammar of non-standard dialects are far more difficult either to discern or to maintain than that of standard English, since they are not codified. *It has higher prestige, certainly, but this has no connection with its linguistic structure*: the distinctive linguistic structure of standard English, including its grammar, idiom and range of styles, compared with non-standard dialects, contributes to the prestige which standard English enjoys because of the functions which it is thus enabled to fulfil.

If we wish people to become articulate speakers of English, we can best do this by encouraging them to be confident and fluent speakers of their own dialect – but the overwhelming majority of critics of standard English, including the Milroys, Pinker and Trudgill himself, claim that people already speak their native dialect fluently – *rather than wasting time and undermining confidence by persuading them to become speakers of [standard English]*: the idea that learning standard English is a waste of time confirms the argument of this book that prominent British academic linguists have worked to deny or reduce access to this especially valuable variety for British children.

In November 1992 the *Times Higher Education Supplement* printed a letter on the National Curriculum over the signatures of 22 university professors of English – including high-status figures like Gillian Beer, who is also head of a Cambridge college – and the same letter was reprinted in June 1993, this time having been signed by 576 university teachers of English, including 42 from Oxbridge, and (says Professor Cox) many who were "known to be traditional in their sympathies": the great majority of them were in fact specialists in literature rather than English language studies. They viewed "with dismay" the government's proposed reforms of the teaching of English in schools. Though they expected sound grammar and speaking from their students,

> the Government's doctrinaire preoccupation with these skills betrays a disastrously reductive, mechanistic understanding of English studies . . . Similarly, its evident hostility to regional and working-class forms of speech in the classroom betrays a prejudice which has little or no intellectual basis, and which is seriously harmful to the well-being and self-esteem of many children.

The letter had been drafted by Terry Eagleton, a leading Marxist who is also a professor of English literature at Oxford, and it went on to attack the proposals as "philistine" and "ill-informed", threatening "to reduce a living language to a dead one". The idea that these proposals were intended to increase the accessibility to working-class pupils of the standard English in which most of English literature has been written, is simply not mentioned, and the incident provided the cautionary spectacle of large numbers of well-meaning but naive academics being led by the nose.

I must state candidly that I deplore the government's treatment of Professor Ronald Carter and the teaching materials expensively developed by his LINC (Language in the National Curriculum) project which, whatever their flaws, were a great advance on existing resources. But it must also be admitted that some of the presuppositions underlying those materials laid them open to criticism. In July 1991, one of the regional co-ordinators of the LINC project wrote to the *Times Educational Supplement* to attack an article by journalist Janet Daley in that journal a few weeks before, in which she took the sort of line that I take in this book, that an underprivileged child's acquisition of standard ('correct' or 'proper') English constitutes a "ticket to freedom". He challenged this assumption:

> Who believes that? She writes as if 'correctness' of language were completely independent of who decides what counts as correct, as if there were something intrinsically superior about standard English. One aim of the LINC project was to show that this is *simply a prejudice*, and that it is *connected with power*.

Thus one Professor Carter's lieutenants shot himself – and the project – in the foot.

The idea that the principles of an acceptable National Curriculum for English could be compatible with the orthodoxies of academic linguistics as propounded over the past thirty years is thrown into serious doubt by the many quotations from such authorities that have been cited in this book. And the list goes on. In 1995 Professor Richard Hudson, a respected and usually common-sense specialist in sociolinguistics at University College,

London, published, with a colleague, a study which examined the spoken English of 350 11- and 15-year-olds in four regions of England: Merseyside, Tyneside, the South West, and London. They found that 32 per cent of these pupils used no non-standard forms, while the other 68 per cent used at least one non-standard form (e.g. *them books*, or *have fell*). Girls used fewer non-standard forms than boys at both 11 and 15, and 11-year-olds actually used fewer non-standard forms than 15-year-olds, which tends to confirm the view of non-standard usages as a sign of macho assertiveness and as a badge of educational resistance which develops during adolescence. A particularly interesting finding was that the majority of a fairly small range of about a dozen forms was used in all four regions, again confirming that much of the non-standard spoken English which children bring to school has little to do with the historic regional dialects, but rather with largely urban 'sociolects' whose function – as we saw in Chapter 3 – is partly to express a value-system associated with closed communities based on the accident of birth and residence.

Hudson's willingness to publish these findings was attacked in the professional journal of British specialists in applied linguistics by Dr Euan Reid, a member of the staff of the University of London's Institute of Education, one of the most prestigious and influential centres of teacher education in the English-speaking world. Reid found it "hard to understand how, with his extensive knowledge and experience in the socially contextualised study of language in general, Dick Hudson could have been responsible for such a study. There is, after all, a clear alternative direction: to argue for a more complex, accurate and constructive approach to the use and meaning of spoken English, and to refuse to engage in a way of talking about 'Standard English' which neglects *the historically and socially constructed nature of this concept* . . ." In other words, Reid is attacking Hudson for not disparaging standard English for being an élitist middle-class imposition on working-class children since the nineteenth century, as the revisionist historians have claimed it to be. Here, *historically constructed* means that nineteenth-century middle-class intellectuals foisted it on the working classes, as per Raymond Williams, Harris and Crowley; and *socially* means 'not for them', because properly belonging only to the middle and upper classes.

One of Reid's other main criticisms is that "I cannot help seeing this kind of work connecting to *a continuing public discourse about the imposition of authority* on pupils and teachers"; and herein lies a clue to another of the grounds of hostility to the emphasis on standard English in schools, the persistent disparagement of authority which some teachers would claim has, in the past three or four decades, seriously undercut school discipline and the possibility for many children of making something of their school studies.

Meanwhile another senior British linguist, Dr Jim Miller of Edinburgh University, had been explaining (1993) that the real reason why researchers find that children from an early age appear to associate the prestige of standard English with intelligence and leadership, is to be found in "the speed with which children learn at primary school what opinions will gain public approval, and what ones are best confined to their close friends".

As we saw in Chapter 4, the American linguistics professor James Tollefson attacked the Kingman Committee for ignoring the *class* basis of standard English and its association with economic élites, and for its unwarranted assumption that participation in British society is dependent upon knowledge of standard English, or that standard English is 'normal'. His complaint that making standard English central for school instruction gives *unfair advantage* to children whose home language is standard English has been voiced by many other critics of standard English, including Professor Trudgill. Also in that chapter, we noted Robert St Clair's contention that standard English in the United States is used against minorities by the *power élite* in order to *deny them full access to mainstream culture*, and to guarantee the success of their own (middle-class) children.

Donna Christian, writing on language differences in an official publication for American teachers and committed to the proposition that "dialects are inherently equal", proclaims that teaching standard English is *a discriminatory action*, and Professor Trudgill has also publicly associated himself with the proposition that for the teacher to correct a child's non-standard English constitutes the oppressive imposition of an alien dialect. Dr Viv Edwards of Reading University, who believes that standard English owes its status to "the emergence of one social group with a *stronghold* [*sc.* stranglehold?] *on power*, extends this notion to the education of children of West Indian origin in Britain: to teach standard English without sympathetic appreciation of the status of creole would, she says, "inevitably be seen as an *act of oppression* in a climate where Black patois usage is a symbol of Black unity." This shows up a real problem: how can the teacher demonstrate sympathetic appreciation of this variety, knowing the way it is used by some as a symbol of anti-educational values and attitudes, of sexist prejudices, and of racial exclusiveness? The Milroys claim that this variety of English must be handled by the teacher in a "non-evaluative way", but the central argument of their book is that forms of non-standard English persist *because* of evaluations associated with them – their *raison d'être* cannot be understood without such evaluation. This affects not only 'Black English': similar reservations affect the way the teacher handles features of all the 'ghost' dialects whose (mainly grammatical) traces stand between their pupils and a confident use of standard English.

Dignity, celebration and reality

Linguists rightly point to the adverse effects of making children ashamed of their own language. These are similar to those involved in classroom discussions – in social history, sociology or literature – of social class differences, where some children are embarrassed to realise some of the implications for their own status of these class labels. In fact, teachers of English need to walk a tightrope, indicating that they reject the usual stigmatising attitudes towards non-standard speech, yet at the same time trying to suggest that there are limitations to such usages in present-day Britain, especially outside the child's immediate community. Indeed, teachers should always try to find occasions to *celebrate* dialect forms, especially where the historic regional dialects are concerned, where there is least chance of appearing patronising. In some communities it is possible to find elderly speakers, perhaps the grandparents of pupils, whose distinctive speech can be recorded and discussed. But the teacher cannot avoid a responsibility to point out the greater variety of functions which standard English fulfils in a modern community. Yet how do you tell pupils sensitively that their own non-standard variety has no literary tradition, has a limited range of styles and social functions, and that the most educated among its native speakers no longer use it? In a grammar school where I taught in the early 1960s, a boy told me, in a quite matter-of-fact way, that he had never had a bath or shower in his life – he grew up in a rural cottage with no bathroom. The opportunity to take a shower at school after games appeared in no way shameful to him, nor in any way damaging to his self-esteem. In this way, his school simply supplied a valued facility. There is always the potential for damaged self-esteem in the comparisons between the culture of the home and that of the school, yet the great majority of pupils have always managed to cope with it. But to give a phoney dignity to non-standard varieties of language which children will come to see is in reality patronising, is ultimately degrading and insulting – a phoney dignity, because it it can never correspond to the evaluations of any society where there is a general respect for education and competence. The question is not whether self-esteem is important, but whether self-esteem is more important than anything else.

Studies in the United States have shown consistently that speakers of the Black American dialect score lower on achievement tests in mathematics, reading and 'language arts' than their white counterparts, and need special assistance to make the transition to reading and writing in standard English, skills which are an indispensable entrée to the whole curriculum. As Einar Haugen has admitted, learning another dialect of English is, because of confusing similarities, in some ways more difficult than learning another language; moreover, these difficulties increase as the learner grows older. As Professor Trudgill himself has told us, "it is a rare adult that successfully masters the speaking of a new dialect in all its details". Yet the majority of teachers of non-standard English speakers, in both the United States and Britain, are not trained to recognise the way forms of dialect interference operate. Above all, these pupils need teachers who are themselves models of standard English usage.

There is also evidence from the United States that failing schools in deprived neighbourhoods can be 'turned around' by a crash programme of exacting workloads and rigorous testing in the basic skills, including grammar, spelling and general knowledge, though there is always likely to be opposition from some educationists to offering a 'rich man's curriculum' to Black children – the 'not for them' argument we have encountered before. In the 1980s, quoting the fact that "Language scholars long ago denied that the myth of standard American dialect has any validity", educationists were demanding a programme of what they called 'Dialect-fair' instruction for minorities. Its first principle is that "literacy is independent of any language or dialect", so every school textbook must be re-written in all the different varieties of Black English and other dialects, and instruction in standard English is to be available only as an option.

It is well known that many middle-class parents in both Britain and the United States give an unfair advantage in life to their very young children by reading to them. Many working-class children, including in the United States many Black children, grow up without this advantage. If you want to equalise life-chances for all these children, you can either invent penalties for middle-class children who have had these advantages, or you can extend the benefit to the deprived children by forms of compensatory reading provision. A third option is to invent reasons why children should not be read to, on the grounds that reading is a Bad Thing and 'not for them'. Something of this form of logic has entered into linguists' discussions of standard English, and their net effect in both Britain and North America has been the creation of an underclass which is unteachable and unemployable.

Students' perceptions of language variation

In his 1995 paperback on standard English, Jeff Wilkinson maintains that "because of home and peer-group pressures, teachers can have little hope of changing how pupils speak". This is a defeatist view which not all the parents and teachers of today's younger generation will readily accept. Moreover, there is evidence both in this country and abroad which suggests that many students may themselves arrive at a vivid appreciation of the real implications of different varieties of English.

Perhaps the most fascinating study on this comes from Canada, where John Willinsky carried out research on English teaching in a big-city high school, which he published in book form as *The Well-tempered Tongue* (1988). His early chapters in particular deserve to be relished, as a classic statement of the extreme position among linguistic theorists which has been frequently cited in my pages, which ascribes the status of standard English entirely to its being the property of a *class*, an élite group who hold their favoured status by virtue of their ability to work this prestige form, which they impose on lower-class children as part of "a strategy of exclusion and [class] consolidation"; moreover, standard English (Willinsky claims) would have little value if separated from the prejudices that support it. Thus, learning to read in school may simply be "another process of initiation and acceptance into a white, male, middle class world". (It has, of course, traces of all those three characteristics, but what is crucial is that it also involves a great deal more.) In order to begin his task of "exploding misconceptions about language differences" and showing that non-standard English is as valid as standard, Willinsky admits that he is "making language over into a political struggle". He gives no serious consideration to the possibility that there might be qualitative or functional differences between standard and non-standard English. For Willinsky, standard English derives its status solely from indefensible but widespread prejudices relating to the class system.

In the context of a school system in which up to 45 per cent more students stayed on for a full high-school course compared with thirty years before, the Ontario high school studied by Dr Willinsky had adopted an unusually liberal policy about expectations of 'correct' English, quoting the doctrines of modern linguistic theorists that "there are no absolutes of right and wrong", though in practice teachers tended to defer to the usages favoured by the "majority of educated Canadians".

Willinsky says that he set out to show what meaning the concept 'standard English' had for his students at this high school, by examining a group of 84 who represented both the ablest and the less able students, divided between 'Academic' and 'General' (i.e., non-academic) streams. Willinsky painstakingly analysed their opinions across this divide. Students showed remarkable percipience about the need for standard English – time and again they stressed its connection with educatedness – and about what it could do for them; when a progressive teacher tried to discourage the expression of favourable attitutes to standard English, students defied him and wrote about "proper" English. One (weaker) student commented that speaking standard English would make him "a better person"; other weak students said that it would make them sound "fuddy-duddy and strange" or not genuine – underlining their awareness of the observable fact that among the functions of non-standard English are certain forms of oral expressiveness for which standard English is less effective. Willinsky implies that some students, having learned the standard dialect, might feel insecure about their acceptance in the new social groups to which they now had access; but one said "It's fine if you can speak both ways – you can really speak a cool way to your friends", and he then mentioned the need to be able to speak in another way to teachers and in connexion with jobs.

Willinsky is amazed that students tend to associate "care in expression" with "notions of propriety and grammar" – and he comments that this "can only be explained by social perceptiveness"! Many students show, without even being taught so, that they recognise that non-standard English is suitable for *informal* rather than formal contexts – "working-class talk is the talk s*poke at home*" – and that standard English is more appropriate for abstract uses. To his chagrin, Willinsky finds that, despite the best efforts of the school not to denigrate non-standard English, students who are learning to speak standard English come to "regard care with language as a matter of deference and politeness" and to view standard English as representing "intellectual, expressive and *moral* qualities which they are without" but which they respect. Some of these 'General' students cannot imagine standard English as representing less than "being able to express onself, be smart, and be good".

Jane, an "inarticulate" Black student, deduces for herself, without being taught it by the school, that she would not only become a higher achiever as a student, but would be able to express herself more successfully, if she could use standard English. Therefore these non-standard English speakers come to realise that standard English is a *threshold* requirement not only for handling the academic demands of the school, but also for self-expression. Thus, a working-class boy explains how he is given a *sense of power* by being able to use 'good English' even when writing a letter or song or poem to his girlfriend. One General student underwent in Grade 10 a "literacy conversion"– what Willinsky calls his "redemption out of the darkness of a poorly grasped language and into the glory that is literature"; another student similarly shows gratitude to his English teacher who "introduced me into reading and hence into English", which he clarifies by adding "into standard English". Student Bob shows a "classic symptom of a literate concern" – i.e., a sense of 'correctness' – which he says helps him to command respect from other people from a wide range of backgrounds. Students also associate this sense of 'correctness' with "good manners". Annie, a Black student, also from an underprivileged background and, in her case, not interested in the literary uses of standard English, elaborates this principle: "I just think standard English is important because it *gives you more respect* and it makes you *feel good about yourself*", and other students make the same point about associating standard English with earning, and expecting, "a certain respect". They also recognise that the "distinct Black way of talking" English is a form of rebelliousness, just as they recognise that "Pop music is a statement against the school".

Willinsky intended this book to be a spirited attack on the school's preoccupation with standard English, but instead it becomes a record of his mounting exasperation as the catalogue of evidence builds up of the students' common-sense perceptions of its superior functions and its potential value in their lives. Despite all the conscientious official propaganda in the school about honouring linguistic diversity, the students arrive at a quite different conclusion about the relative value of different varieties, and the examples proliferate: a girl from the slums finds standard English to be a way of raising herself; another underprivileged boy uses the term *word power* for what he feels his grasp of standard English has given him; a poor Black student is accepted as if from a 'high-class' neighbourhood on the strength of her English. Some of the abler students who do advanced English literature end up with "a fuller sense of themselves and of the world" through it, even though, as Willinsky points out, some critics claim that "literary language is implicated in *the bourgeois installation of the dominant language form*."*

* Willinsky also makes the bizarre claim that "literature owes little to standard English – it is quite the reverse". The claim is of course absurd. Only a tiny proportion of what is regarded as literature is written in non-standard English. No sooner has Willinsky made this claim than he supports it with arguments which in fact refute it: you have to know standard English (a) before you can write like James Joyce, etc., and (b) before you can appreciate word-play, etc. and enjoy the upset expectations that non-standard English then provides.

Despite the fact that his book has ended up as a brilliantly per-suasive tract in favour of standard English, Willinsky seems to have learned nothing from his own evidence,* and he concludes with a call to teachers to challenge "the hierarchy of language forms: the whole ineluctable common-sense positioning by language must be shaken"; he urges teachers to expose the prestige of standard English to their students as an artificially contrived prejudice "with a history and a contemporary significance". Here we recognise the words *history* and *contemporary significance* as being coded refer-ences to the notion of a middle- and upper-class dialect which grew out of élite origins between a hundred and five hundred years ago (cf. Williams, Crowley, et al.), and is thus not appropriate for lower-class students today to use.

What neither Dr Willinsky – nor any of these other authors who believe that the teaching of standard English is part of an élitist, middle-class plot against the lower classes – tells us is why those élites should want to force it on the masses. As I have already claimed, the logic of speaking a privileged form of language is that one should refuse to extend that privilege to others, yet here we have the 'ruling classes' insisting on sharing it with every child, indeed making a big issue of its availability to every under-privileged child in the land. Denying access to poor children and to Black people would be a much more obvious strategy of exploitation and oppression. Anne Barnes, a prominent member of NATE, the professional association for teachers of English

---

* It cannot be regarded as irrelevant that Dr Willinsky's disregard for the conventions of standard English is even more blatant than Dr Crowley's. Willinsky confirms his own sense of 'solidarity' with the weaker students of the General stream by falling into the same kinds of 'schoolboy' mistakes, often repeated with some consistency, and uncorrected in later editions. The text is littered with the author's idiosyncratic spellings: accessable (*passim*), ennunciate, valadity, transcendal, noteable, humourous, reminescent, bourgeios; 'they were mislead'. Yet this book received a grant for its adaptation from a doctoral thesis, and was published by a university press. Willinsky's later book on the Oxford Dictionary was likewise littered with mis-spellings, malapropisms and misuse of historical evidence.

whose hostility to the teaching of grammar has already been
mentioned, was reported as having made the following comments
on the government's proposals in 1993 to institute regular testing
in standard English for pupils of various ages:

> If you can make a series of hurdles which children have to
> jump over to speak and write correct English in an acceptable
> way, it is a good way to control society. Society is much more
> difficult to control if you make everyone articulate and fluent.

But this is to stand logic on its head: it would clearly be much
easier to control or manipulate 'society' – the mass of the population – if one could restrict or (ideally) prevent access to the most
authoritative and power-laden forms of language in that society,
and by making everyone articulate and fluent in those forms of
language (as her second sentence acknowledges) one would in fact
be ensuring their empowerment.

In May 1994 Prince Charles was quoted in the media in Britain
and around the world as having drawn attention to the success of
what he called a form of 'political correctness' in making people
doubt the common-sense arguments in favour of three things, two
of which are relevant to the discussion in this chapter: the value of
'good English', and the effectiveness of teaching grammar. On the
evidence I have put forward in these pages, it would seem that the
Prince hit these two nails on the head.

If I have anything to boast of it is that I sincerely love and speak truth with indifferency whom it pleases and displeases.

John Locke (1632–1704)

A reader in a hurry would be well advised to skip this chapter, which is simply a brief account of an episode in the recent public discussion of the issues surrounding standard English in the educational system – an episode which is, however, profoundly instructive on the methods used by certain linguistic scholars to restrict discussion of these issues.

I had come to know Brian Cox and A. E. (Tony) Dyson in the 1950s, when we were fellow-students at Pembroke College, Cambridge. After distinguished first degrees they were now both doing research in English literature, and I was a freshman reading a different subject, but the absence of a separate graduate common room in those days meant that there was no apartheid between undergraduates and graduate students. It was an interesting generation, I think, at that delightful college, and also included the poet Ted Hughes, and indeed a few years later another of the names mentioned in this book, David Tomlinson, studied there. (Disciples of Foucault might find all these links to be evidence of something sinister.) I was working abroad in teacher education during the heyday of the Black Papers, but on my return to Britain, and again working in teacher education, I was in touch with Professor Cox and around 1980 I addressed a conference of the National Council for Educational Standards, of which he was at that time one of the principal organisers. My main concern in those days was with what I saw as flaws in the pattern of teacher education in Britain, and an imbalance of emphasis between initial training and in-service components, which meant that an unacceptably high proportion of school teachers were, in practice, not sufficiently competent (I gave the figure 13,000; in 1995 the senior chief inspector was to say 15,000). The fault lay not so much with the teachers, most of whom were (and are) committed and caring individuals, but with the *system*, by which the crucial appraisal of their skills takes place essentially before they have had a proper chance to display them in practice. I also coined the term 'MoTs for Teachers' – taken up since by other educationists – to dramatise the need for some form of regular assessment and updating of teaching competence (I favoured five-year intervals) largely on the basis of self-assessment and of evaluations by fellow-teachers.

As a result of this renewed contact, Professor Cox invited me to write a monograph – an extended pamphlet – for a new series which he was then editing (the Kay-Shuttleworth Papers on Education), and he gave me *carte blanche* as to its subject and made no attempt to influence what I wrote. My contribution, *The Language Trap*, appeared in the spring of 1983. It was given respectful attention by journals such as the *Times Educational Supplement* and *The Times*, though many news reports, on the radio and even in serious newspapers like the *Guardian* (not to speak of tabloids like the *Daily Express* and *Daily Mail*) could not resist the temptation to misrepresent it as crudely disparaging of non-standard English. After a few weeks it might have passed into oblivion: since it was not published by a commercial pubisher, few would-be readers knew how to get hold of it, and most libraries, including all those which are monitored for purposes of Public Lending Right, did not bother to acquire copies, so it is now something of a collector's piece. But among academic specialists in linguistics, it caused a furore.

My argument in *The Language Trap* was essentially the same as the one elaborated, in far greater detail, in this book: I listed a number of statements reflecting the academic orthodoxy on 'linguistic equality', and made two points. First, I questioned whether this dogma was in fact tenable in the ways in which it was repeatedly asserted; and secondly I claimed that in the way this dogma and its corollaries were mediated to the general public (especially teachers), they had caused considerable harm, both in the insecurity they caused to teachers who were now unsure about correcting children's spoken or written English, and also among other educationists, who used the dogma as an argument against teaching standard English at all in schools. In support of my case, I included my fundamental criticisms of the plausibility of Labov's famous article. *The Language Trap* was in places provocative in style and tone, and its call for the wide availablity of standard English for underprivileged pupils was infused with passion.

Unusually, the professional journal of British specialists in applied linguistics – the *BAAL Newsletter* – devoted not one but two reviews to it, in the same issue. The first was a long and angry demolition job, heavy with ridicule, by Professor David Crystal, who had been stung to find himself named in the pamphlet. He denied that linguists had ever been implicated in the promotion of the view that "anything goes" in English usage; he was angry at my criticism of his quoted views on 'linguistic equality' because *in a quite different book*, addressed to a different readership, he had emphasised the value of standard English. But he did not attempt to show that linguists had not, in fact, been quoted to the effect I claimed, nor did he offer any evidence they had ever dissociated themselves from these harmful views. He attacked me for quoting mainly "popularisations and secondary accounts" – "sixth-form books" – rather than from the primary sources in which linguists had (he claimed) made the necessary qualifications or reservations, and he charged me with "misinterpretation of the linguists' position". He excused the faults of the Labov paper on the grounds that it had been written *in a historical context* – fifteen years before – when Labov's approach was the only way non-standard varieties like Black English could succeed in attracting serious research, therefore it was 'gall' on my part that I dared to question its scientific method. Quoting my statement that the whole of the education system is posited upon standard English, he denied that linguists had disputed this. In fact, almost nothing in *The Languge Trap* was true: he claimed that he had not known any case of a teacher denying the value to children of standard English; he denied my claim that "there are almost no 'pure' dialect speakers left in Britain"; he denied the validity of my reference to "the inability of our schools to turn out pupils with satisfactory standards of English", countering that most of his university students speak and write a language called English. The idea that experts have claimed or implied that languages are *equally good* is (said Crystal) a myth. Specifically, he denied my suggestion that a powerful school of linguistic thought had grown up, dedicated to disparaging standard English. My "technique is to attribute absurd and extreme views to linguists, and then demolish the absurdity". However, it is now fair to ask, since my statements were verbatim quotations, how was I misrepresenting them? If Crystal was correct in that criticism of *The Language Trap*, it must also apply to this book, since my case is essentially the same: that linguists have said things which have been widely interpreted in ways which do harm to schoolchildren, and they have not taken steps to correct those harmful interpretations.

The other reviewer in that journal was Professor Richard Hudson, who has already been quoted in this book (page 135). He deplored the negative comments on non-standard English in press and media reports which had been provoked by its publication. But he found several points in *The Language Trap* which he could positively applaud, especially its call for the teaching of explicit knowledge about language by teachers who were properly qualified to teach it, and as we have seen (Chapter 2) he admitted that linguists had got into a muddle over their claim that all languages varieties are 'linguistically equal'. He suggested that these issues deserved to be investigated and re-defined by linguists (he has since taken an important initiative) and that I had every right to point out the weakness of the linguists' position. But he regretted the publication of *The Language Trap* on the grounds that it was "a prize example of demagoguery – telling the uninitiated what they want to hear, and letting them think you've got respectable arguments to show that they, with their 'common sense' (alias prejudice and ignorance), were right after all, and that the experts got it wrong". We must return to this kind of argument in Chapter 10, but it should be noted that Professor Hudson's review was essentially fair and balanced.

I have no complaint about the Crystal review – its polemical tone and knockabout style were in response to equally provocative ingredients in *The Language Trap*, and the effect of his arguments seemed in many ways to confirm my general case. Moreover, with characteristic courtesy he had sent me a copy of it in advance so that I could write the reply which he assumed his review would draw, and which the *BAAL Newsletter* had already arranged to insert in its next issue. In that reply I underlined what I felt were the harmful effects on schoolchildren of what linguists were preaching. I also challenged Crystal to reply on a number of specific points, but he chose not to do so, and bowed out of the contest – thus allowing it to be thought that there might perhaps be substance in at least some of my points.

The general reaction among linguists was mainly – and under-standably – one of resentment at what they saw as an injury to their professional *amour propre*. Looking back on these events four years later, a professor of theoretical linguistics who had not been involved in all this wrote in the *Times Literary Supplement*: "The general tenor of the responses suggested that what linguists chiefly objected to in Honey's pamphlet was not intellectual error but vulgarity: it was distasteful to the profession to find its principles called into question before laymen." Perhaps I should have fore-seen this basic fact of human psychology. But in any case, if one wants to challenge and break through what one is convinced is a powerful but harmful orthodoxy, the alternative – a series of gentlemanly arguments in the pages of a learned journal – would have had little effect. However, as it was, my confrontational approach had limited effect anyway, especially in view of the campaign of damage limitation mounted by my opponents.

I began to hear, on the grapevine, that Professor Crystal's review was being circulated gleefully among advisers on English teaching for local education authorities and among English teachers – but without, of course, any reference to my published reply to it. It was arranged to print Crystal's side, but not mine, in *English in Education*, the official journal of NATE, and when I wrote to ask if my reply could also be printed, the editor declined to reprint it in full, but grudgingly allowed a small ration of space. In one and a half pages (compared to my opponent's eight) it was impossible to develop the kind of case which his detailed criticisms deserved. Signs of my critics' tactics were beginning to emerge: at first, a refusal to debate or discuss my criticisms publicly, and this was soon to be followed by an inclination where possible simply to suppress or to rubbish my whole case.

Five years after the publication of *The Language Trap*, two Open University specialists in language and education published an article which examined the controversy aroused by it, and by the media coverage at the time of its publication. David Graddol and Joan Swann began by conceding that "there are a number of naturally occurring language varieties which must be discreetly passed over" if one is to try to preserve the integrity of the doctrine of linguistic equality, but that linguists rarely feel able to tackle these issues in public, and "there seems to be a professional consensus that the tenet of 'linguistic equality' should be presented to the lay public as a simple and uncontroversial fact" – thus they decisively contradicted one of the main points of Crystal's attack. Graddol and Swann went on to try to "examine how linguists responded to a direct challenge both to one of their core beliefs and to their professional responsibility: many of the contributors [to the debate] saw [Honey] as a *dangerous insurgent*. Most were concerned to defend their own professional integrity, or the reputation of the [linguistics] profession" against "a polemical attack on the whole body of sociolinguists and their professional responsibilities".

Having made that point, however, Graddol and Swann went on

to declare that my pamphlet was "essentially a *political* polemic which required a strategic response"! They supported this contention by pointing out that several of the contributors to the debate, in the columns of newspapers like *The Times* and *Guardian*, could be shown to be conservatives. They identified a comprehensive school headmaster whose letter in the *Times Educational Supplement* supported my case, as someone "known to be a right-wing educationist". *The Language Trap* had commended the example of the miners' leader Arthur Scargill, who grew up in a household where his father read eight books a week (his models were the Bible, Shakespeare and the standard English dictionary): "he says your life depends on your ability to handle words". The fact that this favourable reference to Scargill was taken up by a columnist in *The Times* who was "recognised for [his] right-wing views" became for Graddol and Swann the occasion of a sinister political link, since, as they pointed out, Scargill "was engaged in a protracted and damaging national strike" a year after *The Language Trap* appeared. These hypothetical connexions caused Graddol and Swann to summarise "the nature of this debate in Britain" as follows: "On the one hand we had well-known right-wing supporters of the Honey pamphlet putting forward views which clearly fit the policies or intentions of the Conservative government. Against their position were the rallied ranks of academic linguists . . ." Then, claimed Graddol and Swann, because linguists are thus forced into this anti-right-wing stance, "they confirm the public impression that they belong to the radical left".

This article was the prelude to a new phase of the discussion by linguists of *The Language Trap*, in which criticism could now be concentrated on its being represented as a production of the political right. References to 'conservative' and 'right-wing' were gradually transmuted into the more sinister 'New Right', in a way which will be explored later.

The whipping-boy

One contribution to this debate which was not discussed by
Graddol and Swann, though it had come out two years before
their article, was the book *Authority in Language* by Professors
James and Lesley Milroy, whose first edition appeared in 1985. (Its
general case was analysed in Chapter 6, above.) It would perhaps
be fair to say that *The Language Trap* is used by these two authors
as a whipping-boy for their attack on the critics of policies which
seem to restrict access to standard English in schools. The same
Times Literary Supplement reviewer who commented in 1987 on
the distastefulness for the linguistics profession of "finding its
principles called into question before laymen" in *The Language
Trap*, wrote thus of the Milroys' book: "The Milroys quote
Honey's short pamphlet, perhaps, more than they quote any other
author – though always dismissively, and never giving enough of
Honey's argument to allow a reader to make up his own mind . . ."

The Milroys' technique is effective, and the more so as their
nine references to it involve, in every case, misinformation or misrepresentation. It would be tedious to go through all of these, but
we may note a few examples. They claim that I "apparently
believe" that "the Chomskyan tradition has advocated the teaching of non-standard dialects on schools", whereas (they claim)
Chomskyanism had in fact been implicitly pro-standard. What I
said was quite different: that Chomskyan nativism had lent powerful support to the linguistic equality theory which had then been
misused in order to deny children access to standard English. The
connexion between Chomskyan nativism and criticisms of
emphases on standard English is well illustrated by Chomsky's
disciple Steven Pinker (see Chapter 4, above); moreover, the
Milroys' claim about this is similarly disputed by Professor John E.
Joseph. They imply that it is unreasonable for me to charge linguists
with any responsibility for what has been happening with language
standards, thus making a "scapegoat of the discipline of linguistics
itself", and they further deny that the analytic approach of

present-day linguists involves 'teaching no grammar' or 'abandoning standards of correctness' – yet *The Language Trap* simply showed that these theories have in some cases led in practice to exactly those results, and this judgment is confirmed by the admissions of other linguists.

They call for a "more balanced" discussion of linguistic prescriptivism and single out *The Language Trap* for attack when criticising "the inadequate level at which this debate is sometimes pursued", but offer as critique of that pamphlet references to the reviews by Crystal and Hudson, taking care to avoid mention of the fact that the same journal that carried those two reviews went on to carry, in its next issue, my full-length reply to them. It is sometimes difficult, the Milroys claim, to see whom or what I am attacking: "Who exactly are these people who are against clear standards?" (I challenge anyone to read *The Language Trap*, and then my reply to Crystal and Hudson, and not come away with a clear hit-list of names and statements which have contributed to uncertainty among teachers about the place of standard English in schools.) But then, "since *no one seems to have denied the importance of teaching standard English*, the debate was largely an empty one in academic terms". This statement, almost breathtaking in its naivety, gives them an opportunity to put the knife in, and attribute to *The Language Trap* "an overtly political stance": "this suggests that the underlying purpose of the pamphlet was ideological rather than academic".

The Milroys' treatment of the Labov paper 'The Logic of Non-standard English' which was discussed in Chapter 3 (above) is interesting, and again revealing. It is obvious that they have taken note of the serious criticisms of it in *The Language Trap*, and their commendation is now mixed with caution. "Although important and influential, the article is somewhat *outdated* and should be read with attention to the historical context in which it was written." They excuse the fact that it was "polemical in style and intent" by referring to the need to break through the barriers of prejudice against non-standard English. ('Polemical' was used as a serious criticism of *The Language Trap* by its opponents, who did not concede that breaking down the prejudices against *standard* English might justify that approach.) At no point do the Milroys suggest – by even so much as a hint – any sense in which the Labov paper was now *outdated* or how that would affect the way it was read by students. What they are doing is in fact subtly distancing themselves from a paper which they know has been the subject of fundamental criticisms by myself and others, but whose ideological message they nevertheless wish readers to accept.

One point must, in all fairness, be conceded to the Milroys. They claim that the arguments of language scholars of the kind they approve of are not publicised in the press, in the way the views of people like me are. This is, in general, true; the important work of scholars like Randolph Quirk, John Sinclair, Ronald Carter and Geoffrey Leech in codifying the real rules of English usage seldom makes the headlines, except when an old shibboleth like the ban on split infinitives is challenged. But it also true that the media will often give headlines – and a public drubbing – to scholars for whom the Milroys have no word of criticism, like the ones who argue, for example, that "the 'correction' of 'mistakes' by school-children is in reality the imposition of an alien dialect" – a view widely associated with Peter Trudgill – or that standard English should not be taught to non-standard speakers, as it is "not for them".

This insistent urge to misrepresent my arguments sits uncomfortably alongside the Milroys' recurrent protestations that they (and by implication they alone) are concerned to analyse these issues "dispassionately" and to base linguistics "on facts not prejudices". When challenged, during a linguistics conference, for having in their book cited the deeply hostile Crystal review, but omitted reference to my article which answered Crystal's criticisms, the Milroys had no reply to offer. When, six years later, they published a new edition of their book containing additional material, and in it they again suppressed any mention of the relevant answer, they laid themselves open to charges of persistent and intentional distortion.

The 'right-wing' slant

Thus a key ingredient in the linguists' counter-attack was to be the implication that *The Language Trap* was "ideologically" – i.e., *politically* – motivated, a stance which had the supreme advantage that they no longer had to answer the specific arguments in it. Labelling my case as 'conservative', 'politically right-wing', and by later extension 'New Right', was a pointed attempt to discredit it in the eyes of those for whom those terms automatically exclude a proposition from being considered seriously. In general I dislike such facile labels, which often conceal more than they reveal: unless writers proclaim allegiance to, for example, Marxist or socialist ideas, it may be wildly misleading to attribute to them a whole collection of political baggage. Since my own (supposed) political beliefs have been made a matter of public discussion, it would be appropriate for me to give a few facts on this. As it happens, the only political party I have ever belonged to is the British Labour Party, and that was back in the days of Hugh Gaitskell, whose courage and integrity I greatly admired. In recent years I have been a qualified admirer of specific aspects of the policies of Conservative governments, and I would now regard myself as a moderate conservative, probably slightly to the left of Tony Blair. But I also had the highest respect for the Labour Party leader (1992–94) John Smith, and as in Gaitskell's case I felt stunned by his early death. What especially struck me about John Smith, in addition to his obvious sincerity and deep compassion for the underdog, was his beautifully clear use of the English language (he was a Scot) and the way he put this to the service of his fellow citizens: "What's the point of being in politics," he used to say, "if you can't speak up for those who can't speak up for themselves?" His ability to 'speak up' authoritatively on their behalf rested on his command of standard English, and their need for him was partly because of their lack of it. In matters of language, and language teaching, I am a radical and, in the eyes of the linguistics establishment, a dangerous one.

This renders slightly comical the efforts of these critics to dismiss my case by dressing me up as a tool of "the political right". In the introduction to their 1989 book on *Dialect and Education*, Jenny Cheshire and Viv Edwards attacked *The Language Trap* because of the way it had been "used by the political Right as part of a wide-ranging political agenda" and, on the strength of that *non sequitur*, claim that it is therefore "best read as a contribution to the political debate" – in other words, that this absolves them from answering any of the arguments it offers. But in any case, they assert, it is "ill-informed about linguistics and sociolinguistics" (a blanket smear, they give no details). This is an especially interesting charge, given these authors' own commitment to 'linguistic equality' and their admission that this doctrine is ideological, a matter of feeling rather than reason, and their own apparent ignorance of the limited tenability of that theory. They also go on to pretend that in *The Language Trap* I claim that this doctrine has contributed to *declining moral standards* in Britain – this is a complete fabrication and it is surprising that, in what sets out to be an academic book, they should feel it necessary to invent it.* And their fabrication is the more incongruous, in that other contributors to their book give examples of a number of teachers in other Western European countries who, as a result of "insights gained from studying linguistics or sociolinguistics" and specifically the linguistic equality theory, strenuously deny that it is important for pupils to learn the standard language at school, despite the difficulties this produces for those children's learning in other

---

* Suzanne Romaine has described her treatment by a newspaper reporter who interviewed her after the announcement of her appointment as a professor of English linguistics at Oxford: he simply invented a number of details of her clothes and appearance in order to portray her in an unfavourable light. It has been shown that Lytton Strachey similarly fabricated personal details of some of the *Eminent Victorians* he wrote about in 1918 – such as the size of Thomas Arnold's feet – as a technique of belittlement.

subjects. Such examples simply serve to confirm the supposedly "ignorant" argument of *The Language Trap*.

Dr Tony Crowley's book on *The Politics of Discourse*, which was extensively discussed in Chapter 5, also contains, in a final chapter, twelve pages of diatribe against *The Language Trap*. His treatment marks an advance on the previous campaign against it, in two ways. First, he shows himself willing to engage in argument on specific issues, instead of merely dismissing it on specious political grounds. His style of argumentation is – not to put too fine a point upon it – distinctive, and readers are again strongly recommended to sample it for themselves. A few illustrations will suffice to explain why it is so enjoyable for an author to find himself pilloried by a critic whose arguments are so eccentric.

Dr Crowley is unimpressed by the extent of illiteracy and sub-literacy in Britain as referred to in *The Language Trap* and rejects any suggestion that standards of literacy have in any way declined in recent decades. Employers' complaints, references to the inability of insurance claimants to explain coherently the causes of accidents, and the observable illiteracies of advertising cards in shop windows are all ridiculed as unconvincing evidence of decline, and condemned as "a familiar tactic of reactionary thought", since such complaints have been voiced widely during the past century or more. I am thus charged with "dehistoricising the problem", but he does not stop to consider the most import-ant factor which has to be taken into account in properly 'historicis-ing' this issue, which is the record of the enormous increase in investment, in real terms, in education over that period which has failed to cure this degree of failure of literacy. During the period of over a century which Dr Crowley refers to, the length of formal schooling for every pupil has been more than *doubled* – from five years around 1890 to at least eleven years today, while for around a third of the population who receive higher education it has been more than *trebled*, involving a national investment of between £4 and £5 billion a year in education. Yet none of this appears relevant to Dr Crowley.

He ridicules the idea that any formulation of the linguistic equality theory could ever be regarded as 'threatening' or 'menacing', having entirely missed the point of the argument, which is the way these theories were used in order to deny access to standard English to the underprivileged. In any case he sees no problem with linguistic equality: any limitations in a language are taken care of by its capacity for instant adaptation. He attempts to defend the questionable research methodology of Labov's famous article by claiming that, among a variety of possible interpretations of his evidence, Labov is as entitled to his own interpretation as I am to mine – which fails to recognise the crucial point that for Labov's conclusions to have scientific validity, one and only one interpretation of it – Labov's – must be shown to be valid. But by far his most revealing passage is a long section in which he tries to justify Professor Trudgill's claim about the adequacy of all languages or varieties to meet their speakers' needs. By a convoluted species of logic he implies that we are not entitled to comment on the linguistic needs of economically backward societies because we are somehow implicated in the reasons for their backwardness.

The second advance in the demolition strategy against *The Language Trap* is the extension of the 'political right' or 'rightwing' label, which in Dr Crowley's book takes the form of repeated references connecting it to "the new right". This term, "new right" (often capitalised), has come to be used of a movement of ideas which became influential in Britain, North America and Western Europe in the 1980s. Dr Robert Bocock of the Open University, whose views were quoted earlier, has summarised the "main emphases of the New Right" which, in contrast to the admittedly 'directive' (i.e., oppressive) nature of Marxism in practice, he is forced to describe as 'liberal'. According to Bocock, the New Right stresses: (a) freedom from unnecessary state interference in the lives of ordinary citizens; (b) freedom of expression in speech, in broadcasting, in the arts, and in publications; and (c) freedom to organise in social movements, and to dissent openly from the government. My response to Dr Bocock's definition is that if this is *really* what is meant by 'the New Right' as used by Dr Crowley and others, then certainly I'm all for it, but in fact the political ideology associated with the term 'the New Right', especially in the United States in the 1980s, typically has other features which are far too extreme to be applicable to me. In an American context, the term 'New Right' frequently relates to the political pressures exercised by financially powerful religious fundamentalists, whose beliefs and agenda are foreign to my own religious position. In Britain the term has been used in connexion with some of the most hard-line groups who tried to influence Margaret Thatcher, whereas in the context of continental Europe, its connotations are even more extreme: in Germany, for instance, the volume on the Hitler period in a new history of Germany is reported to have been written by a "spokesman of the new right" – it plays down the horrors of the holocaust and the guilt of its perpetrators, so 'new right' used here seems to mean simply neo-Nazi.

Aside from such possible imputations, and the specific misrepresentations by these various authors, the general reaction of the linguistics community to the criticisms in *The Language Trap* was perhaps predictable. It followed the usual pattern of sanctions which, among academics, are visited upon dissent, and was not substantially different from what can happen to a Keynesian economist in the heyday of monetarism, or a theologian who comes to seriously unorthodox conclusions about the doctrine of the Trinity. Thus it will happen that, even if you have scarce qualifications in a needed specialism, you will never be invited to become an external examiner for any other university's degrees in this area, nor to sit on any of the many accrediting committees or on the editorial board of a journal, nor to address conferences. Indeed, existing invitations to address academic audiences will suddenly be withdrawn without credible explanation; your offers to review books for specialist journals – usually welcomed for this thankless task – will be spurned or just ignored, and there will be similar treatment if you offer to contribute to an international seminar on a specialist topic in which you have highly relevant publications. At conferences, not only can you expect to be cold-shouldered by some delegates, but you may find yourself button-holed and insulted, in front of bewildered outsiders – indeed you may be the recipient of discreet expressions of surprise that you even dared to show your face and to risk this treatment in such gatherings. Perhaps you will encounter other academics, who after listening to you contribute to a discussion group, come up to you to tell you of their amazement at finding that you had no horns or forked tail and did not seem to be the monster of bigotry which the earlier comments of your fellow-professionals had led them to expect.

I refer to these sorts of experience without bitterness, recalling that in a sense I 'asked for it', in issuing a challenge to the whole profession of linguistics (more especially the sub-discipline of sociolinguistics); and remembering, instead, those fellow-professionals – including scholars named or implicated in my accusations – who made a point of continuing their friendship and furthering my professional career. Fortunately, being relatively 'small fry' academically, I was spared the fate of much more con-siderable figures such as Professor Basil Bernstein, once the darling of the conference circuit, who after his 'disgrace' found he had become almost a 'non-person', at least until recently. I mention these experiences simply to show how academic conformity is asserted when the equivalent of 'political correctnesss' takes over.

Here is an example of the kinds of pressure that may be brought to bear. A group of European scholars planned a major publication in linguistics and wanted to include a variety of views on the rela-tionship of standard language to dialect in educational systems. Because of the views expressed in *The Language Trap* they invited me to contribute an article on this. Two British professors in the field of linguistics attempted to blackmail the editors into drop-ping my article, by threatening to withdraw their own contribu-tions if mine went in. The editors (all of whom, incidentally, would be proud to call themselves firmly left-wing) preferred to put free speech and the integrity of knowledge before political ideology, and the book came out with my article and not those of my opponents.

Much of the support I received was very discreet. An overseas scholar in the field of linguistics, whose work I greatly admired, used my name on an application for research funding in another country. Afterwards she wrote to thank me, saying,

> You will understand, I hope, that while I am happy to draw on your services with great thanks from this distance, I am unable, alas, to associate my name with yours in the United Kingdom because of the vilification that you have received. In mitigation, let me say that I think you are not right all the time, but are immeasurably 'righter' than those who vilify you.

At the same time, it was chastening to watch the enemies of standard English prosper. Professor Trudgill went onwards and upwards through professorships at Reading and Essex to a chair in Switzerland, thus becoming one of the highest-paid professors of English linguistics in the world, and Jenny Cheshire achieved similar status at two other Swiss universities. Viv Edwards was given a professorship at Reading University. Most ironically of all, Dr Crowley was appointed in 1993, largely on the strength of a degree thesis and a subsequent book which have been analysed in Chapter 5, to a prestigious chair of English at Manchester University – the very post which had been held with distinction, for nearly twenty years, by that marvellous teacher of English literature and sensitive user of the English language, Brian Cox. (It must be admitted that my own career also prospered, though I had to leave the English-speaking world for this to be possible.)

I end this chapter with a reference to an article in 1989 which carried comments on another publication of mine, by Dr Raphael Salkie, who has a senior post in linguistics at Brighton University. He began with a reaffirmation of the principle of linguistic equality: "The fact is that no dialect of English is better than another on purely linguistic grounds" – and differences between them are just reflections of the diverse histories of the English-speaking peoples. He went on to observe that, according to John Honey, those people (such as Trudgill, the Milroys, etc.) who wish to change national attitudes to non-standard forms, try to do so by "suppressing all serious public discussion of the reason why such prejudices persist." To that suggestion he offered this answer:

> The idea that linguistic theorists and progressive teachers have the power to do this is ridiculous, unless there really is a secret mafia of sociolinguists who ring up newspaper magnates and threaten to *knee-cap* them if they print any articles about [non-standard speech forms]. Informed public discussion of [these forms] is essential if attitudes are to change, and it is *dishonest* of Honey to pretend that people working to this end seek to prevent such discussion.

This chapter is intended as a commentary on that statement, and as an explanation of the way that 'academic knee-capping' in the discipline of linguistics actually operates.

CHAPTER TEN

A National and International
Language

The root function of language is to control the
universe by describing it.

James Baldwin

Most people – ordinary people – find it difficult to believe that
anyone, least of all an 'expert', could deny that certain forms of
language are to be regarded as 'correct' and moreover that any sane
person could deny that some people, on some occasions, use language carelessly or incorrectly. It has been the purpose of this book
to show that in respect of a number of major issues of this kind
involving linguistic variation and its implications for education, the
orthodox position among the experts in academic linguistics over
the past thirty years has been intellectually untenable and, in its
practical consequences, actually harmful. It has further been
argued that this orthodoxy has been maintained by means of a
sustained campaign of suppression and misrepresentation against
dissident views. (By that same process, it is unlikely that this
present book will be allowed to feature on student reading lists.)

We noted, in Professor David Tomlinson's discussion of grammar teaching (Chapter 8), the strictures of linguistics professor
F. R. Palmer on the 'flat-earthers' who cling to discredited beliefs
like the value of teaching grammar, and then (Chapter 9) Professor
Richard Hudson's criticism of *The Language Trap* as a piece of
"demagoguery" – letting "the uninitiated" think there are
respectable arguments to show that "they, with their 'common
sense' (alias *prejudice and ignorance*) were right all along, and the
experts got it wrong". Geoffrey Thornton, the schools inspector
for English quoted in Chapter 8, was likewise full of strictures on
"the vast majority of the population" who remain "linguistic flat-
earthers at heart", tied to a "naive linguistic model" which implies

that grammar should actually be taught, and who are little influenced by the recent work of linguistic scholars.

My suggestion is that the ordinary 'woman or man in the street' does not necessarily deserve the contempt which all these linguists have shown for them. It is true that on many specific aspects of language, 'folk-linguistics' is misleading or simply wrong, but this popular idea that some forms of language are 'better' than others is not as crazy as many linguists have loudly asserted in recent decades. This book is littered with quotations from 'experts' in branches of linguistics – especially applied linguistics and socio-linguistics – who say things which are highly dubious or downright wrong. Moreover, they continue to say them. We saw the cavalier rejection by Oxford's Professor Jean Aitchison (end of Chapter 6) of the popular idea that language change should be kept under control, and another Oxford professor in the field of English linguistics, Suzanne Romaine, has had similarly disputable things to say about some of these issues. After apparently rejecting as a 'medieval' idea any notion of correctness – "that there are right and wrong ways of using words" – she asserts that "Standard English represents *nothing more* than the development of a variety which was once a regional dialect associated within [*sic*] the south-eastern part of Britain." This statement is seriously misleading, since that 'development' involved a process of elaboration which created a variety which is, for important modern functions, very different from, and in fact far stronger than, any other variety. And, in a recent paperback addressed to the general public, "What causes a particular way of speaking to be perceived as superior is the fact that it is used by *the powerful*." This may be true, but the point should not be made without also stating that 'the powerful' may actually *derive* their power from their ability to handle such forms of speech.

Romaine's account of how standard languages come about deserves close consideration. According to this, standardisation is a "deliberately and artificially imposed characteristic", not arising from a 'natural' course of linguistic evolution, but "created by conscious and deliberate planning". As with the standardisation of coinage, weights and measures, etc., "the aim is to *remove* variation and establish *only one system* to serve as a uniform one *for a group*."

The ordinary citizen, whose education contains almost nothing on the history of his language or on how it works, deserves a more balanced account than this one, which does not fit the historical facts of the evolution of standard English. One is bound to question its stress on the notion – with its echoes of Crowley and Foucault – that standard languages like English are not a natural, but instead a conscious and deliberate, creation, and to dispute its mistaken assertion about total uniformity – with its sinister implication that it is imposed in the interests of an unspecified 'group'.

Many such pronouncements by these professional 'experts' on language give the lie to the assumption of superior wisdom compared with the the ideas of the humble 'woman or man in the street'. Linguistic scholars are, in fact, remarkably fallible, and certainly at least as fallible as any other group of scientists. We may take an example from the best-known introductory university textbook on linguistics for American university students, by Fromkin and Rodman, first published in 1974 and revised in several new editions since then: it owes its commercial success largely to its use of strip-cartoons to illustrate serious points about language. Not only has it popularised a crude version of the linguistic equality theory, but its many editions continue to put around the myth that the standard accent in British English is given the name Received Pronunciation (RP) because it is the one which is "received" (i.e., accepted as 'proper') *at the royal court*. Other scholars have shown that Fromkin and Rodman's account of the process called phoneme segmentation is simply wrong. We ought also to question the linguists' dictum – repeated in the Kingman Report – that our language is in *constant flux*: in reality, the more important fact is the high degree of stability of standard English, which enables us to understand texts written several centuries ago; there have been many changes, but they have been absorbed gradually. When the pace of change threatens its general stability, then a language – any language – is in real trouble.*

Many of the confident statements by linguists quoted in my book turn out to be highly questionable. Having clearly mis-represented the 'élite' origins of standard English, Dick Leith goes on to claim that standardisation involves "the cultivation by the élite of a variety that can be regarded as exclusive", but this is the opposite of the truth: as we have seen, it is non-standard English which serves to exclude outsiders. Professor Trudgill continues to attack the efforts of the British government to (as he puts it) "*force* all schoolchildren to speak standard English" – efforts supported by misguided people actuated by "the *mistaken* assumption that standard English is somehow endowed with greater 'adequacy'" and who "have not yet understood that all dialects are structured grammatical systems of *equal clarity and adequacy*". Or we may turn to a recent book edited by Professors James and Lesley Mil-roy, this time on the grammar of some of the dialects in Britain – its contributors include Viv Edwards and Jenny Cheshire. It is given the title *Real English*, as if to imply that by comparison with standard English, these non-standard dialects are the only genuine or valuable ones. In it, Dr Jim Miller, reader in linguistics at Edin-burgh University, commits himself to the highly questionable statement that "every geographical variety of English has an edu-cated version in addition to the 'broadest' version". He gives the example of Scottish English, for which it is obviously true, but for many other geographical varieties it is clearly not – like Cockney, whose educated speakers prefer to express themselves in standard English; or the Black Country dialect of the English midlands, whose version of the Old Testament, of which an excerpt is given in the book, is extremely unlikely to show us how English is in fact used by educated Black Country folk. Its opening chapter of

---

* In *Gulliver's Travels*, Swift represented the language of the people of Struldbrugg as being always in flux, with the result that people "of one age do not understand those of another", and thus live "like foreigners in their own country".

Genesis begins: "Ter start evvrything off, God med the wairld. Mind yo', 'e cudn't see ennythin' cuz it wuz all dark, soo 'e sed, 'let's a' sum lite' and the lite cum, an 'e wor arf plaised wi' it . . ."

So while it is true that in respect of many specific aspects of language, 'folklinguistics' is misleading or simply wrong, the popular notion that some forms of language are 'better' than others is not as ludicrous as many linguists have loudly proclaimed in recent decades. Linguists have been unwilling to justify their position in public argument or to produce solid evidence to prove their case: instead there has been a tendency to ridicule or vilify those who have asked awkward questions about the emperor's new clothes. We would do well to remind those who disparage the views of laypersons about language, of William Cobbett's famous rebuke to Van Mildert, future Bishop of Durham: "Your Lordship is very much deceived in supposing the People (or the *Vulgar*, as you are pleased to call them) to be incapable of comprehending argument."

For this reason, linguists should not be surprised to find themselves less loved by the world than they think they deserve. "When sociolinguistics was emerging as a separate discipline in the 1960s," wrote one such scholar, "many extravagant predictions were made about what could be achieved if teachers had access to the same information and insights as linguists. Sadly, many of the promises of this era have not been fulfilled." And in 1995, Jenny Cheshire could write ruefully of "the growing disdain with which our expertise is treated", but also with little apparent awareness of the way in which that popular contempt was earned.

If public confidence in this fundamentally important discipline – the science of language – is to be restored, there must be a renewed willingness to discuss openly the limitations (in grammar, vocabulary, styles, and functions) which are involved in the use of non-standard varieties of English, and the constraints on their scope for adaptation by incorporating standard forms. The notion of linguistic *deficit*, which (as has been argued in this book) was in the early 1970s swept under the carpet by the arbitrary decision of linguistic scholars that they would not recognise its existence, will require to be brought out again into the light of day and subjected to fresh analysis, as the indispensable basis for beginning to remedy the real educational disadvantages which speakers of non-standard varieties experience because of the functional limitations of their language. If the knee-jerk reactions to the word *deficit* which have been built up over three decades require it, then the word *disadvantage* should be used instead.

Indeed, there are signs that this kind of revaluation is beginning. Though Janet Batsleer and her socialist fellow-contributors whose comments were noted in Chapter 5 attack "the reinvigorated promotion of standards, canons and traditions in education and cultural life", another of their comments is significant, their suggestion that the work of Basil Bernstein, "first welcomed and then harshly repudiated by progressives, and even denounced for helping to reinforce the linguistic subordination of working-class children, may now be coming to be seen only to enjoin a *necessary realism*." Moreover, John E. Joseph offered some very fair comments on *The Language Trap* in an article in 1992, despite his general support for Crowley – the 'vitriol' of whose attack on it he also noted. "Honey deserves credit for drawing attention to the inadequacy of language education and the fact that it has short-changed students and undercut the role of education as a social leveller . . ." In the same year, Ben Rampton was among a group of British linguists who declared that "it is now quite widely recognised that the idea of linguistic equality was overstated . . . Negative attitudes to non-standard varieties tended to be treated [by linguists] as prejudice or ignorance of 'the objective facts'." Nevertheless he dismissed *The Language Trap* as "demogogic counter-reaction purporting to speak up for common-sense against a conspiracy of linguists". It was in the same book that Deborah Cameron considered it "rather awkward" that Black American scholars with radical credentials should deploy "a sort of John Honeyesque, *Language Trap*" argument in complaining that the practical effect of Labov's doctrines was simply to increase the disadvantages of inner-city children. However, in her often perverse – but nevertheless important – book *Verbal Hygiene* (1995), Deborah Cameron gives a much more sympathetic account of the issues which *The Language Trap* tried to raise.

The distribution of social 'goods'

It remains instructive to examine the way these and other issues have been discussed in a much-cited book by James Gee, a professor of linguistics in Southern California, widely read by students on teacher-education courses both in Britain and the United States. In an echo of the linguistic equality doctrine, Gee tells us that if the history of the United States had turned out differently and Black people had achieved power, then Black English would have become the standard form of English. But he fails to tell us that if that had happened it would have been a very different form of Black English, since it would have had to develop the grammar, vocabulary and styles appropriate to the functions of such a standard. For Gee, the teaching of English is about the distribution of social 'goods', such as status, wealth, power, control; and about the fact that schools have in modern times served simply to replicate the status quo and to empower élites. Schools socialise their lower-class students (he claims) not to literacy as such, but to 'literacy tasks' which carry with them mainstream, middle-class values of quiescence and placidity, stressing discipline, time-management, honesty and respect, whereas among upper-class pupils they cultivate verbal skills in order to empower those élites. (Why, if this is so, he wants schools to be discouraged from extending this latter benefit to lower-class children, is not explained.)

Writers such as Plato, Bakhtin, Freire and Mary Douglas have all shared the belief that literacy empowers people when it renders them active questioners of the social reality around them. However, acknowledgment of this fact does not, inexplicably, make Professor Gee wish literacy to be more widely available to those people whom it might liberate from unlettered homes into which they were consigned by the accident of birth. This is partly because he does not believe that a speaker of non-standard English – who, for example suffers discrimination and exclusion for writing *have did* for 'have done' in an office communication – can ever acquire a real facility in standard English, for which one has to be brought up in a middle-class (preferably white) home. (This assumption is, of course, disproved by the experience of millions of children in the United States and Britain who have successfully acquired standard English – in Britain it was one of the important functions of the grammar school, especially in the twentieth century, to facilitate this by causing non-standard speakers to incorporate a relatively small number of grammatical changes, and vastly expanding their vocabulary and range of styles, sometimes with the help of some Latin and other languages.) His reservations are also because such adaptation, if it can ever take place, is likely to be at the price of active complicity with the (middle-class) values of the school, which conflict with those of home and community: individuals who do adapt 'sell out' to the dominant cultural values. Again, this view is surprising, because Gee also acknowledges that 'meta-language' (i.e., *knowledge about language*, which of course includes grammar) "is *power*, because it leads to the ability to manipulate, to analyse, to *resist*" – which is a central argument of the book you are now reading.

Far from wishing to expose children to great literature as a model of admired language, Gee in fact feels an urgent need to protect children from contact with it, since one of its traditional functions has been to suggest that human affairs are 'natural' and part of the universe, whereas we all know they are "conventional, historical, cultural, or *class-based*". For a child to read a story-book in school "leads to the incorporation of a set of values about the naturalness of middle-class ways of behaving", and English Literature courses, under the guise of teaching works supposedly 'neutral' and 'universally recognised as good', have often been, in reality, "apprenticeships into middle-class values, thinking and interactional styles." Fortunately, says Gee, literary criticism today, instead of involving "privileging authoritarian texts" is "no longer centred on 'great books' or even just on 'literature'": instead it analyses "all sorts of written and oral texts to *lay bare* how they relate to social structure, and how all texts are part and parcel of the workings of *knowledge, power and desire* in society"; and he argues for this approach to be the new basis of *language and literacy* classes for everybody.

Gee rightly states that "real people really get hurt by the workings of language and power": what he fails to point out is that real people also get *helped* by the workings of language and power, and that certain kinds of language can be turned into power. He repeatedly proclaims the ethical principle by which he is himself motivated, a moral imperative to question social theories (in his case about English language teaching) which actually or potentially harm other people, and it is precisely the same moral imperative which underlies my writing of this book. The question which he rightly says any teacher on a literacy programme must ask will always be this: "*What sort of social group do I intend to apprentice the learner into?*" (his italics). My answer, and that of many teachers, would always be: "Into the social group of the educated and thereby empowered."

The connexion between the most acceptable forms of English and *literacy* or *educatedness* cuts no ice with Professor Gee, for whom 'correct' simply means "how those people think and write who are viewed by élites in society as intelligent and educated", and literacy serves to "undergird the hegemonic process in Western society". The so-called 'literacy crisis' in the United States – and, by implication, in "most Western capitalistic countries" – merely shows that the products of the school system do badly at those skills which schools choose to reward. Moreover, "the idea of functional literacy is conceptually incoherent", and is "another term for the literacy of the colonised"; and Gee is unlikely to be impressed by the literacy survey which found that huge numbers of American citizens could not even understand the instructions on a bottle of aspirins, for he believes that "there is no one correct reading of the label on an aspirin bottle".

Gee's views on literacy are significant because they reflect a revulsion against both of the features whose identification with standard language have been claimed as earning special prestige for the standard – literacy itself, and educatedness. The extensive claims for the intellectual and other cultural implications of the development of literacy which developed in some (but not all) societies – or even the later modified but still decisive form of those claims about literacy – have proved unpalatable to some scholars because they create a yardstick by which some societies will inevitably be judged superior to others. To the citizens of countries with large illiterate populations these claims are even more obviously invidious. Their feelings were forcefully expressed at an international conference of specialists on literacy in 1987, when a professor from India spoke up to complain that to acknowledge the 'superiority' of literate over pre-literate societies constitutes oppression – such suggestions of superiority have a disabling effect on 800 million illiterates of the world who are thereby branded as second-class citizens. He went on to explain that there are, in any case, some benefits to be derived from a non-literate society. Under conditions of orality, people identify and solve problems by working together, whereas literacy brings about a break in togetherness, permits and promotes individual and isolated initiative in identifying and solving problems. Literacy brings about a different kind of togetherness, cutting across social groups, establishing new interest groups that have the potential to manipulate the illiterate for their own selfish interests.

This kind of reaction has caused some scholars to re-define literacy, and the case for it, in ways which avoid the unpalatable implications of the model which proclaims the crucial cognitive implications for literacy as a catalyst in society. Prominent among these scholars is Britain's Professor Brian Street, an anthropologist working in the field of education. He and others (like Professor Gee) would have the invidious 'cognitive' model replaced by an 'ideological model', in which literacy is held to have no special merits in itself and apart from its social context, and Street appears, following Graff, to be claiming that literacy "is only important for specific positions if that is how they are defined in that particular society". Street represents the popular respect for literacy as being due primarily to "hegemonic practices" by people (such as teachers and other members of educational bodies) who have a vested interest in promoting literacy and in "establishing the authority" of particular educational institutions. For him, literacy is essentially a reflection of power relationships – whereas it could be maintained with equal force that power relationships are a reflection of literacy. In the light of these theories, the aim of educational programmes is now to produce what some of these revisionists call 'the new literacy' and some, including Gee himself and Street, call 'social literacy'. Professor John Willinsky, whose own grasp of the existing literacy was referred to in Chapter 8, has written a book advocating *The New Literacy*. Its ingredients are much as can be expected from the above description of Professor Gee's views, which I have quoted from his popular textbook *Social Linguistics and Literacies*. The disabling flaw in this new species of 'literacy' is that it cannot endow the users of its distinctive forms of language with the special dignity which attaches to standard English because of its persistent association with the most respected forms of knowledge.

Yet here is a real problem. How can one express one's respect for educatedness and for the values associated with the whole culture of literacy, without appearing to disparage those for whom education and bookishness have little appeal? Gee claims that the set of values propagated by our school system in advanced Western countries, with its emphasis on literacy, "privileges" those who have mastered certain forms of language and, because it does not succeed (and, he claims, cannot succeed) in giving these to *all* students, thereby does "significant harm" to those others. It is hard to see how this could be otherwise, since ascribing value to one quality (or 'good') may inevitably cause the absence of that quality to be perceived as inferior. It is true that, for example, high levels of performance at playing musical instruments are not, in reality, available to all children, but does this mean that if we try to develop them in those who appear to benefit from them, we are doing "significant harm" to the rest? Are footballers who do not make the first team, but only play for the second or third, "robbed of their human worth"? President Mandela has called for "a culture of learning" in the new South Africa. But in terms of James Gee's philosophy, if that learning turns out to emphasise 'educated' forms of language – and its recipients will feel cheated and patronised if it doesn't – then Mandela's programme will simply have the effect of creating an *oppressed class* of people who do not respond as hoped to the offer of knowledge and literacy skills.

The question has a real urgency, since we know that the particular values which dominate our educational systems, which have to do with the cultivation of the mind by reading, by trained methods of thinking and observing, etc., are not in fact found interesting by a significant proportion of people in our society. They may defer to these interests in other people but do not desire them for themselves, indeed they may feel the symbols of educatedness to be threatening. This applies particularly to books. The former England cricketer who became Bishop of Liverpool, David Sheppard, has described his early days in charge of a pioneering type of 'mission' church in the East End of London. Its organisers came to realise how important it was to respect the 'distinct culture' of Canning Town: "We realised how bookish the Church often is, and how much that added to the gap which our neighbours sensed between them and church life." He had begun by placing the conventional bookstall just inside the entrance to the church, but soon became aware of the adverse first impression this created on those who entered – the impression that "being a proper Christian involves reading a lot of books". In most homes in Canning Town, "books were not part of the scene"; the bookstall shouted a message that "the Church was a foreign culture", and it was quickly moved to a less conspicuous place. That hostility to literature is not untypical of sections of British society is suggested by the term used by a British professor of education when commenting on figures comparing the academic achievement of British 16-year-olds with Taiwanese 12-year-olds: he referred to "Britain's deep aversion to learning and education".

Education as the fault-line

What this evidence confirms is that modern Western societies are now divided less by wealth or class than by the single factor of culture, and most specifically by those cultural variables which relate to literacy (in its more advanced forms) and literate language. President Clinton declared in 1995 that "Education is the fault-line in the world today" – indicating a fault-line both within societies and across the globe – and the division along this boundary is likely to become sharper as the 'information superhighway' becomes a reality touching everyone's lives. Our computerised, globalised society proceeds on the basis of standard English, and this will persist even after the book is eventually replaced as the main medium of learned communication. Though the initial effect of this new technology may be to give a fillip to local literate languages, the long-term result will be to marginalise still further those who cannot speak and write a standard form of a national language and indeed an international language, especially English. Meanwhile, employers in both Britain and America complain that students leave school unable to compute, read, communicate, or spell, and one American business leader says that only 20 per cent have the education and skills to compete in the global economy.

But we must also look more closely at some of the implications of the concept of educatedness, which in this book has been identified as a defining quality of those forms of spoken and written English which are regarded as standard, and which is the touchstone of prescription. First, educatedness is a *changing* concept which must be recognised as reflecting the way the most educated members of society actually speak and write English in the present day – those members to be identified by objective criteria, rather than by a circular process which effectively identifies the educated by their use of those forms which have in the past been associated with the educated. There was at least a grain of truth in Raymond Williams's complaint that "the level indicated by *educated* has been continually adjusted to leave the majority of people who have received an education below it . . ." Secondly, the concept carries the potential for some unpleasant implications. Respect for educatedness is, for some, a licence for intellectual arrogance: that is not what it is essentially about, but there is always that potential, and it must be recognised and dealt with when it occurs. It also imposes the obligation to find ways of valuing those people who do not regard literacy and education as important factors in their own lives.

I believe it is possible to have a value-system which keeps both the educated and the less educated in appropriate perspective. I must confess here that in my own scale of values, educated people are not the most admired category: it so happens that at the top of my personal list are the parents of handicapped children. But I also know that behind the outpouring of love and self-sacrifice by those parents there stand the knowledge and expertise of doctors, nurses, teachers, scientists and others concerned with their diagnosis, care and remediation. The founder (on earth) of my religion chose as his key agents mostly unlettered fishermen, but his message only took hold because it was committed to writing, and then spread, by more educated people.

Society has a duty to make hard choices about the valuation that is to be placed upon education, in the face of a philosophy which has had some influence in teacher education on both sides of the Atlantic. This is the relativism which we have already seen in the work of postmodernist scholars like Tony Crowley and James Gee, expressed also in the principle which was used by journalist Melanie Phillips as the ironic title of her hard-hitting critique of

British education, *All Must Have Prizes* (1996). The psychologist Liam Hudson has shown how the intellectual bases for these ideas were being propagated at the University of Chicago around 1945 onwards – including the belief that differences in ability between individuals or groups are either illusory or the product of oppression. It is seen as injurious to people's self-respect to compare them with others and find them wanting. Nobody is to be considered ridiculous or bad or disgusting, except only the person who seeks to measure or compare – "the very processes of measurement and comparison being seen as the outward and visible signs of an incipiently fascist mind-set".

This kind of relativism has spilled over into art, literature, and into the idea of what constitutes worthwhile knowledge. Richard Hoggart has quoted the examples of the university teacher at Oxford who declared that lavatorial graffiti are not to be distinguished, in any qualitative way, from the drawings of Rembrandt, and of an Arts Council discussion paper which proposed that Wedgwood pottery and Elgar are no better than Tupperware and Bob Marley – "they just belong to different clubs". The notion that there is no such thing as absolute 'truth' and that all knowledge – including the principles of science – is equally good, is used to disparage academic disciplines as simply 'social constructs', projections of the selfish interests of élite groups: "all cultures and sub-cultures are equally good in their own terms." It thus becomes not only intellectually but also *morally* wrong to suggest that one is better than another. But of course they do not really believe this, just as Labov, Gee, Willinsky and others do not really believe that all varieties of English are 'equal': they would be horrified if their own children proved unable to handle the standard form. The Oxford geneticist Richard Dawkins has exposed the sham of relativist claims of 'all knowledge as equally good', in his famous challenge: "If it gives you satisfaction to say that the theory of aerodynamics is a social construct, that is your privilege, but why do you then entrust your travel plans to a Boeing rather than a magic carpet? Show me a cultural relativist at 30,000 feet, and I'll show you a hypocrite."

It can be argued, too, that relativism has contributed to a climate of opinion in which important issues related to social inequality cannot be properly and openly discussed in the academic community. *The Bell Curve* is a now famous book by two American scholars, Richard Herrnstein and Charles Murray, which in 1994 offered to explain the low status and adverse prospects of minority groups, especially Blacks, by reference to the tendency for those of low intelligence to have more babies, and at earlier ages, than those of higher IQ. The book envisages a bleak future in which the highly intelligent join with the rich to enjoy high-quality education and other services in protected enclaves while the masses rot in inferior education and public squalor. In a brilliant review article in an American sociological journal, Douglas Massey of Pennsylvania University has laid the blame for the apparent plausibility of this book on his own profession: its case could never have been made (he says) if sociologists had been more forthright in studying human intelligence over the past two decades.

In that period, research into the causes of urban poverty and racial disadvantage ran up against politically controversial issues of culture, intelligence, sex, marriage, etc., on which the public had strong but not necessarily well-founded views. "The way to confront theories you do not like," writes Massey, "is to confront them directly, test them rigorously, and prove them wrong. However, in adopting this course, you must accept the possibility that an explanation you perceive as noxious might, in fact, be correct." But rather than accepting such a possibility – either that culture might in some way be implicated in poverty, or that differences in IQ might help to account for variation in social outcomes – "sociologists stuck their heads in the sand and hoped the unpleasant ideas would just go away."

This was bad enough in itself, but was made worse by many academics who also sought to ensure that *no one else* would investigate these sensitive issues. In a variety of ways, the examination of social differences in culture and intelligence was discouraged. "For those who were slow to catch on, object lessons were made of Oscar Lewis and Daniel Patrick Moynihan, and after the treatment these two prominent social scientists received, no one could miss the point." The published findings of both these sociologists – the first investigating the urban poor, the second the negro family – implied a possible contribution by the poor to their own poverty. "For this heresy, both men were excoriated by liberals throughout the social science establishment": their arguments were travestied, they became "racists" who "blamed the victims" of an unjust society rather than the forces of oppression that were in fact responsible. All this had a chilling effect on social science for two decades: sociologists stopped studying controversial issues related to race, culture, and intelligence, and researchers who persisted met resistance and risked being ostracised in their profession.

As a result of this, "significant gaps in the empirical research literature began to emerge on questions that were central to understanding social stratification and racial inequality in the United States". When a conservative political agenda became a reality in the America of the 1980s, the record of research findings which could have refuted the assumptions underlying that agenda in many cases did not exist. Those findings might also, Massey implies, have pre-empted some of the extensive evidence which underlies the main arguments of *The Bell Curve*.

I have to say that I do not accept the depressing central thesis of *The Bell Curve*. Just as with Chomsky and his nativism theory, Herrnstein and Murray are open to the criticism that they over-emphasise the contribution of inherited factors to an individual's language development. I notice that their book proves intelligence to be a largely inherited variable, by methods which themselves presuppose that intelligence is inherited. But, most significantly of all, I believe that one of the most powerful factors contributing to the disadvantage of America's underclass – Blacks and other ethnic groups, and lower-class whites – is in reality capable of being changed: I refer to their ability to handle standard English. A properly funded and effective programme designed to add standard English to their repertoire of speaking and writing skills has the potential to transform the educational and occupational opportunities of members these groups. But a precondition for any such programme is that we discuss the whole subject of non-standard English and its functional disadvantages with an honesty which has been markedly absent from the way many in the academic establishment in linguistics and education have discussed it – or indeed refused to discuss it – for two or three decades.

Moreover, it is time to move away from some of the assumptions which have accompanied the discussion of minorities, which in Britain include a nostalgia for the solidarities of the pit and the shop-floor and the council estate that deserves – as the political commentator Ferdinand Mount has suggested – to be taken in very small doses. The sense of 'community' is a powerful factor in social cohesion and in offering a sense of identity, but we should be ready to move away from the old, arbitrarily allocated, forms of local community, built on the enforced sociability of common poverty or common dangers in the pit or other workplace, and into kinds of association based on freedom of choice. Thus it ought to be possible for someone like Alex Haley to seek to identify as readily with (say) a community of jazz-loving environmental preservationists or vegetarian transcendental-meditationists as with the West African tribe to which his ancestors happened to belong. The vision of society proclaimed by some of the linguistic scholars quoted in this book is based on a new tribalism rooted in the arbitrary particularism of geography and of citizens held captive in an outdated sense of social class.

Furthermore, there are dangers involved in simply celebrating difference and particularity. The political scientist Alan Ryan, working both in the United States and in Oxford, fears a backlash against the demands of minorities, and asks: "How do we square the preservation of national identity with endlessly fragmenting cultural identities?" He goes on to question how, in the face of such demands, a nation can construct a single – yet pluralistic – national ethical and political culture that can absorb and appreciate the formerly excluded: sexual and ethnic minorities, immigrants, non-English speakers, women. The potential for fragmentation might seem particularly real in a country like the United States, where estimates suggest that within just over two decades, Blacks, Hispanics and Asians will comprise 35 per cent of the population. And whereas, a century ago, 60 per cent of Americans were of common ethnic stock – British – now the proportion is smaller than 20 per cent. Yet the American linguistics professor James Tollefson (see Chapter 4) flatly denies that language diversity is inherently disunifying (he gives no evidence for this assertion, and neither Belgium nor Canada features in his book's index). He also flatly denies – again, offering no evidence – that competence in the English language is perceived in America as a measure of a newcomer's loyalty to the nation, or that such competence leads to upward mobility (for example, by better jobs), and even disputes the proposition that anyone who is truly motivated to learn English can do so.

There is much talk nowadays, in both Britain and America, about the need to recreate a sense of community, which is clearly desirable and indeed urgent, though it will be of little value if it is based simply on the 'solidarity' of local particularism, educational deprivation and resistance to learning: the need is instead to overcome cultural differences in a shared citizenship. It is a prominent member of America's Black community, Boston professor Glenn Loury, who insists that "In a democracy, the alternative to force is persuasion and a *common civic culture.*" But Molefi Kete Asante – the adopted name of the chairperson of the African-American Studies department of Temple University – repeatedly asserts that "There is no common American culture . . . A common culture does not exist . . ." and, "Bluntly put, 'mainstream' is a code word for 'white'." Likewise, the linguist James Gee ridicules the claims of what he calls "so-called 'mainstream culture'".* At the same time, the *Economist* reported in 1995 this frightening corollary: "In cities, suburbs, schools, churches, in culture and *even in language*, America is slowly re-segregating."

One of the more curious gaps in Dr Crowley's amazingly select-ive account of the historical development of standard English is his total neglect of the work of the late Ernest Gellner, a distinguished social philosopher at the London School of Economics and Cam-bridge whose influential *Nations and Nationalism* was published in 1983. Readers are referred to that book for the fine detail of its argument, but it is sufficient to note here Gellner's central theme, that by the nineteenth century the European nation-states were being significantly moulded by the Industrial Revolution's changes to education and work, with the result that a common culture and a common standard language, rather than birth, became the touchstone of shared citizenship. It was one of my teachers at Cambridge more than thirty years ago – the anthro-pologist Sir Edmund Leach – who pointed out that "For a man to speak one language rather than another is a ritual act, it is a state-ment about one's personal status; to speak the same language as one's neighbour expresses solidarity with one's neighbour, to

---

* Disparagement of 'mainstream' culture is now common among linguists and educationists in the United States. The editor of a leading professional journal for English teachers writes slightingly of "norms that are tied to the lifestyle of the powerful segment of our society, glossed by the word 'mainstream' (meaning white and middle-class)." James Sledd, quoting the novelist Ralph Ellison, claims that "the metaphor of the 'mainstream' reflects a society where dissenters and other minorities are consigned to the swamps and backwaters." But readers could equally well point to the connotations of 'mainstream' as a broad flow enriched by many tributaries, and in turn enriching its banks on either side. By contrast with the Sledd argument, it was being more convincingly argued from the 1970s onwards by, for example, spokesmen for the disabled in Britain, that to restrict access for the handicapped (or anyone else) to 'mainstream' society was a symptom of oppression, and they demanded "an end to institutions which excluded their participation in the mainstream of society".

speak a different language from one's neighbour expresses social distance or even hostility."

The ability of a common standard language to function as a form of 'social cement' in modern nation states also draws attention, especially when it is absent or uncertain, to some of the nastier manifestations of nationalist feelings. As the journalist William Pfaff has pointed out, historically the most vicious forms of nationalism and instances of racism have arisen in those societies which are least confident of themselves, or are the most divided – by culture, or religion, or *language*. The most frenzied, and the most dangerous, nationalists are marginalised people.

So the question of whether we should foster the use of a common form of language, standard English, or instead encourage minorities to express their particularism through their non-standard forms without regard to how far they also acquire facility in the standard, is an issue with profound implications for the cohesion of our society. Moreover, our conception of 'community' has not only moved away from the neighbourhood or village or housing estate on which we grew up, to the nation, but moved also to the broader region, and to the world at large. And as we enter this new era of global community, the increased reality of internationalism will add to the functions of English as the only readily available international language.

Two international models

So far we have spoken as if there were one model of standard English, but in fact there are two – and some people would argue that there are yet other models. The two undisputed models of standard English are British English and American English, and all varieties of English around the world derive from one of these – those of the states based on territories of the former British Empire in Africa, Asia and the Caribbean deriving from British English, whereas in countries like Canada, Hawaii and the Philippines their variety has grown out of the American model. Until 1945 British

English had undisputed prestige in the world, and was the model for most learners. But by the 1960s, the enormous political and economic power of the United States had led many outside that country's historic sphere of influence to opt for the American variety, which officially replaced British English in the education system of Japan.*

Some language schools, from Western Europe to the far East, even began to specify American English as a qualification for their teachers. During the three decades from the 1960s to the 1980s the influence of American English reached a high point and looked set to rule the world.

What dramatically altered the picture was the downfall of communism in Eastern Europe and the USSR after 1989. Given that English is now firmly established as the first language of the European Union (with German overtaking French as the second most important), and given the ambition of the former communist states of Eastern Europe for admission to, or at the very least association with, the EU, then there will be a strong advantage for British English as the model in their school systems. If we put together the total populations of the European Union, Eastern Europe and the states of the former USSR, as representing this potential bloc in which British English is the model for the English that is used, we have around 900 million would-be speakers. The home base of American English – the United States and Canada – is a population of around 250 million.

If an enlarged EU seems certain to opt for British English as its model, so is Africa, where nearly half the population (48 per cent) already live in states where the British variety is firmly established as a second, and often official, language; and even in the francophone states of West Africa, developing forms of economic union

---

* This had quaint results, since a distinctive feature of American English is 'post-vocalic *r*' – i.e., the *r* in *farm* or *cord* is pronounced, whereas in the standard English of most British (other than Scottish) BBC newsreaders it is not sounded – yet Japanese-speakers have notorious difficulties with *r*, often confusing it with *l* (sometimes with comic effects).

are posited on the adoption of British English. On the other hand South America, originally penetrated by British English, is already being drawn to the American model, and this will speed up if economic links between the United States, Canada and Mexico expand into the rest of the continent, so that both North and South America may be expected to end up as the stronghold of American English. In Asia, the British variety has long been established in at least eight countries, especially in the populous subcontinent of India; and nearly all of Oceania, led by Australia and New Zealand, is inextricably in the camp of British English.

Estimates of world population in the year 2000 illuminate the coming struggle for global supremacy between these two linguistic giants. The combined total for Europe and Africa is more than 1,450 million, while that for North and South America is just over 900 million – a balance of more than three to two in favour of the sphere of British English. Asia will have nearly four billion, with between a third and a half living in states historically committed to British English. The real battleground will be those Asian states, as yet uncommitted, with large populations, like Indonesia (over 180 million) and, above all, China (1.2 billion). China's forty years of fierce antipathy to the US could lead to a preference for British English such as has already been reflected in the enormous success of the BBC's teaching programmes there. But another possibility might be major political change in China leading to a revulsion against former prejudices and an enthusiastic embracing of all things American.

These crude totals may suggest a big advantage in the future for British English, but they also require a number of points of qualification. The really big numbers for British English consist of speakers who have learned English as a second or foreign language, whereas we should rather be comparing the home base of each variety, a point on which American English scores. Its much larger numbers of mother-tongue speakers (concentrated, of course, in North America) and their tendency to devise innovative forms of English – which foreign speakers of a language have less authority to do – give American English a powerful edge. American strength in technology, especially in the technology of communication – for example, in computer software – and the worldwide popularity of American English as mediated by films and pop music, are factors which are to be set against the crude disparity of numbers. Some political commentators (like Yale's Professor Paul Kennedy) have suggested that America's economic and political power will decline over the next fifty years. By contrast, the choice of British English as model has long been motivated by traditionalism, by its association with an historic culture and perceptions of its being the authentic vehicle of great literature and the exponent of admired values.

There was a time when scholars speculated that British English and American English were growing apart to such an extent that they would soon be mutually unintelligible. That view was certainly understandable a century ago, but the likelihood now seems to be that they are growing closer together, thanks to the new technology of mass communication and the culture it gives rise to. Compared with British English, the American variety has a range of well-established and systematic differences, in its generalised accent (for example, *hot, grass, farm*), in its pronunciation of particular words (*leisure, Birmingham, herb*), in a few points of grammar, in vocabulary (*sidewalk, elevator*), in spelling and even in punctuation; and in a mass of idiomatic speech. Yet few of these present any difficulty to British schoolchildren, who acquire an extensive passive knowledge of American English through constant exposure to American films and television programmes. The people of Britain are unlikely to surrender their range of native accents and adopt the readily recognisable (and easily intelligible) American one, but in respect of the rest of American English – pronunciation of particular words, grammar, vocabulary, even punctuation, we can say that modern British English is under siege from American English, which is the greatest single influence on it. (This 'siege' is a one-way process.) Many American grammatical forms are finding their way into English, and the existence of different words means that British speakers end up with access to a number of word-pairs (pavement/sidewalk) and a temptation to use American senses of words, which may be very different from – and sometimes incompatible with – their British English uses, as with *protest* ('he protested his anger') and *slate* ('the performance was slated'); words like *dumb* and *through* can also give trouble.

Guardians of the English language are rightly concerned to try to control the wholesale incorporation of American usages, many of which represent an enrichment but some of which cause confusion and are properly suspect – the ignorant use of *cohort* (Chapter 7) may be an example of an undesirable import, likewise the *may have / might have* shambles. One interesting development in progress in American English is the shifting forward of word-stress on to the beginning of the word – BLOCKade, MILLion-aire, CAMpaign, ALready, HIStoric, CAPsize, INsurance, OBscene, DEcember, ROmance, RObust, OUTnumber, BEloved. It used to be possible to point to the difference in stress between British cigarETTE and American CIGarette, British weekEND and American WEEKend, but the American form is now often heard from British voices. British speakers have for years heard, and often used, the front-stressed American variant REsearch (for reSEARCH), and among American media speakers it is now common to hear REpeat, REcoil, REcess, RElapse, REpeal, REbuff, REsources, REcluse, RElease, REprieve, and the extension of this pattern to many other prefixes including DISpatch (and DISpatcher) DIStrust, DIStaste, DEfault – many of these forms, especially RElease, RElapse, are now often heard in Britain too. A yet further extension is now to collocations (pairs or groups of words), and friendly Americans use the greeting Happy NEWyear, and talk of the three WISEmen, and a HOlywar, a HOLEintheground, and stopping at a REDlight.

As the features of a global community – created and kept together by new communications technology – proliferate, we must expect the two world varieties of English to grow together, and indeed in many respects this is to be welcomed. When the influential news magazine *Asiaweek* announced in June 1993 that it was changing over from British English spelling to the American variety, there were protests from readers in Sri Lanka and elsewhere who pointed out that a large proportion of its readership lived in states where British English had long been enshrined in the educational system. I, as a Briton, would be happy to agree to the acceptance of most of the distinctive – and generally simplified – features of American spelling (*traveler*, *honor*, *center*, *anesthetic*, perhaps even *plow*) and in any case I already have to, since some of the academic books to which I contribute are published simultaneously in London and in the United States and Canada, so the spelling and punctuation have to be made uniform, which means in practice American. This is inevitable because the domestic market for such books is based on a population of a mere 55 million for Britain but 250 million for North America, and publishers have not yet caught up with the implications of the 'Euro' factor I have earlier mentioned, which may only make themselves felt some time in the future.

Some features of American English, however, deserve to be resisted by anyone concerned for intelligibility and clear communication. One of these is the American treatment of the '*t*' sound, which suffers a variable fate depending on where it comes in a word. In most cases it is pronounced in the expected way, but if it appears between vowels, as in le*tt*er and ci*t*y, it becomes almost a '*d*', making it difficult to distinguish between *writer* and *rider*, *bidden* and *bitten*. When a CNN reporter says, "At the UN, delegates are added again", it turns out he means *at it again*. And if the 't' appears after an *n*, it it can disappear altogether, so that Americans often cannot tell the difference between an *inner*-city train and an *inter*-city train. British people think the name of America's president elected in 1992 and 1996 is pronounced as Bill Clin-t'n, but he himself pronounces his name – as for example when he was sworn in for his first term of office – Clin-'n, though most newsreaders heard overseas on America's satellite channels make the effort to pronounce his name with the 't' as spelt, and if they ever do use his own pronunciation, they usually correct themselves, as if they feel that this is too informal a usage. This typical American treatment of 't' has of course nothing to do with Britain's now common (Estuary-influenced) dropping of 't' at the ends of words (there's a lo*t* of i*t* abou*t*) as described in Chapter 7, but its implications for clarity of comprehension are equally disturbing.

There are hard decisions to be made as to how to reconcile these two world varieties, now that the world has effectively decided that English is the world language – at least for the next five hundred years, or until the Martians arrive. Something like a quarter of the total population of the globe now speak, or are trying to learn, English – a proportion without precedent in the history of the world. As well as having two world models – British and American English – between which to choose, there are also the claims of the new Englishes – the localised varieties which have grown up in (for example) the wider region of the subcontinent of India (Pakistan, India, Sri Lanka, etc.), in East, West and South Africa, in the Caribbean, in Singapore and Malaysia and in the Philippines. In many cases these have been used as the vehicle of a rich and vibrant literature which often excites the admiration of both readers and literary scholars and has for many years been represented on the reading lists of students of English literature and indeed, with some success, on the short-lists for literary prizes.

But there may be a big difference between admiring that literature, the bulk of which is written in what is clearly identifiable as standard English, and recognising, for teaching purposes, each separate variety and installing them as models in various educational systems. (Indeed, where does the particular variety begin and end? What are its typical features?) This whole topic has been the subject of an excellent and much publicised debate between the British scholar Randolph Quirk and Professor Braj Kachru, a speaker of Indian English now working in the field of linguistics in the United States, with the latter promoting the case for recognition of the new Englishes and the former pointing out the practical drawbacks. Kachru's case might be thought to be strong in respect of Indian English, which has indeed developed a number of distinctive forms (many of which have passed into the English language generally, to its great benefit). Nevertheless, it is possible to find, in an issue of a leading English-language newspaper like the *Times of India*, articles which are examples of written standard English of the highest quality of style and content, whose only indications of being written outside Britain might be a few typical local words (like *lakh* for a measure of 100,000, or *rupee*). In Singapore, a local variety has emerged, with many distinctive forms, but the kind of English which enjoys the greatest measure of respect at all levels of Singaporean society is the educated English which shows by only a small number of traces of non-standard forms that it is distinctively Singaporean. For either Indian or Singaporean English – or any of the hundreds of alternative Englishes including Black English, British Black English, Chicago English, Chicano English, Ashkenazic English, and hybrids like Japlish (as used in Japan), Chinglish (among Chinese speakers) Arablish (Arabic-speakers), Franglais (French) – to be capable of being used as an alternative model to either British or American English in anybody's educational system, will require that that variety be codified (i.e., that its distinctive usages be listed and described in dictionaries and grammar books); and any forms that are not likely to be used by its more educated speakers are also unlikely to earn respect when used by other speakers.

One result of the cult of diversity by the discipline of academic linguistics in the past three decades has been the creation of uncertainty among teachers of English to foreign learners – comparable with the uncertainty produced among teachers of British and American schoolchildren – about the validity of correcting learner's 'errors'. Thus, teachers of English as a foreign language have also been warned not to make "overly hasty judgments about the language performance of learners", since "language behaviour which at first sight appears to be flawed may in fact be a manifestation of a new – though as yet unrecognised – variety of English".

Many learners of English in Hong Kong, for example, have a problem, because the form of English which has developed among local speakers differs markedly from standard English. The *Economist* in 1996 gave this illustration of Hong Kong English to exemplify the problem: *If anyone interesting to enquiry for more long-time of this problem, please attention to this journalist;* and Professor Roy Harris, who does not believe that there is such a thing as standard English, found that after his encounter with Hong Kong English he was forced to consider the possible truth of a Chinese acquaintance's judgment that this was "the worst English in the world". Perhaps Professor Harris has modified his earlier hostility to the notion of standard English, since, interestingly, his proposed remedy for the weaknesses in the English of university students in Hong Kong is "serious engagement with some of the outstanding works and some of the finest minds that the long tradition of English writing affords", by way of access to "the history-rich language which articulated the tropes, the metaphors, the arguments, the concepts which shaped the minds of some of the world's best poets, scientists and philosophers".

There are similar problems on the Chinese mainland. Writing in 1989 of the expectations which Chinese university students of English there (and indeed their Chinese lecturers) have of the native speakers who come to teach them English, a Chinese professor writes: "It goes without saying that an English teacher should, in the first place, have internationally standard pronunciation and intonation." Unfortunately, he says, "some foreign teachers do not know traditional English grammar well." A British lecturer, arriving to teach in a provincial university in China, found that her students had been told that "Western teachers are good for conversation practice but little else, as they never know anything about grammar", so she taught them about subordinate clauses and the sequence of tenses – a course, "beginning on *the sentence* and going on from there", which many students in Britain would indeed dearly love to have. For Quirk, instead of seeking to institutionalise a mass of different local varieties of English, there is a clear need, around the world, for non-native-speakers who teach English to be able to look for support and guidance to native speakers, and to try to be in constant touch with an acceptable international model of the English language. This is a heavy responsibility, for whereas fifty years ago it was still possible to think of the worldwide activity of teaching English as being personally conducted by British, North American and other expatriate teachers, the task of teaching English to the world is, by the end of the twentieth century, firmly in the hands of non-native speakers. Fortunately the most advanced modern technology is beginning to make access to native-speaker guidance and support a practical possibility even in remote parts. A bigger problem is the economic one in the Third World, where access to adequate-quality tuition in 'good' English is a luxury available only to the well-off minority, producing the unacceptable situation in which facility in internationally valid English becomes a marker of social and economic privilege. Yet the alternative is also stark, since failure to provide people in a number of key occupations with that internationally valid English can actually cost lives. For example, several disastrous air crashes in the 1980s and 1990s – including at least two in 1996 alone – were blamed on breakdowns of communication between pilots and ground controllers due to poor English.

It is not only the notion of international, as opposed to local, models of English which has given rise to dispute. English is seen by some as a virus which can harm or even kill other languages, which is no more nor less than the truth. As we saw in Chapter 2, every year several languages in the world die, and English is perhaps the foremost killer; and the grammar, vocabulary, pronunciation and even word-order of many languages show signs of being invaded by English. My suggestion that perhaps over the next five hundred or a thousand years some even prominent languages in Europe might succumb to competition from the international language earned me a lofty rebuke from Professor Quirk, but it is not entirely fanciful to think that Gaelic or Albanian may have limited life; when you talk, in millennial terms, of languages like French sharing the same fate, there is real horror and incredulity, but the possibility, at least, is surely there.

'Linguistic imperialism'

An even more obvious danger is the set of values represented by English, which some regard as seriously damaging to other cultures. The foremost spokesman of this case has been Robert Phillipson, a British linguist working in Denmark, whose name we encountered in Chapter 2. His *Linguistic Imperialism* became something of a cult book soon after its publication in 1992. For Phillipson, it is a matter of great scandal that English has become the dominant international language, and thus the "cornerstone of the world capitalist system". This dominance is "asserted and maintained by the continuous *creation* of cultural inequalities between English and other languages", essentially by hogging an unfair share of teaching resources. A crucial weapon in this domination is Phillipson's concept of *linguicism*, by which he means, in effect, attributing to one language (for example, English) favourable attributes and denying similar attributes to another. Linguicism has "taken over from racism as a more subtle way of hierarchising social groups", and of promoting social inequality. From the theory advanced in Phillipson's book, the late Kwame Nkrumah, who argued strongly for the use of English as a means of promoting the new nation state of Ghana and for combating what he saw as the evils of tribalism, must now be condemned both as a 'linguicist' and as racist, since 'tribalism' is treated by Phillipson, on totally unconvincing grounds, as a politically incorrect, indeed racist, term.

Phillipson gives copious examples of the domains in which English has become predominant, as the language of international communications, science, technology etc, as a direct result of the creation of myths about its special usefulness, etc. Those who teach English are usually the unwitting stooges of neo-colonialism, indeed of what he calls "neo-neo-colonialism", whose true nature he feels impelled to "unmask".

Not until nearly the end of his book does Phillipson reveal his own theoretical starting-point, which (as we saw in Chapter 2) turns out to be our old 'friend' the doctrine of linguistic equality. "Linguists are trained to see any language as potentially fulfilling any function, hence not intrinsically superior or inferior to any other language." That crucial word "potentially" poses the fundamental question: what processes does the language of a preliterate Third World community have to undergo in order to be able to perform for its speakers the range of functions in (for example) modern science and technology or any other aspect of modern thought? What kinds of elaboration or 'development' (Phillipson's word) are necessary in order to create the vocabulary, the range of styles and 'genres', and all the other other features that make possible its use as what some some scholars, following the distinguished Philippine linguists Gonzalez and Batista, have called an 'edulect' – a form of language which can be the vehicle of modern education? What is the time-scale, and the cost, of all this? We know, of course, that in some circumstances, and to some extent, it can be done: Swahili, Hebrew, Bahasa Indonesia/ Malaysia and Tagalog have made the attempt. Arabic, Russian, Japanese, starting from a high base-line and all backed by huge financial resources, have had to struggle to keep up, and the textbooks now used for advanced degrees in fast-moving disciplines in some universities in Japan and other countries are in English – there is no other economic way of keeping abreast of world knowledge.

But can this realistically be done for *every* language and dialect? In Papua New Guinea, there are over 800, spread among 38 million speakers. Namibia is a favourite example of Phillipson's, because he was a consultant to SWAPO in its guerrilla period but was snubbed when the decision, applauded by other African leaders, was taken at independence to adopt English. Of around eight 'main' indigenous languages, the one that used to be called

'Bushman' has, in its present form, massive limitations in its sound system, vocabulary and stylistic range for purposes of extended education. How much money is available to produce secondary school textbooks in (say) physics and chemistry for those speakers, not to mention university-level books? How rational is it to give priority to that exercise over the thousand other pressing needs of a developing country? These sorts of question are simply not touched on. Nor does he seriously attend to the problem that to take resources away from English teaching and put them into the development of a local language simply creates a different kind of linguistic imperialism, with attendant inequalities as between (say) Swahili and a score of other East African languages, between Hindi and many Indian rivals, between Tagalog and numerous major and minor languages of the Philippines, or between Oshiwambo (Phillipson's favourite) and other Namibian languages, including 'Bushman'. As the British linguist John Swales has put it, "decisions to use a particular language inevitably confer advantage on some and disadvantage on others".

As Phillipson has since shown, he simply has no answer to any of these objections, but his book gives other clues to his underlying attitude to the whole idea of giving modern forms of education to less developed societies. The deplorable growth of demand for English has come about because of "the new gods of efficiency, science and technology, modernity, etc." He likens Britain's project of collecting surplus textbooks for the benefit of Third World countries to the *dumping of poisonous chemicals*, and argues that teachers in those countries, instead of writing syllabuses for their students, should be taught to make paper from banana leaves. His objection to the extension of English is therefore based essentially on his hostility to the forms of modernisation which the language makes possible. This recalls that other phase in the history of Marxist struggle, the Cultural Revolution in Mao's China, when (as readers of Jung Chang's *Wild Swans* will remember) official slogans attacked the whole idea of modernisation: acquiring foreign technology became "sniffing after foreigners' farts and calling them sweet", and in education the slogans proclaimed "We want illiterate working people, not educated spiritual aristocrats." And in Kampuchea the regime of Pol Pot liquidated people simply because they wore spectacles: they were assumed to be educated and thus dangerous to the Marxist state.

All these flaws crucially weaken what would otherwise be the very strong case Phillipson would like to make about the world-wide spread of English, which is the extent to which the language carries cultural baggage which the rest of the world should hesitate before accepting uncritically. Many teachers of English are rightly concerned about the value-system that is implicit in the teaching of both the language and its literature, and much attention has been paid to the uses of English as a voice for writers from non-British cultures. Like many issues in Phillipson's book, it cries out for proper and balanced discussion. Is cultural imperialism inevitable? Or is it possible that, globally, the more people speak English, the less it remains culturally the exclusive property of one group?

A leading Black South African academic, Professor Njabulo Ndebele, has claimed that the very concept of an international, or world language, was "an invention of western imperialism", and has expressed the hope that English as spoken in the new South Africa will be open to the possibility of becoming a new language, making grammatical and other adjustments which reflect its proximity to indigenous African languages. But that kind of hope is not shared by linguists like Professor Jan Svartvik, a Swedish scholar who is also a world expert on English grammar, who in opposition to Braj Kachru's arguments for recognition of many 'new Englishes', has pointed out that these kinds of fragmentation frustrate the whole purpose of having an international language.

In recent years, at least one major African writer has vowed no longer to publish in English, a self-denying decision which will of course seriously limit his readership and influence. Even thirty years ago, in the Zambian Copperbelt, the anthropologist A. L.

Epstein commented on the use of English by young African men as an expression of a growing awareness of themselves as Africans in a new multiracial society, and of "their desire to enter fully the modern world". Professor Adrian Roscoe, an Englishman who has devoted his career to fostering appreciation of writers in English from the developing world, reports from South Africa the comment of a young African poet that English has *empowered* him, enabling him to seek to have influence globally. The Black South African writer Es'kia Mphahlele has suggested that the Black man (or woman) in his country "has vested interests in English as a unifying force. Through it, the continent of Africa can be restored to him and, together with French, English provides a Pan-African forum, [and] widens his constituency. English is therefore tied up with the Black man's efforts to liberate himself."* Mphahlele's efforts to facilitate that liberation include giving unofficial classes in the deprived township of Soweto, in which he tries to "restore paraphrase, précis and sentence construction" (which "today's teacher usually ducks") and to expose students to examples of good English prose.

Fantasies, reinterpretations and power

Coping with these and other problems of the place of English within the educational systems of Britain, the United States – and each and every other country which feels the need to teach English as the international language – can only proceed on the basis of a proper understanding of the nature of language, and of the relationship between the standard and non-standard varieties of any language, and thus depends heavily on the accuracy and credibility of the discipline of linguistics. The argument of this book has been that that important discipline, as it has been widely taught in British and American universities and teachers' colleges in recent

---

* The decision in the new South Africa to have eleven official languages renders it absolutely certain that in practice English will become virtually the sole official language.

decades, has offered a distorted message, tainted by a particular ideology, and that few of the 'experts' have spoken up against this. Canada's Professor J. R. Edwards, in what was apparently the only learned journal to give *The Language Trap* a proper review, felt bound to concede some parts of my case, but one particular sentence of mine was dismissed as "unwarranted and emotional". I had written, "We have seen how a great industry has grown up, dedicated to disparaging standard English, and we have seen how far that industry, manned by mutually supportive theorists, has been based on fantasies, fabrications, and unproven hypotheses." Readers must now be allowed to judge, on the evidence offered in this book, whether any of those charges of *fantasies, fabrications, and unproven hypotheses* have any substance.

Over the past fifty years, many areas of history have been subjected to the work of 'revisionist' historians – they include topics like the causes of the French Revolution and of the English Civil War, the nature and causes of Britain's Industrial Revolution, and the nature and function of childhood and the family in the West. Almost always the radical re-interpretation is offered by some professional historian, but occasionally a gifted amateur may stray in from some different discipline and in due course have their findings validated by a majority of academic historians, and so a new consensus tends to develop. Not all would-be revisions of history turn out ultimately to be credible, some die at birth. Though some of the revolutionary revisions offered concerning the social and economic conflicts of the seventeenth and eighteenth centuries have turned out to be, in major respects, quite wrong, it is extremely doubtful whether the propagation of these new theories ever did anyone any harm. But, by contrast, it is at least arguable that the Crowley thesis – now propagated by other linguistic scholars – can actually have caused harm to hundreds of thousands of children, in supporting the case which belittled the importance to them of access to standard English.

Though many of these theorists on standard English are committed ideologues of the far left, the majority of the people who have supported that case against the need for standard English in schools have just been good-hearted old-fashioned socialists, or indeed people of no particular political commitment at all, who have simply taken on trust the claims of the experts. The result, though, has been the same: a reduction of the opportunities for the least privileged children to gain the advantages enjoyed by those same ideologues who, having drunk their fill, now turn off the tap for others.

There is now also an abundance of convincing evidence – from Britain, the United States, and a wide range of other countries and cultures – that women consistently outdo men in tending to use standard forms of language, especially grammar and accent. Prominent among several factors that may be at work here is the awareness – conscious or unconscious – that, in societies characterised for many millennia by male dominance, this constitutes a subtle method of grasping a small share of that power.

So the proposition that *language is power* which has been asserted by this book is indeed not a new one. Many disadvantaged men and women have in the past become convinced of it and struggled to acquire the kinds of language which most effectively embody that power, though it was not until recent years that their obstacles were added to by the corollary of the linguistic equality myth – the Big Lie that this kind of language was *not for them*. Nearly a century and a half ago, a humble Englishman (Marcus Davis) wrote a little eighteen-penny grammar book whose title expressed "the need for the ordinary citizen to understand *Everybody's Business*" – the "essential practicalities of their rights". The principles of grammar – which, unlike Professor Gee, the author considered were attainable even by those with "almost the meanest capacity" – allowed their possessor to feel "on a footing of equality with those on whom chance or fortune has bestowed the choicest favours" in material terms – or "even Governors or Princes".

The ability to speak fluently and scientifically, he declared, is the very aristocracy of mental possessions. The art of speaking and writing correctly is founded upon *rules*, which decree *you were* and *you are* rather than *you was* or *you is*. These are not immutable laws of grammar, he said: "they may be altered at any time if the majority of literary persons so decide", so ordinary people are to be encouraged to read "works of repute" as well as grammar books. Without this kind of knowledge, we are totally unaware of the powerful weapons of attack and defence, and of the resources for advancement in life, that are inherent in the attainment of a knowledge of grammar. And why are working men and women denied their rightful place in society? Why do some have to live on starvation wages and resort to crime, and suffer contempt at the hands of officialdom?

> Because they have not that command of language which imparts confidence, not only to assert our rights, but to defend them. They have not the capabilities to make their wrongs known . . . the power to make [themselves] heard.

All over the world, and in the very heart of our own society, the disadvantaged and the oppressed are struggling to make themselves heard. This book has tried to identify some of the forces which stand in their way, and some of the means available to them to regain their rightful voice.

Bibliography

(Place of publication is UK unless otherwise stated)

Sylvia Adamson, 'With double tongue', in Mike Short (ed.), *Reading, Analysing and Teaching English*, 1988

Sylvia Adamson, 'Varieties, stereotypes, satire', in Ikegami and Toyota (1993)

Jean Aitchison, *Teach Yourself Linguistics*, 1979

Jean Aitchison, *The Language Web* (BBC Reith Lectures 1996), 1997

Paul Atkinson, *Language, Structure and Reproduction*, 1985

Richard W. Bailey, *Images of English*, USA 1991 (UK 1992)

Stephen Barbour and Patrick Stevenson, *Variation in German*, 1990

John Barrell, *English Literature in History 1730–80: An Equal, Wide Survey*, 1983

Dennis E. Barron, *Grammar and Good Taste*, USA 1982

John D. Barrow, *Pi in the Sky: Counting, Thinking and Being*, 1992

David Barton, *Literacy*, 1994

Janet Batsleer, T. Davies, R. O'Rourke, and C. Weedon, *Rewriting English: Cultural Politics of Gender and Class*, 1985

A. C. Baugh and T. Cable, *A History of the English Language*, 4th edn, 1993 (1st edn, 1951)

C. Bereiter and S. Engelmann, *Teaching Disadvantaged Children in the Preschool*, USA 1966

Paul Berman (ed.), *Debating PC: The Controversy over Political Correctness on College Campuses*, USA 1992

N. F. Blake, *A History of the English Language*, 1996

Leonard Bloomfield, *Language*, USA 1933

George Blue and Rosamond Mitchell (eds.), *Language and Education* (BAAL conference papers 11), 1995

R. Bocock, *Hegemony*, 1986

Dwight Bolinger, *Language: The Loaded Weapon*, 1980

Christopher Brumfit, *Language in the National Curriculum*, 1995

Bullock Report: *A Language for Life*, 1975

Kenneth Burke, *Language as Symbolic Action*, USA 1966

J. D. Burnley, 'Sources of standardisation in later Middle English', in J. B. Trahern (ed.), *Standardising English: Essays in Honour of John Hurt Fisher*, 1989

Deborah Cameron, 'Demythologising sociolinguistics', in J. E. Joseph and Talbot Taylor (eds.), *Ideologies of Language*, 1990

Deborah Cameron, E. Frazer, B. Rampton et al., *Researching Language: Issues of Power and Method*, 1992

Deborah Cameron, *Verbal Hygiene*, 1995

Ronald Carter (ed.), *Linguistics and the Teacher*, 1982

J. K. Chambers and P. Trudgill, *Dialectology*, 1980

Jenny Cheshire, *Variation in an English Dialect: A Sociolinguistic Study*, 1982

Jenny Cheshire, 'The relationship between language and sex in English', in Trudgill (ed.), 1984, pp. 33–49

Jenny Cheshire, Viv Edwards et al. (eds.), *Dialect and Education*, 1989

William Cobbett, *Grammar of the English Tongue*, 1818

William Cobbett, *Autobiography* (ed. W. Reitzel), 1933

David E. Cooper, 'Labov, Larry and Charles', *Oxford Review of Education*, vol. 10 no. 2, 1984, pp. 177–92

David Corson, *The Lexical Bar*, 1985

Florian Coulmas (ed.), *The Handbook of Sociolinguistics*, 1997

Cox Report: *English for Ages 5–16*, 1989

Brian Cox, *Cox on the Battle for the English Curriculum*, 1995

Tony Crowley, *The Politics of Discourse*, 1989 (USA: *The Politics of Standard English*)

David Crystal, *What is Linguistics?* 1968 (and later edns)

David Crystal, *A First Dictionary of Linguistics and Phonetics*, 1980

David Crystal, review of *The Language Trap* in *British Association for Applied Linguistics Newsletter*, no. 18, 1983

David Crystal, *The Cambridge Encyclopaedia of Language*, 1987

Marcus Davis, *Everybody's Business*, 1865

N. Dittmar, *Sociolinguistics*, 1975

Mary Douglas, *Purity and Danger*, 1966

Mary Douglas, *Natural Symbols*, 1970

John R. Edwards, *Language and Disadvantage*, 1979

John R. Edwards, review article on *The Language Trap* in *Journal of Language and Social Psychology*, vol. 2, 1983, pp. 67–76

V. K. Edwards, *The West Indian Language Issue in British Schools*, 1979

W. B. Elley, I. H. Barham, and M. Wyllie, *The Role of Grammar in a Secondary School Curriculum* (NZ Council for Educational Research), NZ 1975

John H. Fisher, *The Emergence of Standard English*, USA 1996

V. Fromkin and R. Rodman, *An Introduction to Language*, USA 1974, 1978, 1983 etc.

James Gee, *Social Linguistics and Literacies*, 1990 (also 2nd edn, 1996)

Clifford Geertz, *The Interpretation of Cultures*, USA 1973

Ernest Gellner, *Nations and Nationalism*, 1983

Andrew Gonzalez and M. L. S. Batista, *Language Surveys in the Philippines 1966–84*, Manila 1986

J. Goody (ed.), *Literacy in Traditional Societies*, 1968

David Graddol and Joan Swann, 'Trapping linguists', in *Language and Education*, vol. 2 no. 2, 1988

Sidney Greenbaum, *Good English and the Grammarian*, 1988

W. Haas (ed.), *Standard Languages, Spoken and Written*, 1982

M. A. K. Halliday, A. McIntosh and P. Strevens, *The Linguistic Sciences and Language Teaching*, 1964

Roy Harris, *The Language Machine*, 1987

Roy Harris, 'Murray, Moore & the myth', in R. Harris (ed.), *Linguistic Thought in England 1914–45*, 1988

Einar Haugen, 'Dialect, language, nation', *American Anthropologist*, vol. 68, 1966, pp. 922–35

Einar Haugen, 'The curse of Babel', in M. Bloomfield and E. Haugen (eds.), *Language as a Human Problem*, USA 1974

Richard J. Herrnstein and Charles Murray, *The Bell Curve: Intelligence and Class Structure in American Life*, USA 1994

Richard Hoggart, *The Way We Live Now*, 1996

John Honey, *The Language Trap* (National Council for Educational Standards), 1983

John Honey, 'The way linguists argue: a reply to Crystal and Hudson', *British Association for Applied Linguistics Newsletter*, no 19, Autumn 1983

John Honey [1988a], 'First language didactics', art. no. 183 in U. Ammon, N. Dittmar and K. Mattheier (eds.), *Sociolinguistics: An International Handbook*, vol. 2, Berlin and USA 1988

John Honey [1988b], 'Talking proper: schooling and the establishment of English "RP"' in Graham Nixon and John Honey (eds.), *An Historic Tongue: Studies in English Linguistics in Honour of Barbara Strang*, 1988

John Honey, *Does Accent Matter? The Pygmalion Factor*, 1989 (2nd edn, 1991)

John Honey, review of Phillipson, *Linguistic Imperialism* (1992), in *RASK: International Journal of Speech and Communication* (Odense University, Denmark), vol. 1, October 1994

John Honey, 'English as megalanguage: the myth of linguistic equality', *Anglistik* (Heidelberg), vol. 7 no. 1, March 1996

Richard Hudson, *Sociolinguistics*, 1980

Richard Hudson, review of *The Language Trap* in *British Association for Applied Linguistics Newsletter*, no. 18, 1983

Richard Hudson and Jasper Holmes, *Children's Use of Spoken Standard English* (Report for School Curriculum and Assessment Authority), 1995

Dell Hymes (ed.), *Language in Culture and Society: A Reader*, USA and London 1964

Dell Hymes, review of J. Lyons, *Chomsky*, in *Language*, 1974

Yoshihiko Ikegami and Masanori Toyota (eds.), *Aspects of English as a World Language*, Tokyo 1993

John E. Joseph, *Eloquence and Power*, 1987

John E. Joseph, 'Modern linguistics in post-modern perspective', *Language & Communication*, XII/2, 1992

P. Joyce, *Visions of the People: Industrial England and the Question of Class, 1848–1914*, 1991

Kingman Report: *Teaching of English Language*, 1988

William Labov, *Language in the Inner City*, 1972

William Labov, *Sociolinguistic Patterns*, 1972

Bernard Lamb, *A National Survey of UK Undergraduates' Standards of English* (Queen's English Society), 1992

Bernard Lamb, *A National Survey of Communication Skills of Young Entrants to Industry and Commerce* (Queen's English Society), 1994

Bernard Lamb, *A National Survey of the Opinions and Practices of Teachers of English to 11-to-18-year-olds* (Queen's English Society), 1996

Dick Leith, *A Social History of English*, 1983

R. A. Lodge, *French: From Dialect to Standard*, 1993

Peter Lowenberg (ed.), *Language Spread and Language Policy: Issues, Implications and Case Studies*, USA 1988

John Lyons, *Chomsky*, 1970 (reprinted 1977)

T. W. Machan and C. T. Scott, *English in its Social Contexts*, USA 1992

M. McLuhan, *The Gutenberg Galaxy*, 1962

M. McLuhan, *Understanding Media: The Extensions of Man*, USA 1964

Bernice Martin, *A Sociology of Contemporary Cultural Change*, 1981

Douglas S. Massey, 'Review essay: The Bell Curve', *American Journal of Sociology*, vol. 101 no. 3, November 1995, pp. 747–53

Ian Michael, *The Teaching of English (16th Century to 1870)*, 1987

Leonard Michaels and Christopher Ricks (eds.), *The State of the Language*, 1980

James and Lesley Milroy, *Authority in Language*, 1985 (2nd edn, 1991)

James and Lesley Milroy (eds.), *Real English*, 1993

Joyce Morris (ed.), *Professional Writers Support the Cause of Literacy*, 1995

Es'kia Mphahlele, 'Prometheus in chains: the fate of English in South Africa', *The English Academy Review* (South Africa), vol. 2, 1984

Lynda Mugglestone, *Talking Proper: The Rise of Accent as Social Symbol*, 1995

Peter Mühlhäusler, 'Language and communication efficiency: the case of Tok Pisin', *Language and Communication*, vol. 2 no. 2, 1982

Njabulo S. Ndebele, 'The English language and social change in South Africa', *The English Academy Review* (South Africa), vol. 4, 1987, p. 3

Gerhard Nickel and J. C. Stalker, *Problems of Standardization and Linguistic Variation in Present-day English*, Heidelberg 1986

W. R. O'Donnell and L. Todd, *Variety in Contemporary English*, 1980

David Olson and Nancy R. Torrance (eds.), *Literacy and Orality*, 1991

David R. Olson, *The World on Paper*, 1994

W. J. Ong, *Orality and Literacy*, 1982

H. Orton and W. J. Halliday, *Survey of English Dialects*, 1962

L. B. Osborn, *Life of John Hoskyns*, USA 1937

Adrian Pennycook, *The Cultural Politics of English as an International Language*, 1994

K. M. Petyt, *The Study of Dialect*, 1980

Steven Pinker, *The Language Instinct*, 1994

Randolph Quirk, S. Greenbaum, G. Leech and J. Svartvik, *A Grammar of Contemporary English*, 1972

Suzanne Romaine, *The Language of Children and Adolescents*, 1984

Suzanne Romaine, *Language in Society: An Introduction to Sociolinguistics*, 1994

A. L. Rowse, *Friends and Contemporaries*, 1989

R. St Clair, 'From social history to language attitudes', in E. B. Ryan and Howard Giles (eds.), *Attitudes Towards Language Variation*, 1982

Geoffrey Sampson, *Schools of Linguistics*, 1980

M. L. Samuels, 'Some applications of Middle English dialectology', *English Studies*, vol. 44, 1963, pp. 81–94

J. F. Savage, *Linguistics for Teachers*, USA 1973

A. Scaglione (ed.), *The Emergence of Standard Languages*, Italy 1984

Judy Schwartz, *Teaching the Linguistically Diverse*, USA 1979

Mark Sebba, *London Jamaican*, 1993

Timothy Shopen and Joseph M. Williams, *Standards and Dialects in English*, USA 1980

Robert F. Spencer, Jesse D. Jennings et al., *The Native Americans*, USA 1977

Barbara M. H. Strang, *A History of English*, 1970

Brian V. Street, *Literacy in Theory and Practice*, 1984

Michael Stubbs, *Language, Schools and Classrooms*, 1976

David Sutcliffe, *British Black English*, 1982

John Swain, Vic Finkelstein et al., *Disabling Barriers, Enabling Environments*, 1993

V. Tauli, *The Structural Tendencies of Languages*, Helsinki 1958

E. Barrington Thomas (ed.), *Papua New Guinea Education*, Melbourne 1976

E. P. Thompson, *The Making of the English Working Class*, 1963 (revised reprint, 1991)

Geoffrey Thornton, *Language, Ignorance and Education*, 1986

M. L. Tickoo (ed.), *Languages and Standards: Issues, Attitudes, Case Studies*, RELC Anthology Series 26, Singapore 1991

J. W. Tollefson, *Planning Language, Planning Inequality*, 1991

David Tomlinson, 'Errors in the research into the effectiveness of grammar teaching', *English in Education*, vol. 28 no. 1, 1993, pp 2–26

David Tomlinson, 'A pioneer investigation into grammar teaching: the Hoyt study and its influence', *Language Issues* (Kumamoto, Japan), vol. 1 no. 1, 1995, pp. 113–15

David Tomlinson, 'Not the last word: the 1974 Elley investigation into the effect of grammar teaching' (forthcoming, 1997)

N. Tredell, *Conversations with Critics*, 1992

Peter Trudgill, *The Social Differentiation of English in Norwich*, 1974

Peter Trudgill, *Sociolinguistics*, 1974

Peter Trudgill, *Accent, Dialect and the School*, 1975

Peter Trudgill, *On Dialect: Social and Geographical Perspectives*, 1983

Peter Trudgill (ed.), *Applied Sociolinguistics*, 1984

John Vaizey, *The Costs of Education*, 1958

Brian Vickers, *Appropriating Shakespeare: Contemporary Critical Quarrels*, USA 1993

David Vincent, *Literacy and Popular Culture: England 1750–1914*, 1989

M. Wakelin, *The Archaeology of English*, 1988

Jeff Wilkinson, *Introducing Standard English*, 1995

Raymond Williams, *The Long Revolution*, 1961

Raymond Williams, *Keywords*, 1983

John Willinsky, *The Well-tempered Tongue: The politics of Standard English in the High School*, USA 1988

Ruth Wodak and Gertraud Benke, 'Gender as a sociolinguistic variable', in Coulmas (ed.) (1997), pp. 127–50

References

Sources are identified by author and date as listed in the Bibliography (page 261). *THES = Times Higher Education Supplement*; *TLS = Times Literary Supplement*. Citations from radio and TV programmes broadcast from the UK, USA, France, etc. are in some cases given with the date of their reception in Japan.

1: Introduction

Page

2 **yous/yees**: pronouns and other forms in non-standard varieties of British English are from J. and L. Milroy, eds., (1993). Tyneside examples are from Joan Beal's article in that volume.
   quite different book: John Honey, *Does Accent Matter?* (1989, 2nd edn 1991).

4 **emotional issue**: Jenny Cheshire and Jim Miller, in J. and L. Milroy, eds., (1993), p. 16.
   quotation marks: Randolph Quirk, *The Times*, 30 December 1994.
   standard English ideology: e.g. R. Lippi Green, in *Language in Society*, 23/2, June 1994, pp. 163–90.

5 **south east of England**: Alan Sinfield, 'Merchants of Menace', *THES*, 15 July 1994.

2: The Language Myth

6 **distinguished British linguists**: Halliday, McIntosh and Strevens (1964), p. 100.

7 **development of its users**: David Crystal (1968 and later edns.), p. 15.
   Lyons: (1970), p. 21.
   Wolfram: in J. F. Savage, ed. (1973), p. 69.
   Trudgill: (1974), p. 20.
   Edwards: V. K. Edwards (1979), p. 105.
   Fromkin and Rodman: (1974 and later edns.), p. 16.
   Sutcliffe: (1982), p. 76.
   Haugen: in Bloomfield and Haugen, eds. (1974).
   Fromkin and Rodman: 1974 etc., as above.

8 **Laycock**: in E. Barrington Thomas, ed. (1976), p. 180.
   Ken Livingstone: *Any Questions?*, BBC Radio 4, 8 January 1982.

8 **twenty statements**: *Anglistik* (Heidelberg), vol 7, no. 1, March 1996.

10 **aesthetic expression**: Hymes in Dell Hymes, ed. (1964), p. 75.
   excuses for discriminating: Hymes, loc. cit.

11 **Navajo language examples**: see Robert F. Spencer et al. (1977), pp.
   48–9; E. Sapir and M. Swadesh, 'American Indian grammatical categories', in Hymes (1964), p. 103.

12 **Nootka invitation to a feast**: Spencer et al. (1977) loc. cit. and pp. 155–62.
   very far away; 40 conditionals: V. Tauli (1958), pp. 29, 129.

13 **language of only 200 words**: Pinker (1964), p. 261.
   lengthy circumlocution: Crystal (1987), p. 356.

14 **resort to gesture for numbering**: Barrow (1992), p. 34.
   great proficiency in it: Barrow (1992), p. 34n.

15 **always tend to be a time-lag**: Mühlhäusler (1982).

16 **'incongruent elements'**: see (e.g.) Edward P. Dozier, 'Two examples of
   linguistic acculturation', in Hymes (1964), p. 511.

17 **bludgeon ... rapier**: quoted by A. A. Hill in 'A Note on Primitive
   Languages', in Hymes (1964), p. 89.
   richness of structure: John E. Joseph (1987), p. 88.
   culturocentric: Joseph (1987), p. 21.
   host of questions ... ideological confidence: Hymes (1974), review of
   Lyons.

18 **critique of linguistic equality dogma ... blistering attacks**: John
   Honey, *The Language Trap* (1983); see below, Chapter 9.
   two powerful critics; 'system' vs. 'use': J. and L. Milroy (1985/91),
   p. 10.
   'the organic fallacy': Cameron (1990), pp. 89–90. See also Honey,
   Anglistik (1996), especially pp. 106–7.
   Robert Phillipson's book: *Linguistic Imperialism* (1992).

19 **invidious comparison**: Trudgill (1983), p. 208.

3: *The Dialect Trap*

22 **Bereiter and Engelmann**: see C. Bereiter and S. Engelmann (1966).
   Bernstein's linguistic codes: on his theory and how it has changed, see
   P. Atkinson (1985); Basil Bernstein, *Class, Codes and Control*, 3 vols. in
   original and revised editions, 1971–77. There is a useful summary of the
   main differences claimed by Bernstein between elaborated and restricted
   codes in N. Dittmar (1975), Chapter 1.

23 **William Labov's famous paper**: 'The Logic of Non-standard English',
   (Georgetown Monographs, no. 22, 1969), was included as Chapter 5 in
   Labov's *Language in the Inner City* (1972), and widely reprinted and
   anthologised from 1972 onwards, e.g. in P. P. Giglioli (ed.), *Language
   and Social Context* (1972).

25 **"accepted without much criticism"**: J. R. Edwards (1979), p. 58.

26 **another popular textbook**: M. Stubbs (1976), p. 119.

29 **Cooper's devastating critique**: David E. Cooper (1984).

31 **Martha's Vineyard**: see 'The Social Motivation of a Sound Change', in Labov's *Sociolinguistic Patterns* (1972).

'close paralect' of RP: see Honey (1989), pp. 80–82.

status, political and economic power: see especially Robert N. St Clair, 'From social history to language attitudes', in E. B. Ryan and Howard Giles, eds. (1982), p. 165.

32 **finely tuned account of solidarity**: Lesley Milroy, *Language and Social Networks* (1987).

33 **many scholars have shown, modernisation, urbanisation, mass education**: see K. J. Mattheier, *Pragmatik und Soziologie der Dialekte* (Heidelberg, 1980), pp. 146–7; and Barbour and Stevenson (1990), pp. 100–3.

'mainstream' norms and values: for a view of methods of 'inducing common expectations among citizenry' see R. St Clair (1982), p. 165.

literacy, importance and limitations: David Barton (1994), p. 48.

work of Goody, McLuhan and Ong: e.g. J. Goody (1968); M. McLuhan (1962, 1964); W. J. Ong (1982).

transform human consciousness: W. J. Ong (1982), pp. 78, 82; see also Honey, 'First Language Didactics' (1988).

34 **Black American gang members**: Labov, *Language in the Inner City* (1972), Chapter 7.

teenagers in Reading: Jenny Cheshire (1982).

young Blacks in London etc.: D. Sutcliffe (1982); M. Sebba (1993).

Greeks and Turks in London: R. Hewitt (1982), quoted in J. and L. Milroy (1985/91), p. 114.

women adapt to standard: see, e.g., J. Cheshire, 'Language and sex in English', in P. Trudgill, ed. (1984).

covert prestige: Peter Trudgill, 'Sex, covert prestige and linguistic change . . .' in *Language in Society*, vol. 1 (1972), pp. 179–95; also Chambers and Trudgill (1980), pp. 98–100.

mainstream forms as in some sense 'right': see also R. A. Hudson (1980), p. 201.

physical violence disciplines deviations: J. and L. Milroy (1985), p. 58.

35 **lost speech through brain damage**: see Robert J. Scholes and Brenda J. Willis, 'Linguists, literacy and intensionality . . .', and other papers in Olson and Torrance, eds. (1991).

Latin or Greek roots: Corson (1985), especially Chapter 2.

not just highbrow synonyms: Corson (1985), p. 48.

seven semantic fields: Corson (1985), p. 59.

35 **poorer working-class children don't use Graeco-Latin words widely**: Corson (1985), p. 74.

36 **differences in active vocabularies by 15**: Corson (1985), p. 114.
essay published elsewhere: John Honey, 'The concept of "Standard English" in first and second language contexts', in M. L. Tickoo, ed. (1991).

38 **scholars at Leeds University**: O'Donnell and Todd (1980), pp. 29–32. The classic description of Yorkshire dialects is in Orton and Halliday, vol. I (1962).
stable and coherent entity?: Sylvia Adamson, 'Varieties, stereotypes, satire and Shakespeare', in Ikegami and Toyota, eds. (1993).

39 **differences between non-standard pronunciation and standard orthography**: this refers to differences which are greater than those presented to all learners from the mismatch between English spelling and standard pronunciation. See M. Stubbs, *Language and Literacy* (1980), especially Chapter II.
clearly established correspondence: see review by Professor Peter Bryant of Oxford University in *THES*, 10 September 1982.
dialect discussion of Keats: Trudgill (1975), p. 80.

40 **kyaan gud iina skuul**: D. Sutcliffe, MEd thesis, University of Leicester, 1978, quoted in V. K. Edwards (1979), p. 47.

41 **Barbara Jordan**: comments quoted are from an article by Sue Anne Presley, *Washington Post*, reprinted in *Japan Times*, 23 January 1996.

43 **children who are exposed to them**: Judy Schwartz (1979), p. 56.
liberals insulate *their own* children from dialect: Deborah Cameron, 'Respect, please . . .', in Cameron, Frazer, Rampton et al. (1992), p. 129.
Maya Angelou: quoted by Vermont teacher Daniel Heller, 'The problem of standard English', in *English Journal* (NCTE secondary section), vol. 83, no. 5, September 1994.
Language is power: Daniel Heller, loc. cit.

4: *Some Enemies of Standard English*

44 **set of mental tramlines**: this and other references to Chomsky's theories are taken from two very useful accounts – from very different standpoints – of Chomsky's work: G. Sampson (1980), p. 235 etc., and John Lyons (1970/77), pp. 128, 135.

49 **although language is an instinct**: Pinker (1994), p. 189.
distinction between everyday English and written dialect: Pinker (1994), p. 289.
constructions not mastered by age four: Pinker (1994), p. 273.

50 **chapter on demolition of prescriptivism**: Pinker (1994), Chapter 12.
even primitive societies have standards of usage: Dell Hymes, in Hymes (1964), p. 74; W. Haas, in Haas (1982), p. 15.

50 **speakers differ in communicating effectively**: Pinker (1994), p. 365.
    dialects have degrees of complexity: Pinker (1994), p. 366.

51 **dignity of vernacular language**: Pinker (1994), p. 19.
    far more complex trains of thought: Pinker (1994), p. 401.
    native speakers of 'good English': Bloomfield (1933), p. 48.
    standard languages with no native speakers: C. J. N. Bailey, in Nickel and Stalker (1986), p. 82.

52 **standard (written) English is nobody's mother-tongue**: Suzanne Romaine (1984), p. 233.
    closer detail in a later chapter: see below, Chapter 8.

53 **small and self-serving élite**: Cameron (1995), p. 42.
    naive social belief: James Gee (1990), p. 17.
    oppressive class relations in Britain: Cameron (1995), p. 42.
    reinforcing social privilege: loc. cit.

54 **male, white, heterosexual**: ibid., p. 27.
    control of economic resources and political power: Tollefson (1991), p. 61.
    unwarranted assumption: Tollefson, loc. cit.
    arbitrary result of domination: ibid., p. 62.
    unfair advantage to children with standard English: ibid.
    narrow, non-common language: Leon Botstein, 'Imitative literacy', in *Partisan Review*, vol. 48, no. 3 (1981), p. 403.

55 **deny minorities access to mainstream culture**: R. St Clair (1982), p. 165, and note 2.
    skimming off . . . depleting lower classes of most favoured members: C. A. Brakel, 'Language structure and social structure', in *Michigan Academician*, vol. 9, no. 2 (1978), p. 163.
    ownership of capital: Leith (1983), p. 56.
    exclusive **. . . a class dialect imposed on populace**: ibid., p. 33.
    correlations with specific social classes: P. Trudgill, *The Social Differentiation of English in Norwich* (1974); Chambers and Trudgill (1980), Chapter 5. K. M. Petyt (1980), p. 164, shows that education was a key variable for his category of social class in his Bradford study quoted in J. and L. Milroy (1985/91).
    prestige transfer: Joseph (1987), pp. 30–32, 40.
    intrinsic qualities undetectable: ibid., pp. 30–32.

56 **mantle of power**: ibid., p. 43.
    overall social status quo: ibid., p. 45.
    prestigious occupations, few in number: Leith (1983), p. 2.
    famous paper in 1969: James Sledd, 'Bidialectalism: the linguistics of White Supremacy', in *English Journal* (USA), vol. 58, no. 9, December 1969.
    black trash into white trash: ibid., p. 1308.

56 **white power will frustrate upward mobility**: ibid., p. 1309.
    another mode of exploitation: ibid., p. 1314.
57 **at mercy of slavers**: Dwight Bolinger (1980), p. 46.
    Black progress in three decades, but class inequality grows: *The Economist*, 8 July 1995, p. 35; 23 December 1995 (Lexington column).
    Marxist theorists and manufacture of class: see Bocock (1986), p. 103.

5: Rewriting History

59 **convict a majority of native speakers**: Williams (1983), pp. 296–7.
60 **first hear of standard English . . . a model language . . . social distinction**: Williams (1961), p. 220.
    new cult of uniformity . . . embalmed: ibid., p. 224.
    ashamed of speech of fathers: loc. cit.
61 **national unity a silly ideal**: ibid., p. 318.
    rather extreme view: C. J. N. Bailey, 'Remarks on Standardization', in Nickel and Stalker (1986), pp. 79–83.
62 **determine what standard usage is**: Harris (1988), p. 14.
    myth of standard English: ibid., p. 1.
    no one quite sure: ibid., p. 17.
    central tenet of official view: ibid., p. 3.
63 **'English par excellence'**: ibid., p. 21.
    neologistically called 'standard English': loc. cit.
64 **direction to proceed**: Crowley (1989), p. 1.
    remain in silence: ibid., p. 2.
    discourse is controlled: loc. cit.
65 **distribution of knowledge and power**: ibid., p. 3.
    Voloshinov and Bakhtin: Crowley's references to these authors are in his pages 3–11, and derive from Voloshinov's *Marxism and the Philosophy of Language* (1930), and Bakhtin's *The Dialogic Imagination*, a translation of Bakhtin's main writings of the 1930s (US, 1981).
67 **not writing a slavish account**: Crowley (1988), p. 10.
    gain specific ends: ibid., p. 89.
71 **'history of the language'**: ibid., p. 28.
    'historical becoming of language': ibid., p. 8.
    rise to rapid hegemony: ibid., p. 29.
    power was still exclusively exercised: ibid., p. 44.
    earliest citation for 'standard language': ibid., pp. 117–18.
72 **B. Smart's 'common standard dialect'**: ibid., p. 132; see also I. Michael (1987), pp. 572–3, and I. Michael, *Early Textbooks of English, a Guide* (Colloquium on Textbooks, Schools and Society, 1993), p. 43.
    writer of educational texts: *The Elementary Catechisms* (1850), quoted in L. Mugglestone (1995), p. 292.

72 'standard' applied as early as 1711: R. W. Bailey (1991), p. 3.
   origins of standard English revealed by scholars: see especially the works of M. L. Samuels (1963), J. D. Burnley (1989), and J. H. Fisher (1996), as cited in Bibiography.

73 this new London standard: Baugh and Cable (1993), p. 190.
   deliberately fostered and taught: quoted from E. J. Dobson, 'Early Modern Standard English', in *Transactions of the Philological Society* (1955), pp. 25–54, reprinted in R. Lass, *Approaches to English Historical Linguistics* (1969), p. 420. See also Honey (1989), p. 15.

74 Harold Macmillan and the hyperlect: Honey (1989), pp. 43–4.
   precept as well as practice: Baugh and Cable (1993), p. 195.

75 Latin words entering English: S. Adamson (1988), p. 208.

76 the King's English: Thomas Wilson, *The Arte of Rhetorique* (1553).
   abusing the Queen's English: Thomas Nashe, *Strange Newes* (1592).

77 John Hart: see Michael (1987), p. 473.
   Mulcaster, Daines, Price: ibid., pp. 372, 522, 433, 549.
   ABC, Bales, Coote, Hodges: ibid., pp. 387–8, 396–7, 131, 429, 479.
   John Newton . . . William Ward: ibid., pp. 143, 533, 579, 472–3, 414–15, 602, 552, 469, 566, 445, 396, 592–3.

78 John Brinsley: ibid., pp. 112, 407.
   Alexander Gill: see his *Logonomia Anglica* (1619), translated by R. C. Alston, *Stockholm Studies in English* XXVI, 2 vols. (Sweden, 1972).
   (footnote) 'cant' in Elizabethan underworld literature: see A. V. Judges (ed.), *The Elizabethan Underworld* (1930, 1965).

79 great mingle-mangle: John Green, *A refutation of the Apology for Actors* (1615, US 1941).
   John White's 1701 textbook: Michael (1987), p. 595.
   read the whole English tongue: for 1705 text, see Michael (1987), p. 394.
   Wilson/Hutchinson, Carter . . . Rhodes: ibid., pp. 512, 416, 592, 522, 555.
   Shelley, Loughton, Turner: ibid., pp. 569, 536, 586.
   Ann Fisher of Tyneside: ibid., p. 457.
   shake off false dialect: for John Carter, see ibid., p. 415.

80 New & Improved, Fenning, Pape: ibid., pp. 527, 455, 537.
   pronunciation in Oxford and London: Elisha Coles, *The Compleat English Schoolmaster* (1674, reprinted 1967).
   Buchanan, Sheridan . . . Batchelor: Michael (1987), pp. 410, 570, 408, 392, 399.
   authority, royalty, universality in dictionaries: for Tobias Ellis, ibid., p. 445; Greenwood, ibid., p. 468; Farro, ibid., p. 452; Fenning, ibid., p. 455; Thomas Chapman ibid., p. 417; James Barclay, ibid., p. 397; William Perry, ibid., p. 540.

81   **emulation of literary works as a matter of course**: ibid., pp. 159–60.
Spectator 'a Standard of good style': Foot, in ibid., pp. 202, 459.
pestered by host of grammars: William Hill of Huddersfield, ibid., pp. 348, 477–78.
'**most approved standard' writers**: on William Johnstone, ibid., pp. 261, 492; on Anon (*Poems*, 1818), ibid., p. 545; J. F. Winks, ibid., p. 599.
Webster on well-bred usage in USA, Oxford, etc.: Barron (1982), pp. 54–5.

82   **intercourse among the learned**: ibid., p. 44.
diffuse an authority: ibid., p. 42.
a million copies: Barron (1982), p. 142. I. Michael, p. 523, citing R. D. Altick, says a million copies were sold by about 1826.
Lindley Murray's criteria of correctness: on Murray's *English Grammar* (1795), see I. Michael (1987), p. 523; Barron (1982), p. 145.

83   **Croft: fixing the *standard***: Barron (1982), p. 36.
standard governs absolutely in England: ibid., p. 37.

84   **chancery clerks as 'the typing pool'**: Fisher (1996), p. 56.
(footnote) **Cable's ten individuals**: T. Cable in 'The rise of written standard English', in Scaglione (1984), pp. 75–94.

85   **Mavor's Spelling Book, 322nd edition**: Vincent (1989), p. 68; Michael (1987), pp. 261, 515.
wonderful stories in choice English: J. Lawson, *A Man's Life* (1932), p. 11, quoted in Vincent (1989), pp. 60–61.
Baldwin's 1928 reference: Crowley (1989), pp. 254–5.

86   **Gloucestershire boy's church experience**: Laurie Lee, *Cider with Rosie* (1959).

87   **extent of popular literacy in nineteenth century**: figures are largely based on Vincent (1989), especially Chapter 2.
postage rose 55 times: ibid., p. 33.

88   **Ruth Puddleputty**: see Vincent, p. 193.
Samuel Laycock and dialect literature: my account draws substantially on the valuable book by P. Joyce, *Visions of the People* (1991). See also Samuel Laycock, *Selected Writings*, ed. G. Milner (1908).

89   *Reynolds' News*: Vincent (1989), pp. 241–2, 251–6.

90   **scurrility most vile**: ibid., p. 253.
Northern Star, 'illiteracy' and popular audience: Joyce (1991), p. 38.
battleground of class: E. P. Thompson (1963/1991), p. 914.

91   **Cobbett's birth of intellect**: Cobbett/Reitzel (1933), pp. 1–19.
want of knowledge of most essential grammar: ibid. p. 26.
apprentices and ploughboys: title page of Cobbett's *A Grammar of the English Tongue* (1818).
dedication to Queen Caroline: ibid., p. 5.

91 **letters of thanks**: Cobbett, *Advice to Young Men and Women* (1830, new edn 1862), Introduction, p. ix.
Cobbett's influence on Clynes: Vincent (1989), p. 295, note 66.

92 **'gateway' to 'rights and liberties'**: Cobbett, *Grammar*, pp. 6–8.
discourse produced a new object: Crowley (1989), p. 108.
totalise English by synthesising it: loc. cit.
English language 'pure and simple': ibid., p. 107.
prevailing linguistic thought: ibid., p. 106.
real life of language: Max Müller, quoted by Crowley, p. 106.

93 **Leeds journalist**: ibid., p. 75.
1890s textbook: (A. West), ibid., p. 147.

94 **non-existent canon**: ibid., p. 122.

95 **anthologies began to appear**: Michael (1989), pp. 159–60.
taste for composition: ibid., p. 412.
most celebrated authors: for *Beauties in Prose and Verse* (1783), see ibid., p. 400.
29 latest poets: Adams's *Parnassus*, ibid., p. 389.
distinguished, eminent, admired, approved writers: ibid., p. 545.
favourite authors in two periods: ibid., pp. 198–236.
1747 textbook: William Foot's *Essay on Education*, ibid., pp. 202, 459.

96 **elaboration of French from thirteenth century**: Lodge (1993), p. 139.
definitions of best French after 1600: ibid., pp. 176–180.
the cultural project: Crowley (1989), p. 129.

97 **'aristocratic' forms of RP**: ibid., p. 203.
lowest vulgarity to the mere provinciality: (A. J. Ellis in 1869), ibid., p. 140; see also p. 131.

98 **primary, central, culturally hegemonic form**: ibid., p. 133.
well-informed: (B. Smart, 1836), ibid., p. 132.
civilised persons: (Sedgwick, 1868), ibid., p. 148.
class delimitation, binary definition: loc. cit.
definition socially specific: ibid., p. 132.
educated came from ruling class: ibid., p. 149.

99 **accent differences of little consequence … grammar, properly understood**: Cobbett, *Grammar*, pp. 14, 15. Interestingly, Dr L. Mugglestone (1995, p. 89), has drawn attention to the fact that Cobbett's son John added a chapter to his 1866 edition of his father's *Grammar* in which he suggested that in some ways pronunciation was perhaps more important than William had implied.
Dean Alford and 'good breeding': Crowley (1989), p. 149.

100 **Milton and Sheridan**: citations on 'breeding' are from the *OED*.
teachers' union pamphlet: (NUT), ibid., pp. 150–51.
vulgar-speaking illiterates: ibid., p. 151.

100 **Mr Wylie fosters dialect**: Honey (1988b), p. 224, citing B. Holling-worth, 'Dialect in school'; *Durham and Newcastle Research Review*, vol. 8, no. 39, Autumn 1977, pp. 15–20.

101 **Elworthy on marked provincialisms**: Honey (1988b), p. 215, citing F. T. Elworthy, *The Dialect of West Somerset* (1875).
experience of 'superior education': A. J. Ellis, in Crowley (1989), p. 146.
public-school system, new sense: Honey (1988b), pp. 209–10.

102 **Ellis: how can he?**: ibid., p. 221.
more prescriptive college staffs: ibid., pp. 221–3.
precisely **the preserve**: Crowley (1989), p. 173.

103 **RP speakers 'a tiny minority'**: ibid., p. 202.

104 **self-images false; preferences and prejudices**: ibid., p. 205.

105 **paradox of 'English par excellence'**: Harris (1988), pp. 21–2.
Bourdieu's single official stroke: Harris (1987), p. 142.

106 **part and parcel of the myth**: ibid., p. 117; and Harris (1988), p. 18.
quoting one's own claim as evidence: Harris (1988), p. 17. There is a similar claim, with slightly different wording ("hardly a more blatant example of attempting retrospective validation"), in Harris (1987), p. 116.
effective social history of a meaning: Raymond Williams (1961), p. 316n.

108 **standard English was 'creation of nineteenth century'**: Pennycook (1994), p. 113.
five centuries too late: John E. Joseph (1992), p. 175.
taken mildly to task: ibid., p. 174.
do not compromise judgment: ibid., p. 176.

109 **Foucault and history of madness, illness, etc.**: the main ideas of Foucault can be found in such of his books as *Madness and Civilisation* (France, 1961; UK, 1967); *The Archaeology of Knowledge* (France, 1969; UK 1972); *The Birth of the Clinic* (1963, UK 1973); *Discipline and Punishment* (1975, UK 1977); *The History of Sexuality*, 3 vols (1976–84; UK 1979–88). Useful introductions are P. Rabinow (ed.), *The Foucault Reader* (1986) and A. McHoul and W. Grace (eds.), *A Foucault Primer* (1993).
Foucault and IRA violence: C. Gordon, review in *TLS*, 21 June 1996.

111 (footnote): **criticisms of Foucault's writings**: see especially Brian Vickers (1993), pp. 27–9, 32–6, etc. Since that book in 1993, Professor Vickers has accumulated a further store of examples of wide-ranging criticisms of Foucault, mainly by Continental scholars in various fields.
(footnote): **Gramsci on dialect**: see his *Prison Notebooks 1929–35* (1971), p. 325.

112 **repression and low standard of living**: Bocock (1986), p. 109.
no opposition allowed: ibid., pp. 109–10.

112 **no evidence to count against it**: ibid., p. 69.
     classes produced by political activities: ibid., p. 103.
113 **long-running debate on dominant ideology versus organisation of production**: see, e.g., N. Abercrombie, S. Hill and B. S. Turner, *The Dominant Ideology Thesis* (1980).
     the same admiring critic: John E. Joseph (1992), p. 166.
     Standard English a class variety: Deborah Cameron (1995), p. 110.
114 **induced to consent to subordination**: Janet Batsleer et al. (1985), pp. 36–8.
115 **improved social status**: R. Harris (1988), p. 19.
     diminution of class-consciousness: Williams (1961), p. 325.
116 **Williams 'never there' for students**: see Lisa Jardine in N. Tredell (1992); also David Caute in *TLS*, 15 December 1995. On Williams's nostalgia for working classes, see Donald Davie in Tredell (1992), especially p. 274.
     fine talking as social handicap: Crowley (1989), p. 161.
     self-serving élite: Cameron (1995), p. 42.
     imposed norm hypothesis: see H. Giles, R. Bourhis, P. Trudgill, A. Lewis, 'The imposed norm hypothesis, a validation', in *Quarterly Journal of Speech*, vol. 60, no. 4, December 1974, especially p. 406; and Giles and Trudgill, in Trudgill (1983). Chapter 12.
117 **gross historical howlers**: these include, in addition to misunderstandings concerning the historical evolution of both state and private education systems in the nineteenth century, his assertion that the study of English "language and literature at the beginning of the nineteenth century was effectively proscribed in the major public schools as a result of the Leeds Grammar School case" (p. 83). There is a serious confusion here about how far this ruling affected the major public schools, or even Leeds Grammar School itself, which by 1824 possessed its own English grammar book (Michael, 1987, pp. 363, 534). Dr Crowley seems under the impression (pp. 236–48) that the Newbolt Report was produced by a (Royal) Commission: in fact it was produced by a departmental committee of the Board of Education.

6: Authority in Language: Anagogy and Prescription

118 **descriptive not prescriptive**: J. Aitchison (1979), p. 13.
     prescriptivisim is pejorative: D. Crystal (1980), p. 283.
119 **successful people used it**: J. and L. Milroy (1985), p. 27.
120 **communicative competence of millions**: loc. cit.
     influential portions: loc. cit.
121 **complaint tradition, reliability, uniformity**: ibid., pp. 34–6.
     norms of everyday English: ibid., p. 37.

122 **model in written channel**: ibid. p. 38.

123 **parasitic upon spoken English**: Gillian Brown, 'The Spoken Language', in Carter, ed. (1982), p. 82.

seen two men: J. and L. Milroy (1985), p. 38.

only one correct way . . . arbitrary social values: ibid., pp. 39–40.

124 **select one and only one**: ibid., p. 17, 22–3; Leith (1983), pp. 32–3; E. Haugen (1966).

126 **minimal variation of form**: Leith (1983), p. 32.

the total uniformity: J. and L. Milroy (1985), p. 60.

127 **claims about 'superiority'**: ibid., p. 40.

one variety as superior: ibid., p. 48.

128 **the 'correctness tradition'**: ibid., p. 39.

moral degeneracy, etc.: ibid., p. 40.

and 'careless speech': ibid., p. 104.

130 **'better' explanation**: ibid., p. 49.

factors actually involved: ibid., p. 56.

131 **prefer status to solidarity**: ibid., p. 59.

solidarity as unacceptable face of exclusiveness: A. H. Halsey, *No Discouragement* (1996), p. 190.

stereotyped markers of social class: J. and L. Milroy (1985), p. 81.

'disease' or malfunctioning: ibid., p. 69.

132 **Plain English Campaign**: in Britain, founded by Chrissie Maher and Martin Cutts in 1974, offers consultancy to firms and public bodies in making their forms and other documentation easily intelligible and reader-friendly.

133 **native speakers have implicit knowledge**: J. and L. Milroy (1985), p. 71.

preferred – or even enforced: ibid., p. 90.

134 **linguistic value system**: ibid., p. 91.

attempt to change language patterns: ibid., p. 97.

rejection of social values: ibid., p. 98.

135 **'dispassionate' approach**: ibid., p. 1 and *passim*.

'in some absolute sense, right': Hudson (1980), p. 201.

136 **a morality of language**: John Simon, 'The corruption of English', in Michaels and Ricks, eds. (1980), p. 38.

'improved in morals and pronunciation': quoted, from Robert W. Malcolmson, in Barrell (1983), p. 138.

137 **King James's Prayer Book**: Alan Clark, *Diaries* (1993), p. 90, entry in August 1984. He presumably meant the 1662 Prayer Book, issued under Charles II; but this was the final version of a liturgy first formulated in the 1540s, revised under Elizabeth I and indeed James I.

139 **American Menomini**: Bloomfield, cited in Haas (1982), pp. 15–16.

crucial defining function: see Bernice Martin (1981), p. 34.

140 **untidy experience**: Mary Douglas (1966), p. 4.
depth and permanence: ibid., p. 36.
values tidily ordered: ibid., pp. 38–9.

141 **defining landmarks**: Bernice Martin (1981), p. 54.
stand outside immediate culture: Mary Douglas (1970), pp. 190–91.
respectability with symmetry: Bernice Martin (1981), p. 57.

142 **ritual and repetition**: ibid., pp. 61–3.
rituals of shopping: Margaret Forster, *Hidden Lives* (1995), pp. 165–7.
boundary and order: Bernice Martin (1981), loc. cit.

143 **embodied controls in lifestyle**: loc. cit.
culture of control: loc. cit.
truth, force, uniformity: Hoskyns, 'Directions for Speech and Style', in Osborn (1937), pp. 103, 115–16.

144 **decay of the language**: Greenbaum (1988), p. 33.

147 **an intrinsic feature**: Haas, ed. (1982), p. 15.
an integral part: M. W. Sugathapala De Silva in Haas, ed. (1982), p. 119.
policing the 'correctness': Margaret Sharpe, anthropologist at the University of New England, private communication (1995).

148 **understand language, not control it**: Lecture 1 of (Oxford) Professor Jean Aitchison's 1996 Reith Lectures on BBC Radio; see Aitchison (1997), p. 19.

7: Safeguarding English

149 **different from/to**: A. L. Rowse (1989), p. 48.

152 **Randolph Quirk and associates**: Quirk et al. (1972).

153 **Ontario premier's 'fulsome'**: letter in *TLS*, 28 September 1990, from Malcolm Page of Simon Fraser University.

154 **Central Committee decimated**: Yuri Modin, *My Five Cambridge Friends* (1994), p. 33.
Lomu destroyed, then decimated: *Daily Mirror*, quoted in *Japan Times*, 22 June 1995.

155 **reticent to commit**: correspondent Andrew Cassell, BBC TV, 22 May 1993.
reticence to break: Misha Glennie, Balkans correspondent, BBC Radio World Service, 11 January 1993.
reticent to believe: US Black civil rights leader, on Martin Luther King anniversary march, voice on BBC Radio World Service, 29 August 1993.
Bennett reticent to try: Julie Carter, *The Literary North*, BBC World Service, 27 February 1990.
reticence to interfere: Claire Harman, *Sylvia Townsend Warner* (1989), p. 124.
Tom Clancy novel: *Patriot Games* (1988), p. 184.

155 **reticence to talk**: J. E. Joseph (1987), p. 82.
American writer on China: Nancy Woronov, *China Through My Window*, (US, 1989), pp. 44, 52.
Oxford professor: Professor Jack Lively, review in *TLS*, 5 January 1990.
American interviewee: BBC Radio 4, 26 October 1996.

156 **réticent de publier**: French TV2, 7 June 1993.
Baudouin accepta: French TV2, 2 August 1993.
infected cohorts in Uganda: Ed Hooper, *Slim: a Reporter's Own Story of AIDS in Africa* (1990), p. 112.
cohort of French thinkers: Tony Judt, review in *TLS*, 19 January 1996.
Thatcherite cohort: news headline, Max Pearson, BBC Radio World Service, 14 November 1990.
Zia and cohorts: N. Sethi, *Independent* (London), 8 August 1990.

157 **Ershad cohorts**: news headline, Oliver Scott, BBC Radio World Service, 11 December 1990.
Mr Baker and cohorts: in *The Economist*, 27 June 1992.
Hilary Mantel: *Eight Months on Ghazzah Street* (1988), p. 26.
John Le Carré: *The Russia House* (1988; paperback edn 1990), pp. 279, 339.
Flashman's cohorts: Alistair Cooke, 'Letter from America', BBC Radio World Service, 7 October 1991.

158 **British professor's trip**: Eileen Barker, 'Don's Diary', *THES*, 22 July 1994.
Ecstasy with water: BBC TV news, 1 February 1996.

159 **if equipment available**: BBC TV news, 17 January 1996.
Jeffrey Archer: on BBC TV news, 13 June 1992.
Italian currency crisis: ITN (Britain) news, 17 September 1992.
high on drugs: Bob Losure on CNN, 23 May 1993.
Robert Black: Mike McKay, BBC TV news, 20 May 1994.
agent Arnold Deutsch: review of Costello and Tsarev, *Deadly Illusion*, in *L. A. Times*, reprinted in *Japan Times*, 29 August 1993.
Catherine Phillips: *Robert Bridges* (1992), p. 90.

161 **American commentator**: John Simon (1980), quoted in J. M. Williams, 'O When Degree is Shaked!', in Machan and Scott (1992), p. 69.
English Today: John Honey, 'A New Rule for the Queen and I?', in issue 44, vol. 11, no. 4.

162 **Alan Bennett's diary**: extracts in *Sunday Telegraph*, 24 January 1996.
hate-words in Sunday newspaper: *Sunday Telegraph*, 24 December 1995, supplementing earlier list in that paper, 17 December 1995.
H. W. Fowler: especially his *Modern English Usage* (1926) and, with his brother, *The King's English* (1906).
Sir Ernest Gowers: *Plain Words* (1948).

166 **is themselves out**: Laurie Taylor, *THES*, 4 October 1996.

166 (footnote) **ne, thon, etc. as candidates for unisex pronoun**: these are among abundant examples in D. E. Barron, 'The epicene pronoun: the word that failed', in *American Speech*, vol. 56 (1981), pp. 83–97.

167 **there's a lot of it about**: John Honey (1989), p. 91.
   St Paws (treatment of *l*): ibid., p. 93.
   Professor Aitchison's ridicule: in her BBC Reith Lecture 1, 1996.

8: *Language in School: The Lost Generation*

169 **quarter of Latin vocabulary**: Barbara Strang (1970), p. 129.

170 **grammatical exercises abandoned**: N. F. Blake (1996), p. 312.
   advice on dating: quoted in Bullock Report: *A Language for Life* (1975), p. 5.
   emotional development: quoted, ibid., p. 6.
   thus *anything goes*: Nickel and Stalker (1986), p. 1.

171 **simply one dialect among many**: Trudgill (1975), p. 28.
   higher status speakers: ibid., 38.
   purely social one: ibid., p. 81.
   teachers' attitudes more positive: as interpreted by J. van den Hoogen and H. Kuijper, in Cheshire, Edwards et al. (1989), p. 224.
   imposition of an alien dialect: Trudgill (1983), p. 205.
   as correct as any other dialect: see, for example, Maura Healy, *Your Language* (I), Macmillan Education (1981), p. 59.
   without the discipline of craft: Cox (1995), p. 10.

172 **dignify their travesty**: ibid., p. 12.
   write a poem: R. Protherough, *English in Education*, vol. 12, no. 1, Spring 1978.
   grammar does not improve writing: Sir Alan Bullock (chairman), Bullock Report (for Department of Education and Science), *A Language for Life* (1975), p. 171.

173 **should be raised**: ibid., p. 7.
   barely a third: ibid., pp. 227, 228.

174 **tight deadline**: Sir John Kingman (chairman), Kingman Report (for Department of Education and Science), p. v.
   great social bank: ibid., p. 14.
   open to all: ibid., p. 7.
   linguistically superior: ibid., p. 43.
   punctuation: ibid., p. 13.

175 **stated unequivocally**: Professor Brian Cox (chairman), Cox Report (for DES and Welsh Office), (1989), §5.41.
   has social prestige: ibid., §5.42.
   liberal consensus: Brumfit (1995), p. 120.

175 **viciously stupid debate**: Colin MacCabe, *Critical Quarterly*, Winter 1990.

right-wing extremists: Cox (1995), p. 29.

elderly emotional traditionalists: ibid., p. 9.

old-fashioned grammar: ibid., p. 5.

176 **developmental approaches**: Jennifer Chew in Joyce Morris (1995), p. 26.

178 **Milton before Shelley**: Dan Jacobson, *TLS*, 4 August 1995.

narrow prescriptive approach: Lamb (1992), p. 48.

the best response: loc. cit.

almost all respondents: all these comments are quoted from Lamb (1992), pp. 45–50.

179 **reports of examination boards**: Lamb (1994), pp. 9–10.

examiners' inappropriate censoriousness: Roger Knight, 'Thinking about "good English"', in C. Sutton (ed.), *Communicating in the Classroom* (1981), p. 86.

minimal number of scripts: Jennifer Chew in Morris (1995), p. 25.

180 **massive 92 per cent**: Lamb (1994), p. 2.

Gallup study: Lamb (1994), p. 8.

181 **instructions from a manual**: ibid., p. 9.

opinions and practices of English teachers: Lamb (1996), especially pp. 5, 58.

182 **1921, 1912 employers complain**: Bullock Report (1975), p. 3; Cox (1995), p. 37.

public spending on education: Vaizey (1958), pp. 70, 98–101.

an educational failure: Hoggart (1996), p. 34.

183 **lag behind German counterparts**: as reported in the British press, e.g. *Weekly Telegraph*, 13 September 1995.

bookstores doubled: Daniel Bell in *TLS*, 9 July 1995.

to near alarming: *THES*, 23 December 1994, quoting A. Shankar and A. Lapointe, *Learning by Degrees*.

rise in SAT scores: *THES*, 20 October 1995.

aspirin bottle: *Economist*, 9 December 1995, p. 37.

most pressing business: ABC News, (US TV), 1 March 1996.

184 **grammar as separate subject**: F. C. Cook HMI, Report on the Eastern Circuit, Committee of Council on Education, *Minutes* (1845), vol I, p. 140.

HMI and poet: Matthew Arnold, in *General Report* for 1876.

speakers' implicit knowledge: J. and L. Milroy (1985/91), p. 71.

185 **teachable content**: Thornton (1986), p. 13.

teaching analytical grammar: Bullock Report (1975), p. 171.

product of class-structure: Thornton (1986), pp. 44, 45.

prestige dialect misleadingly: John Richmond, in A. James and R. Jeffcoate, *The School in the Multiracial Society* (1981), p. 102.

185 **research suggests grammar harmful**: Kingman Report (1988), p. 12.
research studies are so flawed: my account follows closely that of Professor Tomlinson in his three articles (1993, 1995 and (draft) 1997).

187 **different meanings of 'grammar'**: W. N. Francis, 'Revolution in grammar', in *Quarterly Journal of Speech*, vol. 40, (1954) pp. 299–312; P. Hartwell, 'Grammar, grammars, and the teaching of grammar', in *College English*, vol. 47, no. 2, pp. 105–27 (1985); Randolph Quirk, *The English Language and Images of Matter* (1972).
Elley's New Zealand study: W. B. Elley et al. (1975).

189 **treat Elley's conclusions as decisive**: Cox (1995), pp. 9–10.

190 **exercises unrelated to needs**: Kingman Report (1988), p. 13.
major developments in linguistics: Cox (1995), p. 13.
unsympathetic to research: ibid., pp. 13, 33.
Professor Peter Trudgill: *THES*, 2 July 1993, commenting on letter from David Pascall, 18 June 1993.

192 **traditional in sympathies**: Cox (1995), p. 95; *THES*, 11 June 1993.
disastrously reductive: loc. cit.
drafted by Eagleton: Cox, loc. cit.

193 **Who believes that?**: John Haynes, Co-ordinator LINC South-East Consortium, *TES*, 12 July 1991; Janet Daley, *TES*, 10 June 1991.

194 **spoken English of 350 11- and 15-year-olds**: Hudson and Holmes (1995).
historically and socially constructed: Euan Reid, review of Hudson and Holmes (1995) in *British Association for Applied Linguistics Newsletter*, no. 53, Summer 1996, p. 22.

195 **imposition of authority**: loc. cit.
opinions gain public approval: Jim Miller, in J. and L. Milroy, eds. (1993), p. 103.
association with economic élites: Tollefson (1991), p. 61.
unfair advantage: ibid., p. 62.
against minorities by power élite: R. St Clair, in Ryan and Giles (eds.), (1982), p. 165.

196 **dialects are inherently equal**: Donna Christian, *Language Arts and Dialect Differences* (US, 1979), p. 5.
a discriminatory action: loc. cit.
stronghold on power: V. Edwards and A. Redfern, *The World in the Classroom*, (1992), p. 7.
Black patois usage: V. Edwards (1981), quoted in J. and L. Milroy (1985/91), pp. 114–15.
adverse effects of shame: ibid., p. 116.

198 **learning another dialect is more difficult**: E. Haugen, 'Bilingualism and bidialectalism', in R. W. Shuy (ed.), *Social Dialects and Language Learning* (US, 1965), p. 125.

198 **rare adult masters new dialect**: Trudgill (1983), p. 13.
'**rich man's curriculum**': *Economist*, 2 December 1995, p. 35.
'**Dialect-fair instruction**: see Robert Berdan, 'Black English and dialect-fair instruction', in N. Mercer (ed.), *Language in School and Community* (1981), Chapter XI.

199 **little hope of changing**: Wilkinson (1995), p. 11.
property of a class: Willinsky (1988), p. 5.
strategy of exclusion: ibid., p. 32.
prejudices that support it: ibid., p. 129.
process of initiation: ibid., p. 32.

200 **making language over**: ibid., p. xvii.
45 per cent more students: ibid., p. 59.
no absolutes . . . educated Canadians: ibid., p. 38.
insecure about acceptance: ibid., p. 87.

201 **speak both ways**: ibid., p. 88.
'**care in expression**': ibid., p. 95.
social perceptiveness: ibid., p. 99.
for abstract uses: ibid., p. 101.
deference and politeness: ibid., p. 103.
intellectual, expressive . . . and be good: loc. cit.
Jane: ibid., p. 108.
for self-expression: loc. cit.
poem to girlfriend: ibid., p. 112–13.
redemption out of darkness: ibid., p. 114.
gratitude to teacher: loc. cit.
Student Bob: ibid., p. 115–16.

202 **good manners**: ibid., p. 117.
Annie: ibid., pp. 116–18.
rebelliousness; pop music: ibid., pp. 119, 113.
girl from slums; underprivileged boy; poor Black student: ibid., pp. 110, 111, 118.
fuller sense of themselves: ibid., p. 132.
bourgeois installation: ibid., p. 133, quoting E. Balibar and P. Macherey (1981).
(footnote): **bizarre claim**: ibid., p. 48.

203 **concludes with a call**: ibid., p. 141.
(footnote): **mis-spellings etc.**: ibid., p. 100 ('they were mislead').
Among curiosities in this book is the transformation of the famous American linguist Leonard Bloomfield into Leopold. Similar faults of language as well as misuse of historical evidence in this author's *Empire of Words* (1995) are exposed in a review by Anthony Quinton, *TLS*, 21 April 1995.

204 **Society more difficult to control**: Anne Barnes, *Independent on Sunday*, 7 February 1993.

9: The *Language Trap* Debate

205 **senior chief inspector says 15,000**: Chris Woodhead said, on BBC TV News, 5 February 1995, that 15,000 teachers in England and Wales were unsatisfactory, and also in February 1996 that one in four primary-school lessons were unsatisfactory.

206 **MoTs taken up by others**: see, for example, Michael Barber, *The Learning Game* (1996), pp. 221–3.
The Language Trap: subtitled 'Race, class and the standard English issue in schools', published as Kay-Shuttleworth Papers on Education No. 3 by the National Council for Educational Standards, 1983.

207 **angry demolition job**: Crystal (1983), pp. 42–50.

208 **The other reviewer**: R. Hudson (1983), pp. 50–54.
taken an important initiative: On behalf of the Committee for Linguistics in Education of BAAL and the Linguistics Association of Great Britain, Professor Hudson organised a small session of 15 professionals to discuss certain aspects of this issue, and he reported its findings in his 'Linguistic Equality', CLIE Working Paper no. 1, (1983).

209 **In that reply**: John Honey in *BAAL Newsletter* 19 (1983), pp. 37–46.
not error but vulgarity: Geoffrey Sampson, review of J. and L. Milroy, (1985), in *TLS*, 11 April 1987.

210 **NATE journal**: the Crystal review was reproduced in *English in Education*, vol. 18 no. 1, and the short summary of my reply in vol. 18 no. 3.
published an article: see Graddol and Swann (1988), pp. 95–111.
polemical attack: ibid., p. 111.

211 **commended Scargill**: Honey, *The Language Trap*, p. 24.
damaging national strike: Graddol and Swann (1988), p. 103.
ranks of academic linguists: Graddol and Swann (p. 104), actually add 'and educationists', but they do not cite any educationists.

212 **same *TLS* reviewer**: Geoffrey Sampson, *TLS*, 11 April 1987.
Chomskyan tradition has advocated: J. and L. Milroy (1985/91), pp. 9, 26.
disputed by John E. Joseph: see Joseph (1987), p. 12.
making a 'scapegoat': J. and L. Milroy (1985/91), p. 34.

213 **abandoning standards of correctness**: ibid., p. 175.
this judgment is confirmed: Nickel and Stalker (eds.) (1986), Introduction, p. 1.
'balanced' discussion: ibid., p. 100.
who exactly are these people: ibid., p. 181.
ideological rather than academic: ibid., p. 179.
Milroys' treatment of Labov paper: ibid., pp. 152–5.

214 **approved scholars not publicised**: ibid., p. 53.
facts not prejudices: ibid., pp. 1, 6 and *passim*.

215 **John Smith speaks up**: quoted by an MP, BBC TV News, 13 May 1994.
216 **used by political Right**: Cheshire, Edwards et al. (eds.) (1989), p. 7.
   insights gained from sociolinguistics: Cheshire, Edwards et al. eds. (1988), p. 136.
   strenuously deny: ibid., pp. 135, 311.
   (footnote): **Suzanne Romaine interviewed**: Romaine (1994), p. 131.
217 **tactic of reactionary thought**: Crowley (1989), p. 260.
218 **references to 'New Right'**: ibid., pp. 259–60.
   main emphases of 'New Right': Bocock (1986), pp. 17–18, 120–24.
219 **German spokesman of 'New Right'**: THES, 26 July 1996, p. 10.
221 **article by Dr Raphael Salkie**: 'Voices off the Social Scale', in THES, 14 April 1989.

10: A National and International Language

223 **vast majority are flat-earthers**: Thornton (1986), pp. 9, 11.
224 **right and wrong ways ... represents nothing more**: Romaine (1984), p. 233.
   used by the powerful: Romaine (1994), p. 19.
   not natural ... only one system: ibid., p. 84.
225 **accepted at royal court**: Fromkin and Rodman (1983), p. 251.
   phoneme segmentation wrong: R. J. Scholes and B. J. Willis in Olson and Torrance, eds. (1991) pp. 215–35.
   language in constant flux: see Kingman Report (1988), p. 15.
226 **cultivation by élite**: Leith (1983), p. 33.
   equal clarity and adequacy: P. Trudgill in the *European English Messenger*, IV/1, Spring 1995.
   every geographical variety: Jim Miller, in J. and L. Milroy, eds. (1993) p. 103.
   (footnote): **Swift: foreigners in their own country**: *Gulliver's Travels* (1726), III, 10.
227 **Genesis in Black Country dialect**: (as translated by Kate Fletcher), ibid., p. 296.
   rebuke to Van Mildert: Cobbett, quoted in E. P. Thompson (1963), p. 819.
   many extravagant predictions: J. Sturm, in Cheshire, Edwards et al., eds. (1989), p. 304.
   the growing disdain: Cheshire in Blue and Mitchell, eds. (1995), p. 49.
228 **reinvigorated promotion**: Batsleer et al. (1985), p. 158.
   Bernstein welcomed, then repudiated: ibid., p. 39.
   undercut education as leveller: Joseph (1992), p. 175.
   linguistic equality overstated: Rampton, 'Scope for Empowerment', in Cameron, Frazer et al., eds. (1992), p. 49.

228 **John Honeyesque argument**: Cameron, 'Respect, please', in ibid., p. 129.

229 **Black English would become standard**: Gee (1990), p. 13.
status, wealth, control: ibid., p. 23.
replicate status quo: ibid., p. 30.
time-management: ibid., pp. 31, 39.
Plato, Bakhtin et al.: ibid., p. 41.

230 **active complicity**: ibid., p. 158.
dominant cultural values: ibid., p. 179.
manipulate, analyse, resist: ibid., p. 148.
conventional, historical: ibid., 166.
naturalness of middle-class: ibid., p. 167.
apprenticeships into middle-class: ibid., p. 173.

231 **authoritarian texts**: ibid., p. 190.
workings of knowledge, power: ibid., p. 173.
new basis of literacy classes: ibid., p. 174.
people get hurt: ibid., p. xx.
ethical principle: ibid., pp. 22, 28.
What sort of social group?: ibid., p. 45.
'correct' simply means: ibid., p. 18.
undergird the hegemonic: ibid., p. 42.
literacy of colonised: ibid., p. 155.

232 **aspirin bottle**: ibid., p. xix.
modified but still decisive: see, for example, David R. Olson, 'Literacy as metalinguistic activity', in Olson and Torrance, (eds.) (1991), pp. 251–70.
professor from India: D. P. Pattanayak, 'Literacy: an instrument of oppression', ibid., pp. 105–8.
'cognitive' and 'ideological' models: Street (1984), pp. 1–65.

233 **only important for specific positions**: ibid., p. 107; H. J. Graff, *The Literacy Myth* (US, 1979).
vested interest in 'establishing the authority': Celia Roberts and Brian Street, 'Spoken and written language', in Coulmas, ed. (1997), pp. 168–86. The arguments of these two scholars are based on uncritical acceptance of the Leith/Milroy case on the intolerance of variability by standard languages, and the Giles/Trudgill case on the 'imposition' of standard norms; ibid., p. 175.
The New Literacy: John Willinsky (1990).
significant harm to others: Gee (1990), p. 191.

234 **Canning Town church bookstall**: 'The Happy Pagans', article in *Church Times*, 19 August 1994, based on Bishop Sheppard's contribution to P. Watherston (ed.), *A Different Kind of Church* (1994), p. 65.

235 **deep aversion to learning**: David Reynolds, Professor of Education at

the University of Newcastle upon Tyne, in discussion on BBC2 TV, 19 May 1996.

235 **Education is fault-line**: Clinton, on US TV, including ABC News, 13 April 1995.

20 per cent without skills: quoted by Jim Lehrer, US TV, 28 March 1996.

236 **level continually adjusted**: Raymond Williams, *Keywords* (1976).

237 **fascist mind-set**: Liam Hudson, *TLS*, 2 December 1994.

Wedgwood, Elgar and Bob Marley: Richard Hoggart, *The Way We Live Now* (1996), pp. 55, 61.

Richard Dawkins's exposure: quoted in *TLS*, 31 March 1994, p. 14.

238 **Massey's brilliant review article**: my quotations are all from Massey (1995), pp. 747–53.

240 **nostalgia for solidarities**: Ferdinand Mount in *TLS*, 21 October 1994.

241 **single yet pluralistic culture**: Alan Ryan in *THES*, 31 April 1995.

35 per cent of population: item on ABC News (US TV), 11 August 1993.

common ethnic stock: 'Lexington' column in *Economist*, 18 March 1995.

denies diversity disunifying: Tollefson (1991), p. 132.

professor Glenn Loury: speaking on the Brinckley Programme, US TV, 9 October 1995.

no common culture: M. K. Asante, 'Multiculturalism: an exchange', in Berman, ed. (1992), pp. 308, 311.

code word for 'white': ibid., p. 305.

242 **so-called mainstream**: Gee (1990), p. xiii.

(footnote): **lifestyle of powerful segment**: Anne Haas Dyson, editorial 'What Difference does Difference make?', in *English Education* (official journal of NCTE's conference on English Education), vol. 27, no. 2, May 1995.

(footnote): **swamps and backwaters**: James Sledd, in Nickel and Stalker (1986), p. 67.

(footnote): **exclusion of handicapped from participation**: Vic Finkelstein, in Swain, Finkelstein et al. (1993), pp. 36, 42.

slowly resegregating: leading article (on Simpson verdict) in *Economist*, 7 October 1995.

243 **distance, even hostility**: E. R. Leach, *Political Systems of Highland Burma* (1954), p. 39.

culture, religion or *language*: William Pfaff, article in *Los Angeles Times* and *International Herald Tribune*, reprinted in *Japan Times*, 23 March 1996.

244 **undoubted prestige until 1945**: my account of the rivalry between British and American English draws heavily on my article 'Howdee or Hello? – the Future of British and American English' in *THES*, 31 July 1992.

247 **shifting forward of word-stress**: see John Honey, 'Changing Patterns of Word-stress in Present-day English', in *Etudes Anglaises* (France), vol. xlvii, no. 2, April 1994.

248 **a CNN reporter**: Michael Okwu, CNN TV News, 11 February 1996.

249 **Randolph Quirk and Braj Kachru**: important contributions to this debate are Randolph Quirk, 'The Question of Standards in the International Use of English', in Lowenberg, ed. (1988); R. Quirk, 'Language Varieties and Standard language', in *JALT Journal* (Japan) vol. 11, no. 1; Braj Kachru, *The Alchemy of English* (1986); B. Kachru, 'The Spread of English and Sacred Linguistic Cows', in Lowenberg, ed. (1988). A useful updating of this debate is in Tickoo, ed. (1991), Section iii.

250 **Singapore variety of English**: see especially Anne Pakir, 'The Status of English and the Question of "Standard" in Singapore' (and other papers by A. Pakir and by Anthea Fraser Gupta cited in that article), in Tickoo, (ed.) (1991).

as yet unrecognised variety of English: quoted by Quirk in Tickoo, ed. (1991), p. 174.

251 **illustration of Hong Kong English**: *Economist*, 2 March 1996.
Professor Roy Harris and Hong Kong English: see his Inaugural Lecture, Hong Kong University *Gazette* Supplement, 24 April 1989.
a Chinese professor writes: Harry J. Huang, Zhongshou University, in *English Language Teaching Journal*, vol. 43, no. 4, October 1989.
British lecturer in China: Sarah Lawson, Suzhou University, 'Don's Diary', in *THES*, 10 September 1993.

252 **constant touch with acceptable model**: Quirk in Tickoo, ed. (1991), p. 170.
lofty rebuke from Quirk: see his 'Language Spread and Language Variation', in Quirk, *Grammatical and Lexical Variance in English* (1995), pp. 40–41.

253 **cornerstone of capitalism**: Phillipson (1992), p. 10.
hierarchising social groups: ibid., p. 241.

254 **Linguists are trained**: ibid., p. 276.
distinguished Philippine linguists: Andrew Gonzalez and M. L. S. Batista, (1986).

255 **disadvantage on others**: John Swales, *Genre Analysis* (1990), p. 106.
Phillipson has no answer: see *RASK*, vol. 1, October 1994, for my review of Phillipson (1992), and vol. 3, September 1995, for Phillipson's reply to my review, and my rejoinder.
new gods of modernity: Phillipson (1992), p. 247.
poisonous chemicals: ibid., p. 60.
banana leaves: ibid., p. 239.

256 **not spiritual aristocrats**: Jung Chang, *Wild Swans* (1991), p. 618.
invention of Western imperialism: Ndebele (1987), p. 3.

256 **proximity to African languages**: ibid., p. 13.

   one major African writer: Ngugi wa Thiongo's decision and its rationale can be found in his *Decolonising the Mind* (1986), pp. xiv, 3. See also the discussion in Bailey (1991), Chapter 6.

257 **have influence globally**: Adrian Roscoe, personal communication, August 1995.

   black man's efforts to liberate himself: Es'kia Mphahlele (1984).

258 **'unwarranted and emotional'**: J. R. Edwards (1983), p. 74. The reviews in the professional journal *BAAL Newsletter* (1983) are discussed in Chapter 9 (above).

259 **women consistently outdo men**: see especially Cheshire (1984) and Wodak and Benke (1997).

   practicalities of their rights: Marcus Davis (1865), p. 3.

   meanest capacity . . . Governors or Princes: ibid., pp. 12–13.

   grammar altered at any time: ibid., p. 28.

   works of repute: ibid., p. 23.

   power to make themselves heard: ibid., p. 18.

Index